*Creating Worlds Otherwise*

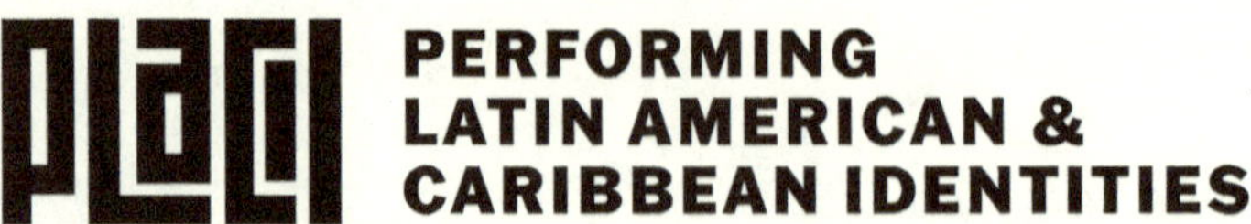


Performing Latin American and Caribbean Identities
KATHRYN BISHOP-SANCHEZ, *series editor*

This series is a forum for scholarship that recognizes the critical role of performance in social, cultural, and political life. Geographically focused on the Caribbean and Latin America (including Latinidad in the United States) but wide-ranging in thematic scope, the series highlights how understandings of desire, gender, sexuality, race, the postcolonial, human rights, and citizenship, among other issues, have been explored and continue to evolve. Books in the series will examine performances by a variety of actors with under-represented and marginalized peoples getting particular (though not exclusive) focus. Studies of spectators or audiences are equally welcome as those of actors—whether literally performers or others whose behaviors can be interpreted that way. In order to create a rich dialogue, the series will include a variety of disciplinary approaches and methods as well as studies of diverse media, genres, and time periods.

Performing Latin American and Caribbean Identities is designed to appeal to scholars and students of these geographic regions who recognize that through the lens of performance (or what may alternatively be described as spectacle, ceremony, or collective ritual, among other descriptors) we can better understand pressing societal issues.

Other titles in the series:

*Atenco Lives!: Filmmaking and Popular Struggle in Mexico* by Livia K. Stone

*Creating Carmen Miranda: Race, Camp, and Transnational Stardom* by Kathryn Bishop-Sanchez

*Living Quixote: Performative Activism in Contemporary Brazil and the Americas* by Rogelio Minana

# Creating Worlds Otherwise

*Art, Collective Action, and (Post)Extractivism*

PAULA SERAFINI

Vanderbilt University Press
*Nashville, Tennessee*

First printing 2022

Library of Congress Cataloging-in-Publication Data
Names: Serafini, Paula, author.
Title: Creating worlds otherwise : art, collective action and (post)extractivism / Paula Serafini.
Description: Nashville, Tennessee : Vanderbilt University Press, [2022] | Includes bibliographical references and index.
Identifiers: LCCN 2021056677 (print) | LCCN 2021056678 (ebook) | ISBN 9780826504555 (paperback) | ISBN 9780826504562 (hardcover) | ISBN 9780826504579 (epub) | ISBN 9780826504586 (pdf)
Subjects: LCSH: Art and social action--Argentina. | Arts--Political aspects--Argentina. | Environmental degradation in art. | Agricultural industries--Social aspects--Argentina. | Mineral industries--Social aspects--Argentina. | Natural resources--Management--Social aspects--Argentina.
Classification: LCC NX180.S6 S48 2022 (print) | LCC NX180.S6 (ebook) | DDC 701/.030982--dc23/eng/20220331
LC record available at https://lccn.loc.gov/2021056677
LC ebook record available at https://lccn.loc.gov/2021056678

*To Fran and Isa*

# CONTENTS

# ACKNOWLEDGMENTS

ONE THING I always aim to do with my research is to work from the stories. This book does not try to prove a hypothesis or evidence a theory; rather, it aims to document the forms of collective action and creative practice that emerge in response to the advance of extractivism, and to offer new, useful tools for understanding them.

The first acknowledgement therefore goes to all the people who were part of this project (those featured in the book and those who are not), who with great generosity gave up their time to tell me their stories and explain what was happening in their territories. This includes the community of Vista Alegre; members of the Asamblea del Algarrobo in Andalgalá; activists and artists from different parts of Córdoba and specially the people at Revolución CC and Casa 1234; organizations like Observatorio Petrolero Sur, Museo del Hambre and La Boca Resiste y Propone, collectives like Proyecto Squatters and Etcétera, and artists like Azul Blaseotto and Eduardo Molinari for continued collaborations that have enriched my work greatly. I particularly thank Sergio Martínez, Milton López, and Revolución CC for their hospitality during my travels.

I would like to thank my former colleagues at CAMEo Research Institute and at the School of Media, Communication and Sociology at the University of Leicester for being fantastic humans and for allowing me to bounce ideas off them. I also thank the Instituto de Investigaciones Gino Germani at the University of Buenos Aires for kindly receiving me as a visiting researcher and allowing me to share the process and outcomes of this project with them. I specially thank Gabriela Merlinsky for her support and friendship during this project and during other shared ventures. I am very grateful as well to the British Academy and the Leverhulme Trust for supporting the period of fieldwork that led to this book, and to my current colleagues at Queen Mary University of London, for supporting and trusting my vision to make this work the basis of new teaching.

A sincere thanks goes to those I regard as my past and present academic mentors (whether they willingly accept the title or not): Mark Banks, Doris Eikhof, Alison Harvey, Tim Jordan, and Ross Parry, all of whom have provided valuable advice as I prepared this book. I also thank Zachary Gresham and Kathryn Bishop-Sanchez at Vanderbilt University Press for their dedication and input from early stages in the development of this book, and Joell Smith-Borne for a careful and detailed editing of this work. And a heartfelt mention goes to the late David Graeber, who generously provided guidance and support on my first steps as a researcher many years ago, and whose brilliant insights and teachings will stay with many of us for years to come.

This work, while based on research I carried out in Argentina, has been influenced as well by conversations, collaborations, and militancy with activists and collectives in the UK, my current home. I am particularly grateful to Shake! and Platform London for many years of shared work and joyful exercises in creating worlds otherwise. I also thank my co-creators at PLANK for wonderful conversations and joint projects, and fellow *actorvists* from BP or not BP? for many years of beautiful and fierce art activism.

Lastly and most importantly, I thank my family and friends in Buenos Aires and London for their love and encouragement always.

# INTRODUCTION

WE FIND OURSELVES in the midst of runaway climate change, in addition to rising inequality, new pandemics, the upsurge of far-right and white supremacist movements in different parts of the globe, and long-standing injustices, such as hunger. Most governments acknowledge the need to tackle climate change, including vows to reduce emissions and transition away from fossil fuels toward renewable energy. However, governments, world organizations, and corporations are not acting fast enough, and furthermore, they frame their responses within a green capitalist logic that assumes the continuation of perpetual growth. This logic rests on ingrained modern ideas of progress and categories that condition our position as humans in relation to other beings and ecosystems, categories that were constituted and enforced through, and as a result of, colonialism.[1] Furthermore, since the turn of the century, we can also identify a further shift from modernity to globality,[2] as advances in telecommunications and free movement (of capital) transformed the global economy, deepening, in many ways, forms of global inequality.

In 2020, as we reached record temperatures, the COVID-19 pandemic emerged as a clear consequence of an unsustainable relationship between humans and their wider ecosystems. The pandemic also exposed some of the crudest forms of inequality and oppression in the world and revealed that the way we organize basic systems for the sustainment of life, such as health care, are deeply flawed. Mainstream solutions to the world's greatest problems continue to be framed within the same paradigms that drove us to where we are in the first place. And indeed, a significant portion of the population is not in fact in denial about the world's problems, but are actually, as argues Irwin, "unsure about what they can do,"[3] given that there is no clear political or infrastructural support for individuals and collectives to contribute to rapid, significant changes in crucial areas from production to welfare.

However, in Latin America, proposals for worlds otherwise are cracking through the concrete, building on and from ancestral knowledge, revolutionary histories, decades of indigenous, peasant, and worker organizing, and more recently, the rise of feminism and of youth climate activism. Furthermore, amid the suffering, the interruption of the system generated by COVID-19 compelled many of us to fundamentally rethink what kind of world we want to live in, and how we can make that happen. Indeed, the pandemic has forcibly created a moment for questioning issues such as prosperity indicators, currently based on economic growth. While capitalism's ability to make the most out of a crisis should not be underestimated, we must also consider the context in which the pandemic found us: already in crisis, and with mass mobilizations awakening. Perhaps we are indeed at a turning point at which we might begin to transcend the paradigm of extractivism, development, and growth following a period of growing tension between the unfulfilled expectations for change by peoples across the globe and the solutions that this paradigm is able to offer.[4]

Considering the current conjuncture, and with the intention to contribute to transitions away from a world driven by the imperatives of perpetual growth and a logic of extraction, this book offers an analysis of the functions of art in anti- and postextractivist movements. It begins from the premise that art has a fundamental role in building and sustaining different forms of collective action, and that some of these functions—such as the generation of narratives, the sustainment of collective identities, and the potential for prefiguration—are common to different movements in a variety of contexts.[5] However, there are also ways art activates mechanisms for transformative change that are constituted in response to a particular context. Here, I examine the functions of art in the Latin American context, taking Argentina as a main site of inquiry and drawing on extractivism as a term to describe the contemporary hegemony in most of the region and as a frame for understanding the social and ecological conflicts resulting from it. It is my contention that in order to understand fully the operations and effects of extractivism and how we can move toward postextractivist worlds, we must look at artistic practice, as this is a realm in which we see the synthesis of forces of resistance and creation.

This book is a contemporary document of the struggles, imaginaries, and actions of people who are, in some way, breaking out of the extractivist hegemony and envisioning and creating worlds otherwise. It offers insight into the creative production of artists, activists, and frontline communities who are taking a stand against the effects of extractivism in their daily lives and challenging the worldviews and structures that underpin and sustain a model of development based on a logic of extraction. Throughout the different chapters, I develop two lines of inquiry: in the first place, I examine the narratives that emerge out of different forms of collective action against extractivism. I look at how different narratives and key ideas frame the conflicts surrounding extractive activities and the wider economic and political model, and how they also point to other ideas and models for other ways of being. I focus on five themes: territory, ecofeminism, human rights and the rights of nature, urban and cultural extractivism, autonomy and sovereignty, and postextractivism and alternatives to development. Second, I look at the role that different forms of art and creative practices have in the fight against extractivism and in imagining and enacting alternative futures. Specifically, I propose a situated framework of analysis for understanding how art and creative practices mobilize counterhegemonic narratives about extractivism and development and how they activate prefigurative socialities and economies and contribute to important ontological shifts. This framework consists of five functions: denunciation, documentation, democratization, deconstruction, and design, functions that respond to the specific context of an extractivist hegemony. In this way, this book aims to join the efforts of other Latin American scholars in bringing to the forefront the planetary dimension of local struggles in the face of a climate crisis, and to fight the "atrophy of the imagination that blockades transformative action" by demonstrating the potential of art to enact radical social change in extractivist societies.[6]

## *Extractivism and Development*

The framework of extractivism was initially developed by scholars and activists in Latin America, and it is used for describing and critiquing the economic model of several Latin American and other Global South countries which base their economies on the intensive extraction of natural resources for export.[7] Extractivism is thus characterized by the primacy of certain activities such as open-pit mining, oil extraction, and agribusiness monocultures. It is associated to the trampling of rights of indigenous and peasant communities, increasingly affected as the extractive frontier advances; severe damage to ecosystems and to the health of communities in proximity to extractive projects; and economic dependency, resulting from the orientation of economies toward the export of fluctuating commodities. Extractivism has also been linked to other issues such as gender violence and to the epistemicide of indigenous cultures displaced from their territories. Indigenous and communitarian antipatriarchal and ecofeminist groups and thinkers have done extensive work on this matter, which I discuss in Chapter 2.

For some, extractivism describes a particular form of economic activity, for others it describes the wider economic model of a country or region, and in recent years, the concept (and its variants, such as "extraction") has been employed to describe the logic behind economic and social dynamics in the current stage of neoliberal capitalism, following a displacement of the frontiers of extraction toward other economic fields and spheres of the social.[8] In this book, I build on the work on extractivism of Latin American scholars and activists, and in particular the understanding of extractivism developed by geographer Horacio Machado Aráoz.[9] According to Machado Aráoz, extractivism is the economic, political, and cultural practice that determines how zones of expropriation and of accumulation function and relate to each other. Extractivism is the pattern of relation established as the base of the modern world, and it is the fundamental basis of the geography and "civilization" of capital, since capitalism is born out of, and expands through, extractivism in Latin America. In other words, extractivism serves to describe the historical form of territorial organization imposed by capital: through the dynamics of primary, export-oriented investments, *inhabited* land becomes *occupied* land, as capital provokes a process of deterritorialization and displacement of local people, their economies, and social fabric.[10] In turn, territorial alienation erodes the capacity for sovereignty and control that people have over their territory. The fight for territory under extractivism is therefore not just a fight for land. Instead, it is the fight for defending ways of being, local economies, identities, sovereignty, and the right to self-determination, issues that are central to the narratives of movements against extractivism, and which I examine in the different chapters of this book.

Machado Aráoz explains that underpinning extractivism is an imaginary based on the premise of a hierarchical division between nature and culture, and the idea that Latin America is a provider of nature—savage, primitive, and underdeveloped—and different from culture and "civility." From the colonization of the continent, the region was subjected to the violent exploitation of bodies and territories, an economy of expropriation that gave way to an era of accumulation. The environmental destruction and violent exploitation of the mines in Potosí and the concentration of the mountain's riches in the hands of the colonists is not only a paradigmatic image of the colonization of the Americas, but it is also an origin story for the current stage of extractivism. Extractivism thus takes place in a context of a perpetuated state of coloniality, a phenomenon that entails the normalization of colonial hierarchies as well as the reproduction of its forms of exploitation.[11]

There have been other terms employed to describe the processes of environmental degradation, violence, displacement, and dispossession resulting from the economic and political models of Latin American and other countries that heavily rely on the extraction of so-called natural resources, such as *accumulation through dispossession* and *expulsion*.[12] However, I frame my analysis primarily through the lens of extractivism for four reasons. In the first place, the framework of extractivism is geographically and historically situated. Because of this, it takes into account the colonial histories of Latin American countries, the incidence of the development paradigm, the conflicting ontologies of indigenous and Afro cosmovisions and the imposed Western paradigm, and the geopolitics of the commodities trade, in ways that other frameworks do not. Second, extractivism is a term used by activists on the ground across the board in Argentina and many other Latin American countries, and since this book is concerned with documenting and analyzing narratives that emerge from the bottom up, it is paramount to engage with the frames used by the actors at the frontlines of struggles. Third, and in relation to the first two points, in a context of political instability in which Latin America has seen a series of shifts to the Right and the Left over the last decade, extractivism cuts across other categories such as "progressive" and "neoliberal" often used to describe the political and ideological inclinations of governments, all of which might champion extractivist models regardless of their position along the Left-Right spectrum. Finally, extractivism is also a term that is elastic enough to frame specific conflicts (e.g., a mining site) or to refer to a systemic issue, and it lends itself to theorization on the social and cultural dynamics that take place alongside economic activity. In Chapter 4, for instance, I develop the concept of cultural extractivism as a way of understanding the ways that the logic of extraction is manifested in the cultural and creative industries, and how these, as a result, reproduce extractive dynamics as part of a wider program of development and modernization.

Before considering the particularities of the current stage of extractivism in Latin America and in Argentina specifically, it is also useful to consider the role of the development paradigm in shaping

Latin American economies and societies since the mid-twentieth century, perpetuating extractivist mindsets and policies. Indeed, as argued by Eduardo Gudynas, "a critical approach to extractivism implies revising the conceptual bases of contemporary development."[13] In Latin America, development is "seen as a discourse of modernization, as well as the environmental degradation that it generates."[14] Even in its so-called "sustainable" versions, development is based on visions of growth and unlimited technological horizons, which are in turn based on the modern idea of progress.[15]

Arturo Escobar explains that from the emergence of the development paradigm in the aftermath of World War II to the beginnings of the current century, development has broadly been thought of and critiqued in three ways. In the 1950s and 1960s, the theory of modernization, which linked development to growth, was prevalent. Then came the theory of dependency in the 1960s and 1970s, which argued that it is the connection between internal exploitation and external dependency that lay at the root of "underdevelopment," rather than a lack of capital or technology. Finally, in the 1980s and 1990s critiques emerged of development as cultural discourse, which proposed that the discourse of development was being deployed in order to construct and sustain the figure of the Third World.[16] As Mario Blaser argues, this perspective responded to the specific way that, since the 1980s, neoliberal development policy was imposed on so-called developing countries by central economies and multilateral organizations.[17] This last approach to critiquing development builds on a poststructuralist perspective, and it gave way to the notion of postdevelopment. This poststructuralist approach highlighted the forms of exclusion that constituted the project of development, including the exclusion of the knowledges and concerns of those who were supposed to benefit from it. What postdevelopment proposes, therefore, is to decenter the development narrative and to center local knowledges and perspectives in our approaches to solving problems and devising other ways of being. This includes incorporating the valuable knowledge that emerges from social movements and other forms of collective organizing, as these are spaces where new socialities, economies, and imaginaries begin to emerge.[18] As Astrid Ulloa also argues, Latin American proposals for alternatives to development "involve other views about nature and spatiality, since they are not only about access, control and effects, but about other ways of being and living in a specific territory."[19] Finally, but not less crucial, post-development also challenges the imperative of perpetual growth that underpins the development paradigm.

We must note, however, that poststructuralist critiques of development have received criticism because of their focus on discourse and imposition from the Global North, and for sometimes failing to consider and engage with local power relationships within development projects, including the different positionings of local groups.[20] Such critiques are important if we want to contribute to a project that aims to deconstruct power and undo oppression in all of its scales and forms.

## *The Extractivist Hegemony*

While extractivism goes back to the colonization of the Americas, it is the period beginning in the mid-1990s that scholars of extractivism are currently interrogating; a period characterized by the incorporation of new technologies of extraction and biotechnologies such as GMOs (which in Argentina date back to 1996), a commodity boom in the early 2000s lasting until around 2012 that greatly benefited Latin American economies, and foreign investment in large-scale extraction projects in mining and fossil fuels.[21] The contemporary extractivist model, sometimes referred to as neoextractivism, was championed by the progressive governments of the "turn to the Left" in the late 1990s and early 2000s, but also by countries that were not part of the wave, as was the case of Colombia.[22] For progressive governments, extractivism was an avenue for development but it was also a way of funding social programs, and indeed in many countries this period saw significant decreases in poverty rates, even if stark inequality still persists.

In recent years we began to see a particular moment of extractivism marked by the violent expansion of the extractive frontier, as

Maristella Svampa explains.[23] This results from the continuous pursuit of growth and is also related to the drop in commodity prices in previous years; the royalties paid by mining companies, for instance, are miniscule percentages that are only profitable in large volumes, and under an extractive logic, declining prices call for more extraction. In this endeavor, techniques that were so far not deployed in the region, such as fracking, are being used in order to access previously inaccessible resources, exposing local communities to new and often unclear types and levels of risk in relation to the integrity of their immediate environment.

Thus far, critiques of extractivism, whether emerging from academia or from affected communities, have remained largely marginal, and tend to be labeled "antiprogress."[24] Extractivism operates as a hegemony in Latin America—for most governments on the Left and on the Right, exploiting the "natural advantage" of resource abundance is an unquestionable economic choice. And indeed, the problem lies in the single economic logic that underpins such decisions—in addition to the geopolitical dynamics that make other pathways more difficult.

In Argentina, the hegemony of extractivism is evidenced by the seamless continuation of the extractivist paradigm from neoliberal to progressive governments and back again from the 1990s to the present date.[25] This hegemony is sustained by, among other things, the epistemological hierarchies that place certain forms of modern, scientific knowledge above all others, as described by Latour.[26] Escobar explains that in the Global South, "science has become the most central political technology of authoritarianism . . . and oppression of peoples and nature. As a reason of state, science operates as the most effective idiom of violent development and even standardizes the formats of dissent."[27] In relation to this, Mario Blaser argues that "as long as debates remain grounded on the assumption of a single 'reality' and on a contest over who produces the most accurate representation of it . . . the very regime of truth that justifies the use of coercion to protect the status quo remains unshaken."[28]

This book supports the project and vision of a pluriverse, or as Enrique Leff puts it, a diversity of "epistemologies, rationalities and imaginaries,"[29] and resists the "hegemony of hegemony," or the idea of replacing one hegemony with another one as a way of achieving social and environmentally just ways of living.[30] However, in the face of a hegemony of extractivism, I choose to describe many of the practices and narratives in this book as counterhegemonic due to their strategic deployment, even when many of them are in fact also post- or alterhegemonic in their long-term visions and in the kinds of processes they facilitate.

## *Ecological Conflicts in Argentina*

While *Creating Worlds Otherwise* seeks to provide new ways of understanding extractivism as a Latin American phenomenon and the role of art at a moment of global crisis and ontological shifts, my interrogations and analysis are situated in one country, Argentina. Contrary to other studies that consider cases from different parts of the Americas or look at the relationship between art and ecological destruction at a global scale, I offer a situated approach that builds theory from the ground up in a way that directly responds to the reality of the site of inquiry and that later can be translocated to other contexts and adapted in each case.

Argentina is the site of multiple manifestations of the extractivist model, from open-pit mining to fracking and monocrop agriculture. Furthermore, its history of social mobilization, autonomous organizing, and creative resistance make it a fertile ground for analyzing the culture of movements against extractivism, as does the fast-changing landscape of such movements, which have in recent years begun to turn increasingly intersectional.

In order to understand the current stage of extractivism in Argentina, we must first look back to the 1990s, when there was a marked shift in terms of legislation surrounding the exploitation of the land and what the Argentine state regards as natural resources. In 1993, the neoliberal government of president Carlos Saul Menem passed a series of laws pertaining to mining, such as the law of mining investments (No. 24.196/93), which guaranteed fiscal stability to mining companies for a period of thirty years, as well as tax breaks and import rights.[31] In 1996, secretary of Agriculture, Cattle Raising and Fishing, Felipe Solá, signed an agreement that gave a green light to Monsanto's experimentation with GMO crops in the country. And in 1997, Argentina saw its first case of open pit mining; the copper and gold mine Bajo de la Alumbrera began operating in Andalgalá, Province of Catamarca, in the northwest of the country.

As part of this new wave of extractivism, or neoextractivism, subsequent governments, with support from multilateral organizations, hailed large-scale extractive projects implementing new technologies as opportunities for development, a narrative that was supported and reproduced by the mainstream media and through cultural production and education texts. Early on, communities in the vicinity of extractive projects were promised employment, wealth, and infrastructural investment. Over and over again, they found that jobs were few and often limited to the first stages of extraction projects, and that the wealth generated was not invested toward the betterment of conditions for local inhabitants. Instead, they were left with polluted lands, health problems, and the demise of local economies.

At the same time, the recent history of extractivism in Argentina wears the badge of popular rebellion.[32] One of the most paradigmatic cases of resistance to extractivism in the country, and in the whole of Latin America, was the case of the Esquel referendum in 2003. That year, the people of Esquel held a referendum to decide whether to accept or reject a project for gold and silver open-pit mining operated by then US American company Meridian Gold. Upholding their constitutional right to previous, informed, and free consultation, the town voted "no" to the mine, with an outcome of 82 percent against.[33] The victory of the movement against mining was so emboldening and symbolic that following this event, consultations for the development of extractive projects in Argentina have become increasingly rare despite this being a constitutional right, as local governments and corporations fear the people's power to self-organize.

Another significant environmental conflict that emerged around the same time concerned the plans of Finnish company Botnia to open a paper pulp mill on the Uruguayan-side banks of the Uruguay River, which marks the natural border with Argentina. Concerns about pollution of the river and the lack of consultation brought together communities from the Argentine side (as well as from the Uruguayan side) to protest against the mill, and resulted in a five-year period of blockades to the international bridge connecting the two countries, between 2005 and 2010.[34] The conflict escalated and made it to the International Court of Justice, and while the mill began operations in the end (eventually leading to a series of environmental incidents as predicted), plans for a second mill were dropped.

A third emblematic case is that of the town of Famatina, in the northwestern province of La Rioja. Maristella Svampa tells the story of their struggle:

> In early 2012 there was an inflection that inserted the issue of mining into the national political agenda: the community of Famatina, in the province of La Rioja, rose once again against megamining. In 2007 they had ejected the company Barrick Gold, which aimed to exploit the mountain, and had secured a provincial law that prohibited megamining. However, in 2008 the law was repealed and it left the conflict at an impasse. [In 2011] the province of La Rioja signed a new agreement with another Canadian company (Osisko Mining). It was then that the community of Famatina initiated a new blockade to prevent the company from accessing the mountain. Soon after, the blockade would turn into an uprising of national resonance, which would force the province to halt the project. This sudden visibilization of the antimining struggle generated sustained solidarity from the big cities.[35]

Most recently, a conflict that has been highly visible since 2017 is that concerning Mapuche indigenous communities in the Patagonia region, who are claiming access and collective ownership of their ancestral territories. Currently, large portions of these territories are in private hands, as is the case of Italian magnate Luciano Benetton, who, through one of his companies, owns 900,000 hectares of land in the province of Chubut. At the same time, within the ancestral territories where Mapuche ancestry and ownership is currently recognized by the Argentine state, conflicts linked to extraction abound, as the communities inhabiting those territories have been dealing with pollution and health problems for decades. In the province of Neuquén, for instance, oil extraction has led to long-standing conflicts over adequate compensation for operation and environmental damage, and this has only worsened with the arrival of fracking and the thousands of related environmental incidents taking place each year.[36]

The resistance to extractivism in Argentina consists of a broad range of actors. In most cases, particularly at the frontlines of extraction, what we witness is an "environmentalism of the poor," in which the defense of the environment is intrinsically linked to human survival, which in turn is underpinned by a lived understanding of the interdependence between different elements of an ecosystem.[37] However, the relationship with the territory is often different for indigenous and settler communities, even if many parallels occur. Ingrained racism has led to decades of ignoring the social and environmental concerns from indigenous and racialized communities, but also as the extractive frontier expands and new conflicts arise, we have seen the systematic persecution of indigenous actors in a way that directly exploits racist tropes, a matter I discuss in Chapter 1. The daily experience of extractivism is also different for those living in big cities, who, while not experiencing certain forms of extractive violence that occur in rural areas, are also exposed to environmental problems and matters of environmental injustice. Within cities, we can clearly see how class dictates geographies of environmental injustice, as the most common environmental conflicts concerning pollution, sanitation, and lack of access to water are consistently located in impoverished areas.[38]

In this book, I engage with the practices and perspectives of a broad range of actors who are differently placed in wider struggles against extractivism, and who belong to different sectors and communities. The works and voices that make up the research the book is based on span different points of the country, from Catamarca to Chubut, from urban to rural areas, and is diverse in its demographic makeup. However, the book is not an all-encompassing survey, and there are certain groups that are not as present as others. Particularly, I would like to highlight the book's focus on the Mapuche struggle for self-determination over other indigenous struggles in Argentina. While there are thirty-eight originary peoples in what constitutes the Argentine territory, conflicts surrounding Mapuche claims to ancestral territory quickly intensified as I began my research, leading to various forms of increased state violence, persecution, and delegitimization campaigns in the media. For this reason, as I wrote this book it felt necessary to highlight this conflict and contextualize the Mapuche struggle within a neocolonial advance of the extractive frontier.

Emerging from different contexts, the perspectives of those featured in this book vary greatly on some matters, but they all represent different positionalities within the subaltern: they are all fighting against a hegemonic model of extractive development that is oppressive, polluting, and leading to dispossession and the violation of rights. They are all aware of the global dimensions of the extractive economy, and of the colonial and imperial roots of extractive dynamics. And they all draw, to greater or lesser extent, from previous and related local and regional experiences of social movements and organizing, which include indigenous resistance, a strong movement for the defense of human rights, and a recent history of autonomous organizing.

Autonomous movements in Latin America are those that question the current form of representative democracy and advocate for other ways of living instead.[39] Autonomy (or *autonomía* in Spanish, as used by Escobar in order to differentiate it from autonomous Marxism) is not about changing the world, but rather about creating new ones. It involves building institutions that are autonomous from the state and tends to have a territorial or place-based dimension, in both rural and urban settings.[40] Svampa argues that there were three key moments in recent Latin American history in which autonomy emerged as a mobilizing narrative. The first was 1994, when the Ejército Zapatista de Liberación Nacional (Zapatista Army for National Liberation) in Chiapas birthed the first movement against neoliberal globalization. The second moment was around 2001 and 2002, when Argentina was submerged in a deep economic and sociopolitical crisis, and assemblies and recuperated factories rejected institutional forms of political representation to organize instead according to an ethos of *autogestión* (autonomous self-management) and cooperativism. And the third moment was in Bolivia toward 2006, when the indigenous demand for autonomy became associated with the project of creating a plurinational state represented by Evo Morales—this project, however, met its limits when the autonomy and self-determination of indigenous and peasant communities was constrained by the state's will to control "natural resources" in those territories.[41]

Marina Sitrin explains that autonomous movements are often anticapitalist, and in all cases, their attempts at creating other forms of being are not oriented toward gaining state power or replacing the status quo with another form of hegemony.[42] Rather, their territorialized social formations and economies put forward contextualized, prefigurative alternatives, demonstrating that other ways of living are possible. Another defining trait of autonomous movements is their commitment to horizontality. Horizontality implies a nonhierarchical and nonauthoritarian form of organizing, and organizers speak of horizontality both "as an end and as a tool."[43] Soon after the 2001 crisis in Argentina, sectors of the new autonomous movements, as well as their practices, were incorporated into the progressive political project of president Néstor Kirchner. However, there were some groups that continued to sustain an independent, autonomous ethos, such as some *piquetero* movements (movements of unemployed workers) and education initiatives run from within recuperated factories.[44] Most importantly for the matters that concern us, the autonomous ethos was carried forward by the environmental citizens' assemblies that make up the Unión de Asambleas Ciudadanas (UAC; Union of Citizens' Assemblies), emerging in 2006.

The UAC is a network of assemblies that spans the whole country and that has become an essential infrastructural element of the antiextractivist movement in Argentina. It is self-organized and its meetings are self-funded, and they follow the principles of autonomy and horizontality in their organizing and decision-making. In their words, the UAC "is a space for exchange, discussion, and action conformed by assemblies, self-organized neighbors, autonomous organizations that are not linked to political parties or to the state, and citizens that come together in defense of the commons, of health, and of the self-determination of the peoples." They also explain that when coming together they "were influenced by global approaches that attempt to explain local realities, denounced with might the new forms of articulation between businesses and the state, and rediscovered socially engaged art and *autogestión*. It became a space of freedom, of relationality, and of origin to a new kind of democracy: a popular one."[45] Autonomous politics and the ethos of *autogestión* are important for understanding the backdrop and background of anti- and postextractivist movements, and I will be expanding on their relevance and influence at different points in this book.

## *Postextractivism and Alternatives to Development*

Given that there tends to be a shared awareness of the connections between extractivism, colonialism, development, and global geopolitics among different social actors opposing extractivism, there is also a shared recognition that targeted reforms are not sufficient, and as a result, movements against extractivism are infused with a desire for radical change. This desire manifests in the form of visions and practices for postextractivist worlds otherwise, which we can understand as part of a history of transition discourse that goes back to the 1970s but has become more prevalent in the last decade with the widespread realization that the social and ecological crisis is linked to our socioeconomic model and the ontologies that underpin it.[46] However, transition discourses vary, and are conditioned by the place of enunciation, its history and the needs of local communities and ecosystems. As Escobar clearly states, "While the age to come is described in the North as being postgrowth, postmaterialist, post economic, postcapitalist, and post human, for the South it is expressed in terms of being post-development, nonliberal, postcapitalist/noncapitalist, biocentric, and postextractivist."[47]

Here I take *postdevelopment* as an umbrella term to refer to most strands of thought and action that challenge the extractivist development paradigm in the Global South. Within postdevelopment, there are two key ideas that have been crucial for Latin American movements: *buen vivir* and the rights of nature. *Buen vivir* originates from the articulation of the Andean indigenous concept of *sumak kawsay* with other social actors such as peasant movements, environmental networks, academic organizations, and movements led by afro-descendant communities, women, and students. It is a perspective that prioritizes dignity and ecology over the economy and follows the principle of biocentrism.[48] The rights of nature, on the other hand, are a juridical attempt to decenter the human by arguing not only that the preservation of ecosystems is important due to their significance to current and future human generations, but that ecosystems should be sustained and protected for their intrinsic value.[49] The rights of nature approach is still relatively new, and therefore there continue to be important discussions to have in terms of its applicability and how it interacts with other forms of societal transformation. I discuss this more in detail in Chapter 3.

*Postextractivism* is a transition perspective that we can locate within or alongside postdevelopment. It focuses on eradicating the dynamics of extractivism at the core of current development models, but it also challenges the validity of extractivism as a sustainable approach to any form of society, economy, or government. The *transitions to postextractivism* model differentiates between various kinds of extractivism, from indispensable to predatory, in an attempt to sketch out stages for transitions away from extraction-centered societies.[50] Postextractivism, argues Martín García, tends to present three main paths of action: the generation of new avenues for tax revenue to replace income from extractive activities, the development of new technologies and knowledges relevant to a diversification of the economy, and the political will and necessary frameworks for ensuring social and environmental justice.[51]

But leaving behind an extractivist model is not only a matter of modelling the transition of the economy and building institutional and legislative frameworks. Extractivism is underpinned by deeply rooted ideologies and understandings of ourselves and our place in the world, including the still prevailing understanding of nature as resource.[52] In this book, I choose to speak about extractivism, antiextractivism, and postextractivism because extractivism as a concept allows an analysis of the material as well as the symbolic, and most importantly, it facilitates an easy route toward discussing ontological issues regarding nature, humanity, and life. Postextractivism, therefore, is also about leaving behind a way of being that is extractive, and about how we learn to do this.

Finally, I take a brief look at *degrowth*, as one of the most prominent ecologically informed discourses at the current time in the Global North. Degrowth and postdevelopment discourses share many points in their assessment of our current predicament and the necessary changes that need to occur at global and local scales in order to limit climate change and ecological collapse.[53] Degrowth scholars argue for an end to the program of unlimited economic growth due to its unsustainability.[54] And indeed, as Escobar explains, "there is likely no other social and policy domain where the paradigm of growth has been most persistently deployed than that of development."[55] However, degrowth has been criticized as being individualistic and not engaging enough with political struggles against capitalism, imperialism, and extractivism. Critics have also pointed to the potential damage of a universal degrowth discourse that fails to consider the circumstances of Global South countries where there are currently deficits in terms of health, nutrition, and shelter. For these reasons, the approaches to degrowth that have the most potential are those that are contextualized and that position themselves alongside other transition discourses. As Padini Nirmal and Dianne Rocheleau put it, both "degrowth and post-development have to be decolonial or nothing at all."[56]

Thinking about transition movements in both the Global South and the Global North, an idea that has become equally widespread has been that of the commons. The commons can be understood as "social systems formed by three basic interconnected elements: 1) a commonwealth, that is, a set of resources held in common and governed by 2) a community of commoners who also 3) engage in the praxis of communing, or doing in common, which reproduces their lives in common and that of their commonwealth."[57] The commons can refer to the shared governance of ecosystems but also to social and cultural tangible and intangible goods. Furthermore, while sometimes it is linked to "resource" language and can therefore be seen as an anthropocentric term, the commons and commoning can also be experienced from the place of interdependence between human communities and the territories they inhabit, making it a useful concept for thinking about postextractivist structures, processes, and governance.[58]

Svampa argues that one of the big challenges facing post-development discourse—or any kind of transition discourse, we could argue—is that of projecting a new vision for what we want our lives to be and for what a "good living" can look like. One of the strengths of the development paradigm, she explains, is how ingrained the imaginary of consumption as equal to quality of life is for most people.[59] It is therefore paramount to spark our capacity to imagine, engender, and enact worlds otherwise. Investigating, cultivating, and activating the cultural, communicative, and creative dimensions of any transition project, I propose, is the way to achieve this.

## *Researching Art and Culture for the Creation of Worlds Otherwise*

The work developed in this book is deeply influenced by cultural studies approaches. Cultural studies centers on the study of conjunctures and proposes that, in this task, looking at culture is key in order to understand the everyday functioning of political forces. This is due to the political nature of cultural production, but also, due to the relevance of art as a place for developing theory.[60] In an article reflecting on the legacy of leading cultural studies figure Stuart Hall, John Clarke explains that for Hall,

> culture was the domain in which people lived—and imagined or understood—their relationship to their subordination. Culture comprised the imaginative, affective, and interpretive maps of the social world and its organization. . . . The enormous depth, diversity, and productivity of the field of culture means that it is continuously traversed by political forces, seeking to forge the connections that would tie political projects into the everyday or commonsense forms of popular thinking. Culture never exists in a "pure" state, outside of these relations—the entanglement is both permanent and constantly shifting as each element changes and/or changes place.[61]

In *Creating Worlds Otherwise*, I follow an environmental (or, I would say, ecological) cultural studies approach, which Kata Beilin and Daniel Ares-López define as one that

> tends to understand socio-environmental processes, events, and actors from a perspective that is, at once, material-corporeal and semiotic. That is, a perspective that recognizes that all knowledge (human or not) is situated and embodied and that life and material processes on Earth cannot be separated from the meanings, social practices, and conceptual frameworks through which life and matter is understood, partitioned, inter-acted with, managed, or transformed.[62]

I also draw from political ecology, a field that emerged in the 1970s from the merger of political economy and the ecologically oriented strands of disciplines such as anthropology, geography, development studies, and the natural sciences, as well as specific theories and approaches including Marxism, decolonial theory, feminism, and poststructuralism.[63] I specifically draw from Latin American political ecology and understand this more as an approach than a discipline, as Héctor Alimonda would put it: one that works directly with movements while being nurtured by different traditions of Latin American critical and decolonial thought.[64]

Importantly, this work takes a cultural politics approach, in which I look at the relationship between culture and power, exploring both resistance and potential for transformation in processes of art making. I follow Honor Fagan in her view that "a cultural politics of postdevelopment is based on the understanding that culture produces power, knowledge, subjectivities and identities so struggle at the cultural level is not only feasible but also necessary."[65] With this in mind, I aim to contribute to a cultural politics of postextractivism by developing a situated analysis grounded on local frames that engages in turn with wider discussions about postextractivism and postdevelopment. At the same time, while I center my study on processes of art making and cultural dynamics (adhering to an understanding of art that is broad and not bound to institutional definitions), I do not assume a clear demarcation between culture and other social spheres, or that conflicts surrounding extractivism have clearly defined facets. I adopt a decolonial perspective that challenges the stark constructions that compartmentalize spheres of human and beyond-human activity. As Ramón Grosfoguel argues, "in the 'coloniality of power' approach, what comes first, 'culture or the economy,' is a false dilemma, a chicken-egg dilemma that obscures the complexity of the capitalist world-system."[66] And, as Escobar puts it, "economic crises are ecological crises are cultural crises."[67]

What we understand as cultural conflicts, argues Escobar, often emerge from underlying ontological differences. We are enmeshed in an onto-epistemic formation that conditions us to be productive, individual, and separate from nature, in other words, "being modern."[68] Because of this, engaging with ontology is paramount, and thus emerges the field of political ontology, which examines the politics of practices that shape particular ontologies or worlds and focuses on the conflicts that result from clashes between different ontologies.[69] Political ontology places the modern world as only one world among many.[70] In this sense, I find Enrique Dussel's concept of *transmodernity* useful for situating Latin America as a site where there is both the presence of a dominant, modern ontology and the survival of nonmodern worlds. This makes approaches to moving beyond modern structures and perspectives coming from this region distinct from European postmodernism.[71]

Approaching environmental and ecological conflicts from an ontological perspective is necessary because the root of such conflicts often lies in different perceptions of the world, of territories and beings, and of how humans relate to other entities in the world.[72] Put differently, "what is at stake in these conflicts is precisely the differing 'things' that are at stake."[73] Epistemological reflections are thus also necessary, in order to allow us to contemplate the different forms of knowledge creation that emerge from actors who are differently situated.[74] While extractivism relies on economic measures of value and certain types of scientific knowledge, resistances often draw from a wider range of knowledge-creation practices and perspectives, including popular epidemiology, ancestral and practice-based knowledge of the land, and art: all vehicles for epistemic and ontological struggles against the neoliberal globalizing project and for the advance of the pluriverse.[75]

The role of the arts in ontological struggles is particularly significant, as art, media and design can be understood as "worlding practices," or practices that allow us to create worlds.[76] Furthermore, studying artistic practices can allow us to identify important social shifts: Hoyos speaks for instance of how contemporary Latin American literature reveals the emergence of a new *transcultural* materialism, one that can be described as postanthropocentric, and through which "the nonhuman aspect of culture is revealed."[77] Indeed, art and cultural practices can allow the creation of new narratives and visions and "languages of valorization,"[78] which, when they go on to question the meaning of value itself, can make ontological interventions in the way we situate ourselves in our environments and in relation to other beings. From this perspective, Tim Ingold argues that art, as anthropology, should play a part in "fashioning a world fit for coming generations to inhabit," as a practice that looks into the question of "how to live." He proposes that art practice be approached with generosity (a kind of investigation that listens and is not extractive), open-endedness, comparison and criticality. Ingold particularly highlights practices like walking, drawing, music, dance and craft, as art forms that do not reproduce but rather *make* sensible.[79] In this sense, *Creating Worlds Otherwise* contributes to a recent body of work (e.g., Gómez-Barris 2017, Demos 2020, Ponce de León 2021) that studies how aesthetic practices denounce and resist dynamics of violence, enclosure, and destruction, and how they "offer diverse approaches to a hopeful futurity."[80] In addition, I take a methodological cue from Macarena Gómez-Barris who argues for a "submerged," decolonial perspective that goes beyond a focus on exposure and denunciation: "if we only track the purview of power's destruction and death force, we are forever analytically imprisoned to reproducing a totalizing viewpoint that ignores life that is unbridled and finds forms of resisting and living alternatively."[81]

Elsewhere, I have examined the relationship between aesthetics and politics by focusing on the processes behind aesthetic-political practices in a range of groups and instances of collective action in the UK.[82] I argued that in art activism, there is a tension between aesthetic and political objectives, one that manifests in the different aspects of a practice, from the way groups conceive of participation to their collective identity processes. In my theorization, I proposed that the tension between aesthetics and politics has the potential of being reconciled when artists and activists adopt a prefigurative approach to their practice, one that foregrounds ethics and underpins both aesthetic and political decisions. As a result, I argued, contrary to some perspectives that distinguish between "interventionist" and "constructive" strands of participatory, socially engaged art,[83] there are ways of developing art activist practices that are simultaneously denouncing and disrupting dominant paradigms and the institutions that uphold them and enacting, in their making, new socialities, forms of aesthetic value, and ethical, organizing principles.

The research I share in this book is a continuation of this work, as it is grounded in this particular understanding of aesthetics and politics and pays attention to the prefigurative character of world-making practices. Here, however, I move away from a more general analysis of the interaction between aesthetics and politics, toward a focus on the particularities of aesthetic practices in a context marked by extractivism.[84] I examine specifically the functions of art in the context of anti- and postextractivist movements, in order to understand more fully the role of art in complex contexts of resistance, environmental and institutional violence, ontological shifts, and the emboldening of visions for worlds otherwise. In this way, I am able to continue contributing to a series of interdisciplinary conversations, initiatives, and instances of theory building around art, extractivism, territory and shifting paradigms emerging from Latin America, including many exhibitions and events covered in this book.[85]

## *Art and Extractivism*

In Argentina, where media conglomerates and sectors of the extractive industries and agribusiness are closely connected and ontologically aligned, mainstream media narratives on the extractive industries tend to sustain the view that extraction is the avenue toward development, progress, and modernization[86]. In recent years, especially since the center-left government of Alberto Fernández came to power in 2019, environmental protection and sustainability have gained a significantly stronger place in political discourse.[87] However, what we see is a discourse that promotes extractivism and sustainability simultaneously under logos such as "responsible mining," which directly contradict the experiences of open-pit mining in the country so far.

In addition to the hermetic character of mainstream media narratives and the discrepancies between political discourse and governmental action, movements against extractivism face other barriers in their task of challenging the hegemony of extractivism: how, for instance, can we visualize and communicate forms of extractivist "slow violence" that are degenerating life in ways that are not easily perceivable, such as long-term pollution of soil and underground water sources?[88] How can we communicate valuable information about the effects of certain industries in ways that are read as legitimate but that are also accessible and engaging? And how do we allow ourselves and others to imagine post-extractivist economies and societies as real possibilities, when the extractivist logic has repressed such capacity for imagination for so long?

In previous work, I proposed that within the context of social movements and community organizing, art has the potential to galvanize collective identities, to generate inclusive and creative political participation, and to transgress boundaries and open up spaces for prefigurative practice.[89] When I began conducting research in Argentina, I identified how these dynamics took place in the work and actions of different artists, activists and grassroots organizations. However, I also began to notice other patterns in the functions of artistic practices, which I identified as responsive to the pressing threats presented by the destruction and violence of the extractivist model, and to the reality of the local mainstream mediascape. Building first from the data and then drawing from different theories on art, politics, communication, and ontology, I combined the mechanisms I observed into a framework that consists of five functions: denunciation, documentation, democratization, deconstruction, and design.

By *denunciation*, I refer to the act of speaking up against injustice. Denunciation involves not only bringing attention to a problem but also pointing to those responsible in an attempt to hold them accountable and to obtain justice. In countries where the mainstream media serve to sustain an extractivist hegemony, alternative media and creative practices are important vehicles for visibilizing conflicts and for pressuring government officials and the justice system to respond to the claims of those affected by extraction. Focusing on climate change, but offering reflections that apply to the communication of several forms of environmental issues and conflicts, Julie Doyle argues that a main challenge in denunciation is "establishing interpretative frameworks," or "informing and making a particular issue relevant." She asks:

> How, then, to make climate change relevant, given the nature of the issue being scientifically complex, based upon predictive forecasting and model simulations? To pose this question is to foreground the more general problems of scientific empiricism, whose validity of observation/ prediction is itself limited by the methodological and epistemological frameworks through which knowledge is presented and authorized.[90]

The mechanism of denunciation is thus a complex one, as it is not only about visibilizing that which has been concealed, but also about challenging which issues are deemed relevant and whose knowledge and standpoint are valid.

*Documentation* on the other hand, refers to practical matters concerning conflicts such as documenting the effects of a particular extractive activity for use in judicial processes. But documentation is also about facilitating processes of memorialization. The aforementioned invisibilization of environmental and extractive conflicts on behalf of the mainstream media and the state means that affected communities, artists, documentary makers, and independent journalists bear the important task of constructing narratives about extractivism that move away from the promises of progress and look instead at the devastating effects experienced by communities and ecosystems. Narratives are paramount to movements for postextractivist futures because they are the way we make sense of the world we live in and the situation we are in: what the problem is, who the actors are, what is at stake.[91] Narrative can be a device for sharing knowledge and for world shaping,[92] helping us begin to imagine other kinds of worlds, as a first step toward designing other futures. But narratives also help us remember and honor those who have passed as a result of both the slow and extreme forms of violence of extractivism. Such processes of memorialization are therefore also important in the construction of movement identities.

*Democratization* refers to the sharing of information as well as to processes of community building that remake social bonds in manners that are nonextractive. It is a meaning-making as well as a social mechanism. In its meaning-making dimension, democratization refers to the opening up of narratives and public debates to include marginalized voices and acknowledge lived experience, art, ancestral knowledges, and popular research as valid sources of knowledge. In its social dimension, it involves creating horizontal spaces through the dynamics of art making, in other words, a political activation of relationality.[93]

*Deconstruction* in turn refers to the critique of constructs and their dissolution. Specifically, I refer to the questioning of hierarchical dualisms characteristic of modern thought, such as nature/culture. Deconstructing such dualisms and their components is a crucial task, because, as Timothy Morton argues, "one of the ideas inhibiting genuinely ecological politics, ethics, philosophy, and art is the idea of nature itself."[94] In my approach to deconstruction I borrow from the way the concept has been developed in different ways by Derrida, but I primarily use deconstruction in the "active" sense as mobilized by feminists in Latin America, in reference for instance to the everyday deconstruction of gender and the patriarchy.[95] Deconstruction therefore means questioning that which is presented as natural and exposing the inner workings of processes that are made to appear neutral as a step toward dismantling power and forms of oppression. The cases presented in this book show instances of deconstruction around concepts such as nature, development and gender. Deconstruction is also about history and scale: in order to deconstruct the elements of a particular conjuncture we must go back to different points in time (e.g., the colonial roots of extractivism, and not only the origins of international development) and think at different scales (from local to global). Important to consider as well is how we approach the task of deconstruction. The concept of *sentipensar*, which breaks down the distinction between thinking and feeling, is key here, as it allows us to break with the cycle of utilizing "the master's tools," as Audre Lorde would put it, in our attempt to undo the structures created by the modern paradigm.[96] In this way, I reconcile the idea of deconstruction with the decolonality project, and argue that deconstruction, in the feminist sense, gives way to the development of decolonial, post-extractivist aesthetics.

Finally, I develop the function of design, drawing from the work of Arturo Escobar and others who have written on both design and ontology. *Design* here is employed in a broad sense, which involves the creation of artwork, of processes, and of organizational structures. Design is thus practical, but it is also ontological: "ontological design stems from a seemingly simple observation: that in designing tools (objects, structures, policies, expert systems, discourses, even narratives) we are creating ways of being."[97] Design is ontological because our inventions alter society, and because through this it contributes to specific ontological shifts that are paramount toward creating worlds otherwise. Design is thus understood within what we could call an ontological turn. The ontological turn manifests an interest in the basic principles behind the ways we understand the world and different beings, the relationships between them, and how humans construct the world.[98]

Throughout the different chapters of this book, I demonstrate how artistic practices in anti- and postextractivist struggles activate these five functions. In the conclusion, I return to the five functions to discuss how they work together and build on each other in the context of antiextractivist struggles, with the aim of creating worlds otherwise.

## *About This Book*

This book has three main objectives. First, it aims to document and visibilize the myriad of creative practices currently taking place in Argentina and in other places in Latin America as part of the resistance to the advance of extractivism and with a view to creating worlds otherwise. By documentation, I mean producing a testimony of the practices and forms of knowledge that are emerging from different sectors that honors and sustains those practices for posterity. I frame this documentation around six key themes that underpin the narratives against extractivism generated by different social actors—which give the book its six-chapter structure—and in this way I situate my analysis of creative practices within the perspectives and frames of those at the frontlines. By visibilizing, in turn, I refer specifically to the aim of making such practices visible to a public beyond Latin America. The second aim of the book is to provide a framework for understanding the role of creative practices in relation to collective action against extractivism, a framework that can help us better understand how these movements operate and the possibilities afforded by creative practices. And third, by looking at different kinds of practices involved in worldmaking, considering their inner workings and processes as well as the kinds of narratives they put forward and the ways they might contribute to ontological shifts, I hope to provide reflections that inspire worldmaking practices elsewhere, ones that move us toward postextractivist forms of living.

*Creating Worlds Otherwise* is the result of twelve years of research and theory building on aesthetics and politics, five years of research in and on Argentina, and over a decade of engagement in socio-environmental movements, art activism, and radical pedagogy projects in Argentina and in the UK. It is the result of trips across Argentina, from the sites of fracking to those of open-pit mining. Of long conversations with inspiring people who opened their homes to me and told me their stories. And of a strongly felt need to make an intervention in the way we study artistic practices in relation to movements for social, political and ecological transformation, proposing an interdisciplinary and contextualized approach. In writing these pages, I tried to present the perspectives and experiences of those at the frontlines as directly as possible, and to build my theorization of artistic practices from the ground up, rather than impose preconceived theories on a body of data. I find it necessary to note, however, that a scholarly work of this kind still involves an act of mediation of those perspectives, and in order to come to fruition, it necessitated an element of distant reflection that is not afforded to those at the frontlines. While I offer this work from a position of continuous engagement, personal investment, and care, I also acknowledge the challenging and often problematic aspects of ethnographic research, especially when based at a Global North university.

This book is the result of situated, empirical research carried out in Argentina, as well as substantial secondary research on extractivism across Latin America. The findings and theoretical proposals I present are therefore primarily situated in the Argentinian context, its history, and imaginaries. However, the everyday realities of extractivism across the region and the movements of resistance to extraction share core similarities that allow us to study Argentine artistic practices alongside examples from other Latin American countries. This means additionally that findings from empirical research in Argentina can be useful in understanding certain dynamics in the wider region. In turn, at a time of global ecological crisis, this type of contextualized research acts as a counternarrative to universal narratives on the climate crisis, highlighting instead the ways extractivism has been generating various forms of socioenvironmental injustice beyond climate change. In this way, *Creating Worlds Otherwise* is a call to recognize the different standpoints from which we join the fight for social and environmental justice and against ecological destruction, as well as to support each other in our transitions to other worlds.

Each of the six chapters in this book is built around a narrative theme and features a range of examples that activate and mobilize such narratives. Through the analysis of these cases, each chapter demonstrates how artistic practices activate the five functions outlined earlier: denunciation, documentation, democratization, deconstruction, and design.

Chapter 1 looks at territory, specifically the ways that territory features in narratives against extractivism, and the ways that creative practices enact forms of territoriality that challenge the extractive logic. Here I draw from Raúl Zibechi's concept of territorialization, which serves to describe the rootedness of social movements in places that have been recuperated through struggles (be that literally or symbolically).[99] I also draw from Svampa's theorization of the ecoterritorial turn, which describes the present environmental dimension of social and territorial struggles in Latin America, contemplating the new languages of valorization generated by such movements.[100] In this chapter, I analyze the series of performance lectures Territorios en Conflicto, the group exhibition *Arte en territorio*, the collective mapping exercises of the duo Iconoclasistas, and the visual and musical practices of young Mapuche artists fighting extraction in their territories. I propose that in their activation of the functions of denunciation, documentation, democratization, and deconstruction, these artistic practices transform the way artists, participants, and audiences engage with the territory.

Chapter 2 looks at ecofeminism in Argentina and the Andean region. I first discuss the different types of (eco)feminisms present in Latin America and then present the recent wave of feminist movements that emerged with the cry of *¡Ni una menos!* The chapter considers how ecofeminist politics underpin the work of visual artists such as Claudia Tula and Pao Lunch in Argentina, and the multidisciplinary practices of the collectives Mujeres Creando in Bolivia and Miradas Críticas del Territorio desde el Feminismo in Ecuador. The analysis of these practices highlights the violence of extractivism exerted on bodies and territories and demonstrates how ecofeminist artistic practices can activate mechanisms of denunciation and deconstruction, specifically in relation to ingrained ideas about gender and the nature/culture divide.

Chapter 3 explores the legacy of human rights discourse and activism in Argentina and examines how the narratives, tropes, and aesthetic resources of the human rights movement have been adopted and adapted by anti- and postextractivist struggles. I first look at the history of human rights in Argentina and then discuss how contemporary movements articulate narratives about the defense of human rights and the rights of nature. Following this, I consider how different artistic practices activate mechanisms of denunciation and documentation. Specifically, I look at the ritualistic protests and performances of the community of Andalgalá, where people are fighting against open-pit mining; the performance actions of Fuerza Artística de Choque Comunicativo (FACC); the traveling *Museo del neoextractivismo* by the collective Etcétera, which acts as a site of denunciation of extractivism and memorialization of antiextractivist struggles; and the images of photojournalist Pablo Piovano, who depicts the effects of the use of agrochemicals on human life. I highlight how these practices activate functions of denunciation and documentation, and reflect on the role of human rights and the rights of nature discourses in the midst of present cultural transformations and necessary ontological shifts.

Chapter 4 engages with the emerging narrative of urban extractivism as a way of understanding dynamics of ecological destruction and social inequality in urban contexts. It looks at the role of the cultural and creative industries in processes of urban change hailed as progress and modernization and proposes the term *cultural extractivism* for naming the reproduction of an extractive logic in the cultural sector and the ways the cultural and creative industries participate in the reproduction of the extractivist model. I illustrate this theory by looking at the case of culture-led gentrification in the neighborhood of La Boca in Buenos Aires. Following this, I consider the cultural practices of resistance that emerge from the local community. I argue that such forms of resistance put forward a different type of logic, one that sees culture as a space for community building and democratization. I look as well at other creative practices that aim to democratize urban spaces, namely the subvertizing collective Proyecto Squatters, also in Buenos Aires, and the political print interventions of activists and artists from Casa 1234, who are fighting extractivism and state violence in the city of Córdoba. I consider their work in relation to the ethos of *autogestión* (autonomous self-management).

Chapter 5 looks at the ways that the notions of autonomy, sovereignty, and self-determination interact in the narratives of movements against extractivism and toward postextractivist futures. The chapter begins with a discussion of the significance of autonomy as an ethos of politically engaged art making in Argentina. It then discusses forms of collective action demanding sovereignty from transnational capital, with an emphasis on artistic interventions against the influence of international and multilateral organizations in Argentina and in Latin America, specifically the exhibition *Malvenido FMI* and the performance action *Procesión pagana del Plumero de La Pampa* during the 2018 G20 summit in Buenos Aires. Following from this, I analyze the artistic intervention United Killers of Benetton, which draws connections between colonialism, state violence, and the power of transnational capital. Toward the end, the chapter revisits the case of the struggle against open-pit mining in Andalgalá, to examine how, over the years, the local assembly has developed a narrative that positions them not only against mining but also for autonomy and postextractivist ways of living. The cases analyzed here give way to a discussion on the mechanisms of documentation, democratization, and deconstruction.

The final chapter of the book, Chapter 6, focuses on ideas and practices that envision and enact worlds otherwise. In other words, the chapter focuses more directly on the alternative social, cultural, knowledge, and economic practices put forward by movements toward postextractivism. In this chapter I build on Escobar's work on design,[101] and I look at how practices like agroecology, environmental education, and autonomous cultural production are designing structures, processes, and socialities that prefigure nonextractive ways of being, contributing to ontological "shifts through design" that challenge the core notions underpinning the extractivist development paradigm. In the final section of the chapter, I look at how the COVID-19 pandemic triggered new proposals for ecological transitions, proposals that are based on years of theory and practice and that responded to a moment of deep crisis by putting forward visions of how to transcend extractivism and social inequality.

The conclusion to the book returns to the five functions of art in the context of anti- and postextractivist struggles, as a way of recapping the findings that emerged from the analysis of the different cases presented. I develop the framework more in depth and describe how all five functions work together, and finally offer a reflection on the potential of transnational collective action for worlds otherwise.

*Creating Worlds Otherwise* aims to make a series of contributions. First, it is an invitation to expand our understanding of extractivism and consider more fully the ways it constitutes a cultural phenomenon. This means considering how cultural production can be extractive in its processes and can sustain the legitimacy of extractivism, but also how culture is a ground for contesting the very roots of extractivism, to weaken its hold in the social imaginary, and to allow the envisioning and enacting of other worlds. In this way, the book is also a call to expand the remits of political ecology and give more space to the analysis of art and culture as political and ecological phenomena that are conditioned by and in turn give shape to extractive societies.

*Creating Worlds Otherwise* also aims to champion an understanding of artistic practice that is contextual and simultaneously considers processes, material conditions, and ontological aspects.[102] Through the provision of a framework that consists of five complementary functions, I propose a way of approaching analysis that is holistic, and that considers these different perspectives in the way that artistic practices develop and to what effects. In other words, the book addresses the question of *how* "submerged perspectives," as termed by Macarena Gómez-Barris, are expressed through artistic practices with a view to creating worlds otherwise.[103]

Finally, in its exploration of the main themes and narratives that frame art and collective action against extractivism, this book contributes to a renewed understanding of Argentine and Latin American politics. It highlights, for instance, the evolution of key concepts, frameworks, and narratives (e.g., rights of nature, *cuerpo-territorio*, sovereignty), including their mobility and the ways they are currently used by different actors. This, in turn, contributes to an understanding of the current conjuncture. Importantly, what *Creating Worlds Otherwise* seeks to achieve is an understanding of how current artistic practices in Argentina and Latin America frame and address matters of ecological breakdown as inherently social and political, providing important lessons for the study and practice of both art and activism at a time of global crisis.

# 1 Territories in Conflict

## *Art and Territorialization*

> The picture that appears, one that becomes increasingly intense, is that the long-awaited new world is being born in the movements' spaces and territories, embedded in the gaps that are opening up in capitalism.
>
> – Raúl Zibechi, *Territories in Resistance*

IN THIS BOOK, I build on political theorist Raúl Zibechi's understanding of territory as the space from which transformational movements emerge. It is also in and through territories that we can "build a new social organization collectively, where new subjects take shape and materially and symbolically appropriate their space."[1] Debates surrounding territory are complex because territory can be approached from multiple perspectives, from cultural to material-economic. Territorial conflicts play out in the judicial and political spheres, but also in the cultural sphere, where important battles over meaning and identity take place.[2]

Indeed, the imaginaries of the different territories that make up the geography of what is now known as the Argentine Republic and that began to emerge with the colonization of the region have been integral to the formation of the national history, a history that has become increasingly contested. The visual arts—from landscape paintings to public art—have been crucial in solidifying and visualizing those imaginaries. This precise theme was at the center of the exhibition *Una historia de la imaginación en la Argentina: Visiones de la pampa, el litoral y el altiplano desde el siglo XIX a la actualidad* (A history of the imagination in Argentina: Visions of the pampas, the Litoral, and the Altiplano from the nineteenth century to today), curated by Javier Villa for the Museum of Modern Art of Buenos Aires in 2019. The exhibition proposed "a journey across land and time" focusing on three axes: nature, the female body, and violence.[3] Featuring the work of one hundred artists and spanning more than two centuries, the show examined past and present depictions of the genocide of indigenous peoples, interrogated humans' relationship to the rest of nature and to the land, deconstructed representations of gender and the body across time, and reflected on the legacy of different cultures and cosmologies across the Argentine territory. The exhibition engaged with ideas of both landscape and territory—which, explains Raffestin, stand for the "seen" and the "lived" respectively.[4] It also posed the question of whether we can abandon a traditional cannon of male landscape painters from Buenos Aires in the construction of territorial imaginaries in Argentina, and instead "trace out a visual lineage arising out [of] a geographic imagination?'[5]

Engaging with this invitation to activate the geographical imagination, this chapter offers a way into contemporary understandings and experiences of territory under extractivism by conversing with the creative practices of a range of actors, from frontline activists to artists and curators. To do this, I engage with three main perspectives on territory: the territorialization of movements, the ecoterritorial turn, and the decolonization of territories. In addition, I look at the particularities of artistic practices dealing with territory in Argentina and the Latin American context, combining the framework of "site-specific art" (art that engages with the physical and/or symbolic characteristics of the space where it is developed or displayed) with the local concept of *trabajo territorial* (territorial work).

In a context in which the global is favored over the local, focusing on the notion of territory—and specifically, Latin American conceptions of *territorialidad*—can be a political, subversive act.[6] Examining conceptions of territory through the lens of creative practice, I propose, allows us to better understand how anti- and postextractivist movements situate themselves in the territory while offering valuable insights into the functions of art within such movements, namely as a vehicle of documentation, denunciation, democratization, deconstruction, and design.

### *The Territorialization of Movements and the Ecoterritorial Turn*

Zibechi argues that the wave of neoliberalism that shook Latin America in the 1980s "ruptured the territorial and symbolic forms of production and reproduction upon which popular sectors' world view and daily activity rested."[7] With this also came a change in the organization, strategies, and vision of political mobilization embodied in a new set of movements and political subjects with distinct identities and strategies, but with a marked territorial approach. These include the Landless Workers' Movement in Brazil mobilizing for land redistribution and agrarian reform, water warriors in Bolivia fighting for access to water as a human right, the Zapatista Army of National Liberation (EZLN) in Chiapas putting forward an autonomous organization and communitarian management of the commons, and the movements of unemployed workers in Argentina promoting horizontal forms of politics and production. In general, adds Zibechi, such movements have a tendency for organizational forms that reject hierarchies and clean-cut divisions of labor and instead emulate community and family life, and a heightened attention to and regards toward the environment.[8]

While territory and "insurgent spatial practices" have always been part of social mobilization, Lopes de Souza argues that this has become more prominent since the mid-twentieth century and begun to accelerate toward the end of it, becoming more and more prominent today.[9] What these movements aim for is a "*genuine socio-spatial development*," in other words, an "emancipatory change of social relations and spatial organization on the basis of collective and individual autonomy as the ultimate goal."[10] These movements are characterized by their engagement in processes of territorialization, meaning that they "have roots in spaces that have been recuperated or otherwise secured through long (open or underground) struggles."[11] Territorialization, argues Zibechi, is the poor's response to the de-territorialization of production and the displacement of popular sectors into new territories (e.g., precarious settlements) brought about by neoliberalism.

Processes of deterritorialization and (re)territorialization can be identified throughout history and across different geographies, though each case carries different characteristics and arguably follows different logics. An often-cited example is the displacement of peasants by the Enclosures Act in England and their subsequent "reterritorialization onto textiles looms as wage-labor in the nascent garment industry."[12] Territorialized movements, adds Zibechi, are also characterized by the search for autonomy, and their political autonomy relies on their material autonomy.[13] They are invested in affirming and revalorizing their culture, be that working class, indigenous, or peasant.

In Argentina, the territorialization of movements can be identified in both rural and urban spaces. The case of the *piqueteros,* a movement of unemployed workers emerging in the mid-1990's, exemplifies the territorialization of protest through the tactic of strategic road blockades and through the surge of workers' cooperatives and associations that aimed to build material autonomy, a trend that continued in the wake of the 2001 economic crisis with the occupied and recuperated factories.[14] Such experiences have been important in setting precedent for other forms of territorialized, popular, urban movements and how they organize, share resources, and sustain themselves.

Nowadays, territorialization processes take place within a complex scenario in which different logics carrying different valorizations intersect, such as those attached to corporations, the state, activists, and communities implicated in ecoterritorial conflicts.[15] In the context of an expanding extractive frontier, since circa the 2000s socioenvironmental movements in Latin America have begun to build a language of valorization of the territory, which Maristella Svampa describes as an ecoterritorial turn. This turn enhances the territorialization process of movements through a heightened awareness of ecology and its connection to various social issues. It involves as well the convergence of different matrixes and languages, including the indigenous community organizational form and the autonomous narrative, and more recently and with great force, a feminist perspective.[16] The combination and centering of these elements has facilitated the construction of common frames for collective action that not only act as alternative forms of interpretation of the current conjuncture, but also act as producers of a collective subjectivity.[17]

These ecoterritorial movements have thus generated a language of valorization surrounding territoriality that is opposed to the resource-centered vision of development upheld by governments, multilateral organizations, and transnational corporations. Some of the issues at the forefront of the ecoterritorial turn are food sovereignty, environmental justice, *sumak kawsay* (or *buen vivir*) and the collective management of the commons.[18] The commons are a key concept here, as they refer to those elements that guarantee and sustain ways of life in a determinate territory; therefore, the struggle over the commons is not about control over "natural resources," but rather, it is a dispute over the construction of a specific kind of territoriality.[19]

Indeed, what we see in today's movements against extractivism and for postextractivist futures are not only forms of organizing that tend toward horizontality and autonomy and that aim to decentralize the management of the commons. What we see is also a rethinking of the notions of the commons themselves and of the relation between humans and the different elements of the territories they inhabit. We see a heightened awareness of interdependence and the merger of indigenous knowledge with political horizons such as autonomy, as well as the use of institutional tools like the claim for territorial rights and the rights of nature, which I discuss more in detail in Chapter 3. In the following section, I examine how the notions of territorialization and the ecoterritorial turn are represented and mobilized in cultural production that engages with contemporary social conflicts by looking at the series of performance lectures Territorios en Conflicto.

## VISIBILIZING TERRITORIES IN CONFLICT

It is not casual that one of the ways that artists have approached the matter of territory is performance. Engaging with the territory and its multiple conflicts involves engaging with its materiality, its identity, the reality of violence, and the multisensory experience of being situated in it. In performance art, the body becomes territory and a channel for the exploration and expression of that situated experience, now recontextualized for an audience.

Territorios en Conflicto (Territories in conflict) was a program of performance lectures at the Teatro Nacional Cervantes in Buenos Aires, which ran from April to November 2017. The program consisted of six shows, each focusing on a different conflict in Argentina and offering different approaches to the understanding of territory and of a series of pressing local (and global) issues. The series was curated by writer, editor, and cultural producer Gabriela Massuh and novelist and critic Carlos Gamerro, who invited artists, journalists, and researchers to create shows based on, or related to, their own practice, combining the languages of critical essay and performance. The six shows of the series covered the following themes, each referring to a kind of conflict framed as territorial: food production, the use of agrochemicals, urban renewal processes and dispossession, the demise of railways, land ownership in Patagonia, and the loss of indigenous culture and languages.[20]

Massuh explains that the aim of the series was to highlight conflicts that are underreported and to provide a platform for voices and stories from the frontlines that are invisibilized by the mainstream media. In a personal interview, Massuh suggested that the media avoids topics linked to death, "such as the cancer caused by glyphosate [a herbicide used in GMO agriculture], the pollution of water caused by cyanide [used in mining], the lack of oxygen caused by the cutting of trees, the uncontrollable construction of buildings, the floods, and above all, the disappearance of languages and cultures."[21] According to Gamerro, another objective of the series was to represent problems from across the country and feature artists from different locations, thus moving away from the media blackout that obscures the socioenvironmental conflicts taking place beyond the city of Buenos Aires.[22] Indeed, as Maristella Svampa notes, there is a stark divide between large cities and rural areas in Argentina, which is particularly evident when it comes to ecoterritorial conflicts.[23] Struggles over mining, fracking, factory agriculture, and indigenous territorial rights, among others, tend to be perceived as contained issues happening at a distance by the majority of those living in Buenos Aires, which houses one third of the country's population in its metropolitan area.

One of the shows in Territorios en Conflicto was titled *El manto* and created by visual artist Eduardo Molinari, whose research-based work includes a strand focusing on soya production. One of the issues that Molinari explores through this work is what he terms the regime of visibility generated by agribusiness, a regime that invisibilizes the effects of the current agricultural model on human health, ecosystems, and cultures, and that constructs an innocuous image for itself.[24] Large-scale GMO soya agriculture, argues Molinari, should be read as constitutive of a broader social, political, and cultural model: a *sojacracia* (soyacracy), sustained through this particular regime of visibility. Molinari argues that "in the *sojacracia*, critical thinking is a negative value."[25] Molinari's regime, which materializes and becomes visible in the shape of endless fields of soya crops, is comparable to Arturo Escobar's reflections on the sugar cane landscapes in Cali, Colombia, where a beautiful landscape obfuscates violent power relations and destructive practices, as well as "the ontological occupation of local relational worlds" by the rational of extractivism.[26]

A related line of inquiry in Molinari's work is territory. In a conversation we had, he shared his belief that one of the problems we currently face is identifying the spatial categories we would like to inhabit, pointing in this way to the conflicting languages of valorization discussed by Svampa:

> In the 1990s, and even during the 2001 economic and social crisis in Argentina, people spoke a lot about the crisis of the Nation State, but I think what exploded was not the Nation State, but rather the

> State of rights; we no longer hold any acquired rights. . . . In my view this ends up becoming a geographical issue concerning the place you inhabit, because there is no guarantee of your rights. That is why territories are in conflict.[27]

Molinari's work is concerned in this sense with practices of territorialization and deterritorialization under the reign of extractivism, an issue he addresses though a research-based artistic practice. He conducts this work in archives and libraries, followed by trips to places he is interested in researching, with the aim of establishing a participatory kind of practice in which he engages in a dialogue with the territory and its inhabitants. His main interest is not portraying the people he encounters, but rather producing a register of the spatial-temporal conditions under which phenomena such as extractive activities develop (see figs. 1.1, 1.2, and 1.3). In turn, he also seeks to understand how people live in territories under those conditions, and how we can break through the regime of (in)visibility to develop new forms of territoriality. Molinari's work denounces the mechanisms that capital employs to naturalize its operations and makes visible the idea of different logics of territoriality.

Through his work, Molinari champions the role of art as a knowledge creating discipline,[28] one that takes an increasingly central role in intervening in public discourse when much scientific knowledge is underpinned by an extractive logic and an economic valorization intertwined with corporate interests. Indeed, much of Molinari's work is embedded in an ongoing collective, artistic research project titled *Arte y territorio: Gramáticas, topografías, cuerpos y poderes* (Art and territory: Grammars, topographies, bodies and powers), which he directs at the National University of the Arts in Argentina. The project proposes "a dialogical dynamic of conversation and commensality with territories and their inhabitants (human and nonhuman), promoting the act of listening through artistic tools and practices that are especially attuned to local knowledges, inhabiting processes of co-teaching and co-learning."[29]

With the ideas of co-production, experimentation, and the knowledge-creation potential of the arts in mind, the series Territorios en Conflicto set out to experiment with the format of performance

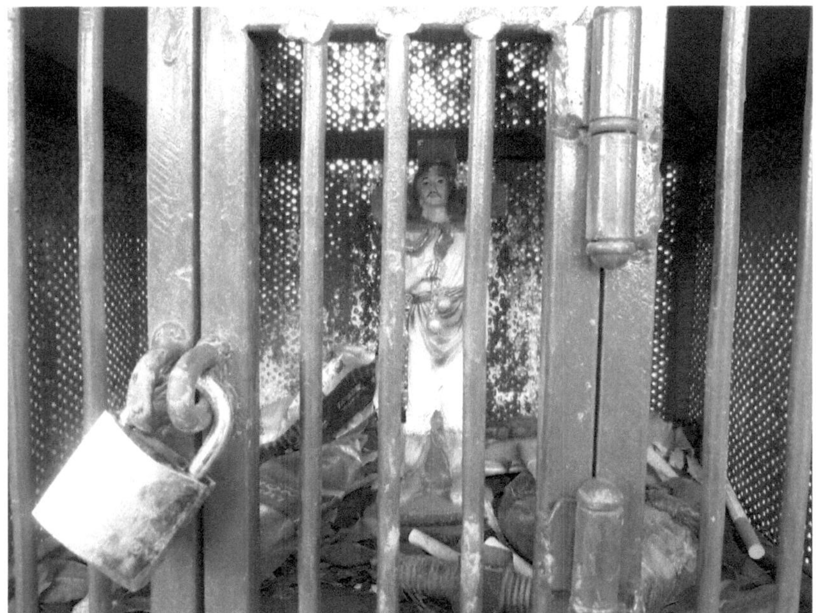

FIGURE 1.1. Eduardo Molinari/Archivo Caminante, *Gauchito Gil*, Tartagal, province of Salta, Argentina. DocAC/2017. Figures 1.1–3 are all from *El manto: Nuevas noticias de la República Unida de la Soja*, part of the performance lecture series Territorios en Conflicto, Teatro Nacional Cervantes, Buenos Aires, 2017.

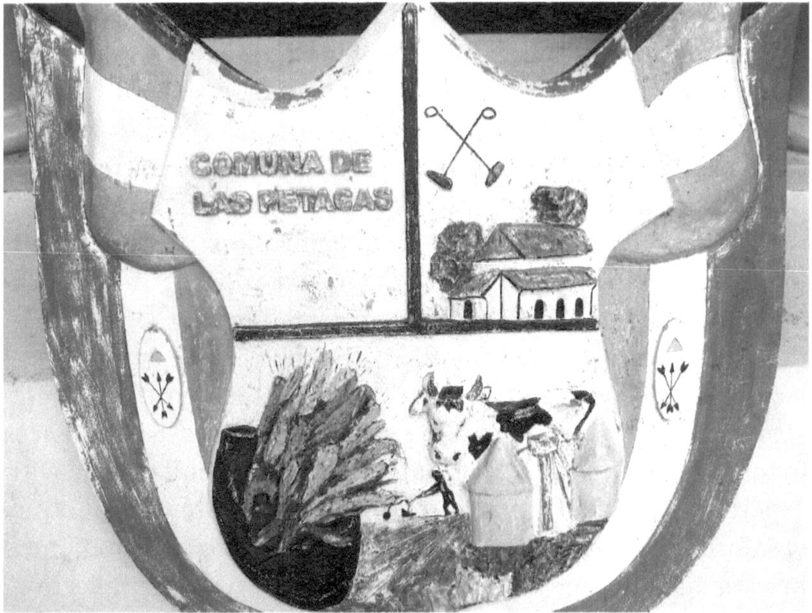


FIGURE 1.2. Eduardo Molinari/Archivo Caminante, *Escudo municipal de las Petacas*, province of Santa Fé, Argentina. DocAC/2017.

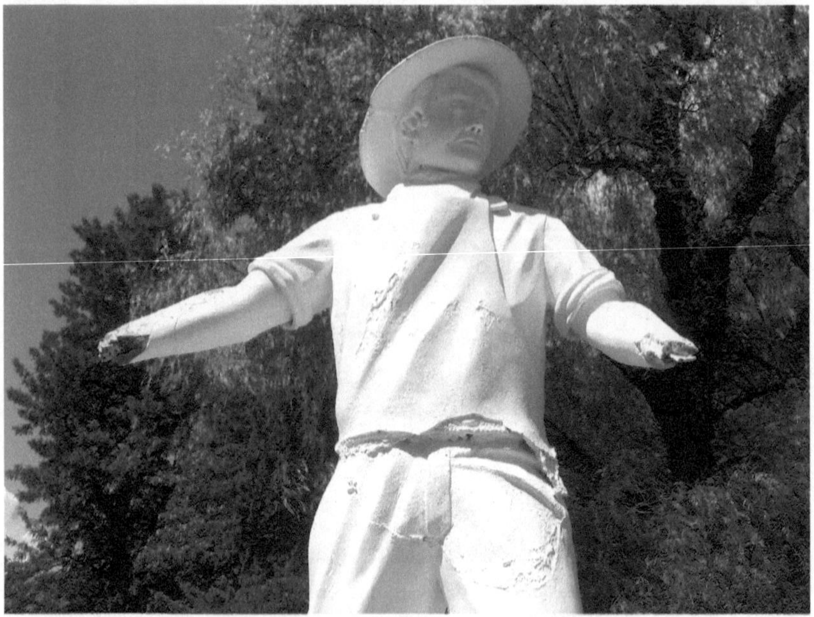

FIGURE 1.3. Eduardo Molinari/Archivo Caminante, *Monumento al sembrador*, San Jorge, province of Santa Fé, Argentina. DocAC/2017.

lectures, one which by then had become familiar in visual art circuits but not so much in the Argentine theatre scene. From Joseph Beuys to Chris Burden, contemporary artists with different kinds of trajectories have used performance lectures "to blur the lines separating art from discourse about art."[30] Performance lectures often build on an ethos of teaching as art and engage in conversation with the framework of institutional critique, starting from "the belief that consciousness stemming from teaching and learning can lead to a new way to live in society."[31] In the case of Territorios en Conflicto, the modality of performance lectures allowed for a number of things. In the first place, it created a space for visual artists and writers to address live audiences for a sustained period. It also allowed them to collaborate with experts from different fields and to communicate vast amounts of information on relatively unknown conflicts to such audiences in ways that offer renewed perspectives and encourage reflection. Thus, while maintaining the languages of the visual and performing arts and the aesthetic considerations that come with them, performance lectures became in this case the embodiment of art as "militant research," a kind of reflexive, political research that seeks to advance movements.[32]

Speaking of the political role of art in a context of expanding extraction, Massuh said,

> I think it is good when theatre has a good reference to contemporary issues. . . . Argentine theatre, literature, and visual arts need a stronger connection to contemporary affairs, a stronger problematization of contemporary issues. Because there is a universalist vision of art that has lost its sense of reference and the problematizing between art and realism. There is a lot of experimentation going on, but content is very traditional. Reality doesn't hurt in this kind of art.[33]

We can interpret Massuh's reflection as a call for an art of denunciation and deconstruction. It is not just about visibilizing and drawing attention to an issue; it is also about doing that in a language that allows people to engage with it and gain a deeper understanding and that encourages the denaturalization of hegemonic narratives. But there are several barriers to this kind of art in a context in which critique and dissent are permitted and sometimes even encouraged, but indirect acts of censorship impose unspoken limits. In my conversation with Molinari, he expressed dissatisfaction at the way Territorios en Conflicto was received by the media and the cultural establishment. In his view, the series was quickly dismissed by many in the cultural sector for failing to live up to the standards of theatre, and at the same time was not recognized for its interdisciplinary and experimental character either. In addition to this, the mainstream media did not offer the kind of coverage expected from a performance program at a reputable national theatre. Molinari shared that a major conservative newspaper interviewed him in relation to his performance lecture but then failed to run the interview, and he believes this was due to his statements about extractivism and the economic sector.[34]

## *Territorial Work / Art in Territory*

Territorios en Conflicto is a valuable example of politically engaged artistic practice operating within the realm of public cultural institutions. But there are other kinds of artistic practices that instead emerge from the sphere of social movements and community organizing and that, as a result, not only think and represent the territory but also facilitate processes of territorialization. Such dynamics are present in the pieces that made up the 2017 exhibition *Arte en territorio* and in the collective mapping work of Iconoclasistas. Before analyzing these cases, I first discuss two concepts that I propose are particularly useful in order to understand creative practices *in* territory: *trabajo territorial* (territorial work) and site-specific art.

In Argentina the term *trabajo territorial* is associated with the *piquetero* organizations of unemployed workers that emerged in the 1990s such as MTD Solano (Movimiento de Trabajadores Desempleados de Solano) and to the subsequent neighborhood assemblies that emerged in response to the 2001 economic crisis.[35] Soon after the mass protests of late 2001, members of the newly formed neighborhood assemblies turned their focus to address the pressing needs of local communities, from the economic to the social and the cultural.[36] Territorial work thus encompasses a broad range of activities, including running popular kitchens and providing health assistance, cultural activities, and different manifestations of solidarity economies, that follow a kind of nonhierarchical, and in many ways anticapitalist, approach.[37] It is based on an ethics of care, and it follows a situated approach that responds to the needs of a particular territory.

In Latin American urban centers, different groups and movements carry out practices that can be framed as territorial work, in what Halvorsen describes as a "context of informal state presence combined with neo-colonial practices of urban 'accumulation by dispossession.'"[38] Territorial work can be autonomous and horizontal or embedded within the dynamics of party politics. Taking the case of Brazil, Lopes de Souza distinguishes between the local manifestations of "luta *de* bairro" (struggle/activism *of* the neighborhood) and "luta a partir *do* bairro" (struggle/activism *from* the neighborhood).[39] The first is usually limited and has a greater tendency toward clientelism and patronage, and the second is a kind of struggle that begins with local problems but goes beyond this to become an emancipatory movement addressing wider structural issues. The latter looks to create systemic change, moving away from extractive, individualist logics and reinforcing bonds of care and solidarity in everyday activities.

In order to understand the ways that art and territorial work merge, it is useful to also consider frameworks emerging from the field of art theory, as is the case of site-specific art. Site-specific art is a term used to describe art that is created for a specific location, responding to the specificities of that site.[40] According to Kwon, site-specific art can be multilayered, if we consider as sites the physical location of an artwork, the art world that frames it, and in addition, the social/political/environmental/economic issues (or "sites') the work addresses.[41] In other words, sites can be both spatial and (inter)textual.[42] Some forms of site-specific art engage with local communities by adopting processes that allow participants to have agency in the development of the work and to use art as a way of exploring and/or transforming their connection to a space.[43] Focusing on the relational aspects of such work, Grant Kester uses the term "dialogical art" to refer to the kinds of participatory processes that allow transformative instances for those involved, giving way to a kind of participation that is grounded,[44] contrary to the more "superficial" forms of participation offered by some artists/institutions.[45] Kester argues that in dialogical art "the particular constellation of forces in place at a given site, brought into conjunction with the consciousness and predisposition of participants, are generative in ways that exceed both the conditions of site and the subjectivity of individual actors."[46]

## *ARTE EN TERRITORIO*

A range of artistic practices embodying the ethos of territorial work and the processes of site-specific art were presented as part of the third edition of the exhibition *Arte en territorio* at the Centro Cultural

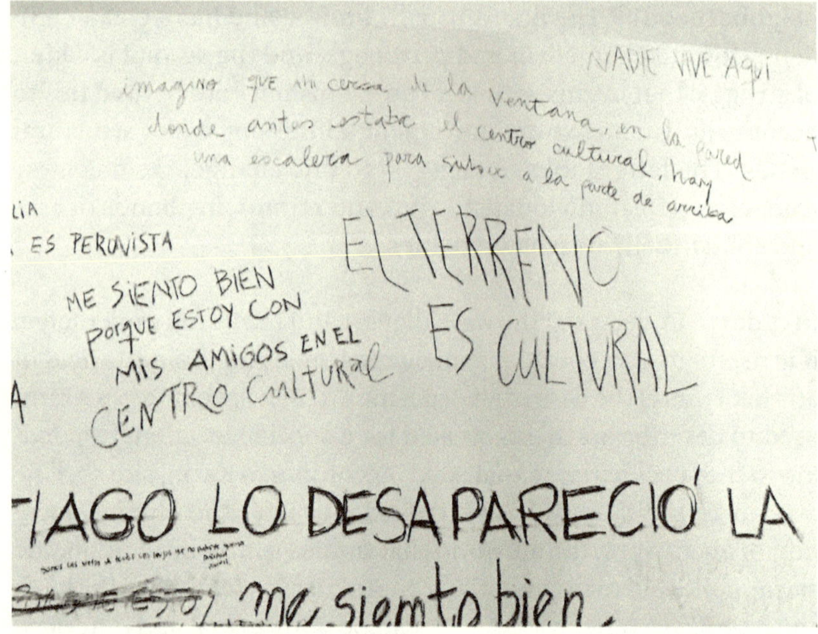


FIGURE 1.4. Writing on the wall from the exhibition *Arte en territorio* reading "The territory is cultural." Photo by the author.

de la Memoria Haroldo Conti, Buenos Aires, running from September 2017 to February 2018. The exhibition aimed at highlighting experiences of art in territory in which artistic practices offer instances of transformation. According to the exhibition's curatorial statement, bringing together experiences of art from different territories is a way of connecting ways of feeling and being in the world. It is to conform a new territory that holds the singularities of inhabited spaces and the potential of creative action.[47] The exhibition brought together the work of a range of artist collectives that engage different communities within different territories, including mural painting with children in a hospital, photography projects where young people produce images of their own environment, and a project for the legal recognition of a space that is already functioning as a community cultural center. In this way, it adopted a flexible understanding of territory that has the potential to include any form of space, that is socially constructed, and in a constant state of flux.[48]

We can understand the kinds of works included in the exhibition as both site-specific art and instances of territorial work. However, the manifestations of these approaches are varied. One of the collectives that took part in the exhibition is Colectivo Cielo Abierto. Their main project is an open-air cultural center called Centro Cultural a Cielo Abierto Armando Labollita (Open-Air Cultural Center Armando Labollita), itself an art project that aims to enact transformations in a precarious block of houses under the Pueyrredón bridge, south of Buenos Aires. The cultural center hosts different sorts of activities, from festivals to markets, meals, and art workshops, and includes an organic community garden allotment. All of these activities respond to the wants and needs of local inhabitants, contributing to community building, training, and professionalization. At the same time, the artists frame the cultural center itself as a socially and politically committed art project. The collective has been active in this space since 2014. Their participation in the exhibition, as stated in the exhibition's website, acts as a public request for the state to grant them rights to the space they occupy so they can build infrastructures that would help them better deliver their activities.[49] In this way, the project puts forward a local initiative in response to the absence of the state that continues to carry on despite this absence. Its day-to-day functioning in the community acts as a performative appeal to the state—complementing institutional vehicles—for the project to be legally recognized and become sustainable in the long term.

Other participants in the exhibition, such as the organization Acción Mutante, the project Ojo de Pez, and the independent publisher Editorial Parador, work with children, young people, and/or families from marginalized backgrounds and areas of the city of Buenos Aires and its suburbs, facilitating opportunities for engaging in forms of cultural production such as photography, film, and books. Ojo de Pez, a project that began in 2007 as part of the activities program of the community organization Centro Conviven, engages with children and young people through photography and film, providing them with tools so they can create images about their environment. Since its inception, the project has operated in a number of neighborhoods in the city of Buenos Aires, with the objective of enacting inclusive social change. In their words, the images produced by participants reveal "that which the official and visible city tends to try to hide . . . through the non-judgmental perspective of young artists. These images shed light on objects, people, landscapes, but also ideas and dreams."[50] This statement remits to Molinari's work on the regime of visibility of extractivism, and the need to make visible that which is concealed. Photography, in this case, gives marginalized children and young people the tools to uncover the workings of the city, and to develop their own ideas about the territory they inhabit and the changes they want to see in it.

Such initiatives aim at activating creative, political subjectivities and emboldening actors, as well as generating platforms for the expression of their views and experiences. Editorial Parador, on the other hand, presented a new edition of a series of children's books that were banned during the last civic-military dictatorship in Argentina (1976–83), now illustrated by children in a transitory shelter and bound by their mothers. The choice of books is not coincidental, as it references the history and territoriality of the exhibiting space: the Centro Cultural de la Memoria Haroldo Conti is located at a former site of clandestine interrogation and torture during the dictatorship. The work thus enacts a multilayered form of site specificity, responding to the needs of particular communities and referencing the painful history of the exhibition site.

*Arte en territorio* follows a holistic understanding of territory that is not only interested in exploring the characteristics of a site—be this a rural area, a city, or a specific institution—but is also invested in producing certain forms of territoriality. The works that make up the exhibition engage with the particular histories and socioeconomic dynamics of the local context, which determine the ways that territories and their imaginaries are produced and the way people experience them. This includes urban dynamics of violence and dispossession, and an extractive economic model that conditions not only the makeup of the country's economy but also a series of territorial dynamics such as the distribution and use of land, the accumulation of wealth, and patterns of internal migration. In addition, territory emerges as a centering element in the work of all these collectives because of the local history of territorial organizing of social movements and communities, which underpins different forms of socially and politically engaged art and community work.

The works in this exhibition put forward a relational understanding of territory, one that is embedded in community bonds and in an experience of territory as constitutive of identities and vice versa.[51] The framework of site-specificity is useful for understanding how such notions of territory are translated into particular aesthetics: in this case, relational, dialogical aesthetics that center process over output and place value on images of quotidian places—in the case of the photography and film projects, for instance—as a way of offering an alternative visualization of urban spaces, one that reflects the experiences of the marginalized. The works in the exhibition thus serve as acts of documentation of people's realities and as democratization of the construction of a public vision of the city. Thinking of these projects as territorial work, on the other hand, allows us to consider them within the social and political context of Latin America, and to articulate artistic creation with wider social phenomena. We could therefore understand "art in territory" as the meeting of site-specific art and territorial work.

## THE COLLECTIVE MAPPING OF ICONOCLASISTAS

Another example of art in territory, one that has become emblematic in struggles against extractivism in Argentina and other parts of Latin America, is the collective mapping techniques developed by Iconoclasistas. In what follows I discuss the duo's history and their process, and then reflect on the affordances of collective mapping as a creative tool of denunciation, democratization and design in the context of territorial conflicts.

Iconoclasistas consists of Pablo Ares (a graphic designer / visual activist) and Julia Risler (a communications researcher / organizer), and it was formally conceived in 2006 with the intention of providing visual resources for the communication practices of political and cultural organizations and social movements. Julia and Pablo realized that a broad range of new sociopolitical practices had emerged in recent years, but the communications language used by these groups belonged to older political traditions and would benefit from updated forms.

One of their first projects was *Cosmovisiones Rebeldes* (2007–2010; Rebel cosmovisions). This consisted of a set of infographics combining visual representations with condensed data in the form of text, and it looked at issues such as "the postmodern city" and "neocolonial looting." Julia and Pablo printed them on cheap paper and then shipped them to environmental assemblies and communities across the country, who used them as educational material or as tools for generating public awareness. From this first form of engagement with assemblies across the country and from the feedback they received and the interest people showed in developing their own maps came the idea for collective mapping tours, which they began to develop in 2008. In an interview, Julia explained that the kind of collaborative cartographical exercises that took place in Latin America until then were led by NGOs working with indigenous peoples, using a top-down approach and following the working dynamics of the state.[52] In order to differentiate themselves from this approach they came up with the term *mapeo colectivo* or "collective mapping." In their own words, collective mappings "energize a critical perception of territories and collective processes of subjectivation and the production of meaning, through the activation of images and graphics."[53] Collective mapping builds on the understanding that everyone has the capability to adopt a bird's eye view of the territory, one that is perceptive, sensorial, and critical.

Iconoclasistas began their collective mapping tours by doing an open call through which they offered to travel to territories in conflict. Julia explained that one of their objectives from the beginning was to work with groups and movements to build "panoramas, cosmovisions, situated stories, in order to amplify a specific conflict or issue into a broader perspective."[54] They began to receive invitations, and so they would take their signs and prints with them on the bus, set up an exhibition of their work upon arrival, and use it as a conversation starter for the collective mapping. In this way, they were able to connect urban and rural conflicts from different parts of the country and start conversations on the common roots of different struggles.

According to Iconoclasistas, "The starting point for processes of collective research are popular, local, and community knowledges, because it is necessary to replenish and work with those perspectives that are invisibilized or underrated by academic and institutional knowledges, through the state agencies that manage interventions in the territories."[55] In addition, Julia shared that the dynamic of the workshops evolved through trial and error. At the beginning, they were exclusively focused on negative things happening in each area, from pollution to the dismissal of workers. But participants were leaving the workshops feeling depressed. So they thought this through, and decided it would be good to look as well at experiences of resistance and organizing and to include these in the maps where appropriate (see fig. 1.5).

Two of such maps that came out of Iconoclasistas's collective mapping looked at open-pit mining and soya production. These were the result of collaborative work with assemblies from across the country, in person during national meetings of the Unión de Asambleas Ciudadanas (UAC; Union of Citizen Assemblies), and then through continued, long-distance conversation with the assemblies and with people with expert knowledge on relevant matters. The maps came out in 2010 for the occasion of the bicentennial celebrations, during which social organizations, indigenous and peasant groups, artists, and movements came together to celebrate the *otro bicentenario* (a bicentennial otherwise), a countercelebration that challenged the persistent coloniality of the Argentine state and its unequal, extractivist model. Iconoclasistas printed the maps and hanged them at the site of the celebration, the square of the two congresses in Buenos Aires, alongside other graphics they had made on the historic processes of rebellion of afro-descendent, peasant, and creole communities. The aim was to visibilize the struggles and resistance that have carried on for hundreds of years since the colonization of the Americas.

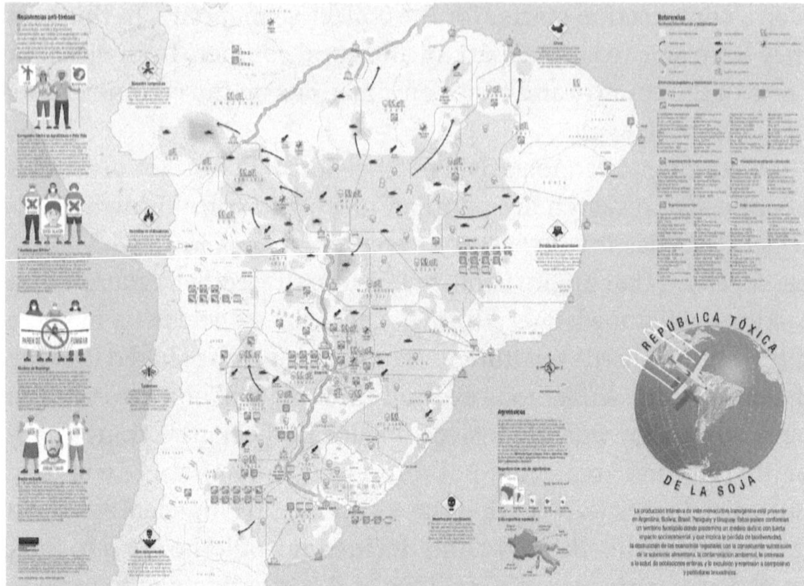


FIGURE 1.5. *República Tóxica de la Soja / Toxic Republic of Soy.* Map resulting from a workshop designed and facilitated by Iconoclasistas, as part of an encounter organized by Acción por la Biodiversidad (Argentina) and BASE-IS (Paraguay), with support from Fundación Rosa Luxemburgo, September 2019, Asunción del Paraguay. Printed in April 2020. Image by Iconoclasistas.

In 2013, Iconoclasistas consolidated the learnings from years of collective mapping and published a collective mapping manual. Mapping continues to be a fundamental element of their work because they see it as "a practice for rememorizing [by] organizing information on a graphic medium, which does not need to be geographic: it can also be a body, an institution, a map of communication discourses on a specific theme."[56]

The collective mapping of Iconoclasistas can be understood as a form of "heretic cartography," which challenges the notions underpinning the practice and the way it is utilized by states and corporations.[57] Heretic cartography adopts mapping tools in order to produce maps that counter hegemonic narratives, and that meet the needs of the oppressed. Furthermore, in the work of Iconoclasistas we see not only an appropriation of tools but also a shift in power dynamics and processes toward a bottom-up, collective approach,

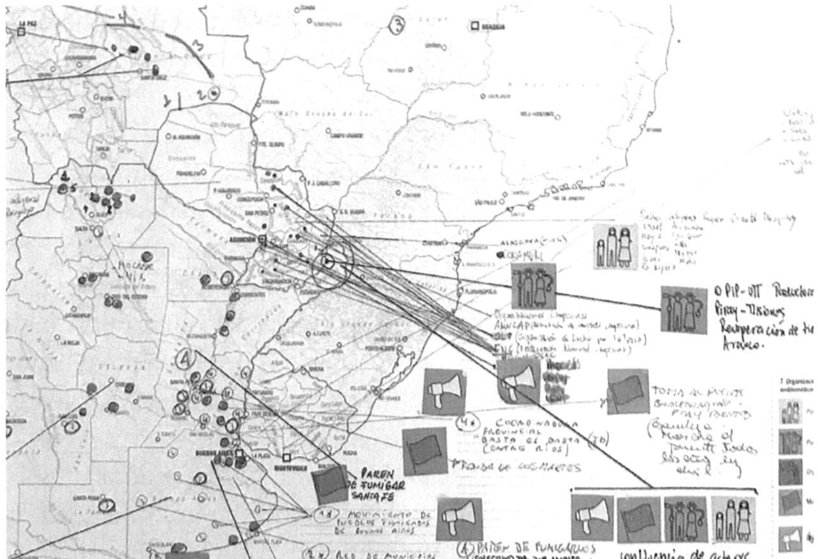


FIGURE 1.6. Fragment of a collective map elaborated during the encounter organized by Acción por la Biodiversidad (Argentina) and BASE-IS (Paraguay), with support from Fundación Rosa Luxemburgo. September 2019, Asunción, Paraguay. Image by Iconoclasistas.

in this way challenging mapping methodologies as well as the use of maps by those championing an extractivist model.

The work of Iconoclasistas is embedded in the ethos and processes of activism, more so than it is in those of the art world, despite the fact that the group has developed a strong and identifiable aesthetic and has gained recognition from the international art world. An important aspect of Iconoclasistas' work is that all their production falls under a Creative Commons license so that anyone can use it and distribute it. In the words of Julia,

> We think a lot about practice, and we work on this because we really like the idea of tactic and strategy, in terms of efficacy. If someone thinks about an action, it should have defined ends, be planned in advance, be grounded territorially in the space where we are working, and respond to one or two concrete objectives. So it is not "I feel the need to express myself, so I will do this with . . ."; no: who we work with, what we want, how we will get there, in

> what time, everything is carefully planned in advance within the possibilities.[58]

In other words, we could understand their mapping work as *dialogically* strategic, facilitating situations of collective thinking and mutual learning in order to achieve specific aims. This approach, in turn, allows them to develop their practice and methodology further. An example of this is the way that their iconography has evolved over time: in each workshop, participants point out things that did not work, terms that were not appropriate, and images that would work better, and as a result, their arsenal of images and icons becomes larger and more inclusive (see fig. 1.6).

The work of Iconoclasistas clearly activates the functions of documentation, democratization, and design. In the first place, their collective mapping allows communities to bring together the different forms of knowledge they hold and to document the present reality of their territories: what is happening, where, what actors are involved, how different processes are connected, and in some cases, what forms of resistance are emerging to extractive processes and how these are distributed. Second, through this act of collective making and knowledge sharing, there is a process of democratization of information. In their words, workshops are conceived as "tactical spaces where the construction of collaborative knowledge develops around the idea of building transformative practices—today, here, now—that respond to the needs of a neighborhood, a community, a collective, or the members of a space."[59] Different actors contribute from their own place and what they know, and learn new information from others. Through the open facilitation of Pablo and Julia, they also have agency in what form the mapping takes, what kind of information is included, and how it is visualized. And finally, in this collective act of visualization, local actors collaborate with Pablo (a designer) and Julia (a communications scholar and practitioner) to collectively design tools that will aid organizing in their local communities and in others facing similar threats. The collective design process is not just one of designing a specific output (a map), but also one of designing visual tools and processes of knowledge sharing and collective decision making. What is being designed here, in other words, are collective methodologies of action, of research, and of communication.

## *Decolonizing Territorial Imaginaries*

Patagonia, a region that comprises parts of what are currently known as Chile and Argentina, has been a contested territory for centuries. Notable in its history of violence and resistance is the campaign known as the Conquest of the Desert led by General Roca in the late nineteenth century, which resulted in the expansion of the Argentine frontier toward the south and involved the murder and displacement of thousands of indigenous people.

Seen as the uttermost part of the earth and the "last frontier," Patagonia "played a significant role in the definition of imperial modernity."[60] In turn, as an exporter of so-called natural resources "in a context of economic and technological dependency," Argentina has long centered nature in "its political, economic, and cultural self-representations."[61] Indeed, the imaginary of Patagonia as a deserted area still serves regional and national governments in justifying the expansion of the petrol frontier and the installation of open-pit mining as the only ways of making this vast land productive toward development and modernization (regardless of the fact that the region is home to numerous other vital economic activities).[62] Nowadays, Patagonia has become an attractive location for exploitation, and the "conquest" of the region is "pursued through a continuous process of territorial purchase [and] piecemeal extraction of natural resources,"[63] under an extractivist model that enforces the separation between the metropolis and its satellites, demarking territories of extraction as subordinate and structured for the consumption and accumulation of the global "centers."[64]

In recent years, following the expansion of the extractive frontier in Patagonia and elsewhere in Argentina, we have seen indigenous actors progressively challenging the political understanding of territory upheld by the Argentine state, as their territories and ways of living are under increasing threat.[65] One of the issues highlighted by Mapuche indigenous organizations is that the understanding of territory that they hold is different to the one imposed by the state, or, we could say, their ontology of territory differs from that of the state. Rather than owning the land, the Mapuche *belong to* the territory, and while they engage in legal fights for the recognition of their ancestral territories—one of the tools they have at their disposal—they do not believe in the notion of private property of the land. Implicit in their position is the rejection of the colonial state as the institution that regulates ownership over territories.

Commenting on the Chilean case specifically, but applicable to the Argentinian context as well, Del Valle Rojas and Maldonado Rivera argue that the struggle of the Mapuche nation is a project of reconstitution of the sovereign fabric. Territorial recuperation is one of the central aspects of the Mapuche political and cultural agenda, because territory is a foundational dimension in their belief and value system or ontology.[66] The dispute around territory positions on the one hand the state and corporate extractivist actors as representatives of capitalism and the coloniality of global power, and on the other, a Mapuche world(view) that values territory as an essential source of life and sovereign reconstruction, inhabited and experienced through relations of reciprocity.[67]

As the extractive frontier advances with developments like the Vaca Muerta nonconventional fossil fuel extraction venture and projects for open-pit mining, conflicts in and around Mapuche territories have intensified. Road blockades and protests are met with increased repression, territories have become militarized, and antiterrorism laws on both sides of the Andes are being used to judicialize activists.[68] In addition, in recent years there have also been ruthless media campaigns delegitimizing Mapuche claims, which have portrayed Mapuche communities as violent and corrupt.[69]

Raffestin argues that "it is impossible to understand territorial production [or processes of territorialization, as Zibechi would put it] without the notions of border or transgression."[70] He adds that transgression "has the value of a cultural mechanism of regulation: culture is a catalogue of limits, and history a catalogue of their transgression. A culture, then, is also a catalogue of possible transgressions: every limit is an opportunity for transgression and thus, in a certain sense, an occasion for creativity."[71] The arts have enormous potential for the transgression of boundaries; not only can artworks use aesthetic means to put forward messages that disrupt the status quo, but also, as I have argued elsewhere, through transgressive and prefigurative processes art can open up spaces for transgressing social norms and experiencing other ways of being in the world.[72] The following examples of Mapuche artistic practice challenge the conception of territory violently imposed by the extractivist, colonial settler state. Through creative, transgressive acts that contribute to the wider Mapuche struggle, these artists attempt to denaturalize long-held conceptions of territory and the history of colonialism, including its contemporary manifestation as extractivism.

## BARBARITY OVER CIVILIZATION

On November 13, 2017, the city of Esquel in the Province of Chubut woke to a multi-site intervention that brought to light the violent colonial history of Argentina and the present violence of extractivism. The intervention was the work of Hugo Fernando Chandía, an artist and student teacher at the 818 Institute in Esquel, who developed the work as part of an assignment in his course. The intervention explored the Conquest of the Desert, the military campaign through which the Argentine state expanded further south into Patagonia, killing, imprisoning, and displacing thousands of indigenous people.

The first site was the bust of the explorer Francisco Moreno, where there was an installation that consisted of human skulls and bones made of plaster, ceramic, and papier-mâché.[73] In an interview with local media, the artist explained he chose this site because Moreno was the first explorer to arrive to the region and make contact with local indigenous communities before General Roca executed the "Conquest."[74] Moreno's bust, as with other monuments of figures that were instrumental to colonization, is a daily reminder of the violence by which colonialism was imposed.[75] The skulls had dates inscribed on them in red, referencing the start and end dates of the conquest, as well as marking the year of the work, 2017. This, explained the artist, alluded to the ongoing persecution of Mapuche people to this day.[76] The installation continued down General Roca street, and ended at the Rural Society, "one of the greatest beneficiaries of this conquest," in the artist's words, given that the land that was taken away from indigenous inhabitants was then mostly destined for agriculture and farming and largely concentrated in the hands of a few.

Chandía's piece is titled *La barbarie sobre la civilización* (Barbarity over civilization), referencing one of the founding slogans of the Argentine nation, "*civilización o barbarie*" (civilization or barbarity), which was the ideological background to the genocide of indigenous people that took place in order to expand the reign of the Argentine state. Following orders from the local government, the police quickly removed the installation. After the backlash received because of this work, the 818 Institute where Chandía was a student publicly defended it. They released a statement in which they situated themselves as "a Further Education establishment with a modality of bilingual, intercultural education that sets out challenges and actions that result in an approach to teaching that is inclusive and decolonial."[77] They also referred to the importance of challenging myths and contributing to an ongoing revision of history, and framed Chandía's intervention as the result of a pedagogic exercise, but also as an exercise of identity.

Chandía's intervention not only denounces the violence exerted upon Mapuche people and their territories for centuries and continuing today, but it also challenges official versions of history that uphold perpetrators of genocide as national heroes. Through a multisite intervention that addresses the past, the present, the role of the state, and the role of the agricultural sector, he also deconstructs ideas about the power dynamics of settler colonialism itself, highlighting the continuation of colonial geographies and institutions to this day, and the role of private economic actors.

This work, like others discussed earlier, can be understood as site-specific. Indeed, in his installation, Chandía maps out in situ the links between different actors who are exerting violence upon peoples and territories, in this way re-signifying the urban space and engaging in an act of reterritorialization. In targeting a monument, we can also read the intervention as part of a global collection of pivotal moments in which public symbols of power are brought into question. This work follows, for instance, the Rhodes Must Fall campaign targeting a statue of Cecil Rhodes in Cape Town, and precedes the more recent wave of statue toppling of slave traders and other contentious historical figures in the UK and the US.

Chandía's work deconstructs hegemonic accounts of the national history by disrupting it and offering an alternative, situated reading. In addition, it aims to democratize history, as his interventions in the public space look to spark conversations among the local population who encounter the work, and indeed, the media coverage the work obtained created an opening for a broader, public conversation.

Chandía's installation is just one example of a growing number of artistic expressions by Mapuche artists in movements against destructive extractive activities and for the state's recognition of indigenous territories and identities. In what follows I discuss another of such cases: the Mapuche Rock band Puel Kona.

## MUSIC, TERRITORY AND IDENTITY

Another form of artistic expression that has found its place in the Mapuche struggle is music, and its most notable example is the band Puel Kona. Puel Kona, which means "warriors of the east" in the Mapuche language Mapudungun, is a ska-rock band that came together in 2007 in the province of Neuquén.[78] It all started when a group of young members of the local Mapuche community who were working on different media projects together (such as a radio station, a film, and a magazine) turned to music in order to experiment with a new form of communication and political action, as told by band member Lefxaru.[79] The original members of the band belong to the Newen Mapu and Puel Pvjv communities in Neuquén, whose territorial origin is in the confluence of two rivers. They are all actively involved in the struggle for the upholding of their rights and the defense of territories currently under threat due to the advance of fracking.[80]

Puel Kona's style is a mixture of rock, ska, folk, and Mapuche sounds. They sometimes refer to themselves as "Mapuche Rock" as a way of differentiating their style from other local genres. Their first song to gain traction was "Malditas petroleras" (Damned oil companies), which became an anthem of the antiextractivist movement in the region. The lyrics denounce the wreckage of oil production:

> Ayer las carabelas,
> hoy son las petroleras,
> la codicia extranjera
> de nuevo en nuestra tierra.
> Gasoductos y pozos
> sangra el Wallmapu abierto,
> no importan las regalías
> si nos dejan un desierto.
>
> *Yesterday it was the caravels*
> *Today it's the oil companies*
> *The foreign greed*
> *Once again in our land*
> *Gas pipelines and wells*
> *The open Wallmapu bleeds*
> *The royalties don't matter*
> *If they leave a desert behind*[81]

Other songs by the band refer to racial discrimination, to the Western paradigm and the capitalist regime, and to the forms of state violence experienced by the Mapuche nation.

Puel Kona's music follows and is part of a legacy of indigenous resistance that goes back to the aforementioned *Conquista del Desi-*

*erto* and that consolidated as a movement in the 1970s alongside a global wave of indigenous movements for self-determination driven by anticolonial and human rights struggles.[82] The movement gained new strength in the 1990s and again in recent years, no longer looking to recuperate land but rather aiming for the recuperation of ancestral territories. This revived conception of territory was molded among other factors by the resistance to neoliberal policies, as argued by Zibechi, and the new connections among local Mapuche communities and with those across the Andes.[83] It led to new processes of territorialization, including certain Mapuche families and groups seeking the status of indigenous communities as recognized by the state with collective claims to specific territories. Toward 2010, the arrival of fracking posed a new threat in a region that had already been marked by oil for decades, and this development, as explains Gutiérrez Ríos, served to once again renew and amalgamate local forms of resistance.[84]

Lefxaru Nawel is a member of Puel Kona and, at the time of our encounter, a spokesperson for the Confederación Mapuche de Neuquén, a Mapuche organization that brings together different communities to fight for recognition of their territories and their cultural identity. I met Lefxaru in the city of Neuquén in August 2017. It was the fourth anniversary of the protest that had brought together Mapuche communities, environmental activists, trade unions, student movements, socialist parties, and feminist groups—collectively known as the *Multisectorial en contra del fracking*, or Multisectorial against Fracking—to try to stop the approval of an agreement between the partially state-owned fossil fuel company YPF and the US American company Chevron for the development of fracking in Vaca Muerta. We met in a café, and Lefxaru shared with me some of the issues they were facing as the extractive frontier advanced into their territories. Lefxaru explained that in their territories "there is a situation of exploitation that precedes fracking, a situation of looting and contamination, which has caused disease, not just for people but of the whole *Wallmapu*, which under our conception of territoriality is not just what is up here but also what lies underneath the place where we exist."[85] He explained as well that the effects of fracking in the territory develop on different scales: the use of water for oil extraction in fracking and the expansion of the extractive frontier represent "a reality that is very harshly experienced in the fruit producing areas, but also in the residential areas. Today people compete for water with the oil industry."[86] He added, however, that the conflict is not about "yes or no to fossil fuels." It is about the situation of the province and the country, about the neglect of indigenous and working-class people, about generating a plan for moving away from extractivism, and developing sustainable forms of energy production for all.

Speaking of the experience of being part of the Multisectorial against Fracking, Lefxaru celebrated the coming together of different social actors, from student and feminist organizations to trade unions and environmentalists. However, he pointed out that Mapuche communities, being at the frontlines, are the ones whose bodies most often face violent repression, given that the armed forces do not only repress protests but also carry out unauthorized raids of Mapuche territories with the aim of intimidating communities. In addition, Mapuche communities regularly face various forms of symbolic violence, which include the deliberate invisibilization of their claims by the mainstream media and, as noted earlier, the constant framing of their protests as both violent and illegitimate. Indeed, racism and state violence are also issues addressed in Puel Kona's songs. In this context, Lefxaru emphasized the possibilities of art as a communication tool: "we are happy to see the power that art has, because sometimes actions we do and statements we put out don't reach people, but songs on the other hand do. And art has its own life beyond the impulse you give it, it even has a strong informational and educational role."[87]

In a similar way to Chandía's public intervention, Puel Kona's songs denounce ongoing forms of extractive and colonial violence experienced by Mapuche communities today. Their lyrics mark the links between the colonization of the Americas and the ongoing exploitation of territories. But also, Puel Kona is an exercise in identity, an act of irruption into the public sphere and of democratization of public narratives through the arts—what could be framed as a "redistribution of the sensible."[88] Puel Kona's intervention in the national and regional musical sphere is significant not only because of their lyrics, but also because of the symbolic significance of a Mapuche band being unapologetic about their identity and achieving success in doing so.

## *Creating Territory*

The works discussed in this chapter all engage in one way or another with territory, be that through site-specific work that emerges from frontline struggles for territory, the visibilization of territories in conflict, or the rethinking of what territory is.

The series Territorios en Conflicto experimented with interdisciplinary performance lectures that embraced the stage as a space of denunciation where a light is shed on different conflicts taking place across the country. Here, artists, journalists, and other actors used the frame of territory to highlight the connections between phenomena such as the current agricultural model, processes of urban dispossession, and the death of indigenous languages.

The exhibition *Arte en territorio* on the other hand, presented works of "art in territory," what could be understood, I proposed, as the meeting of site-specific art and territorial work. In this work, we can broadly identify three functions in place: documentation, democratization, and design. First, many of the projects engaging children and young people with the arts encourage them to record their surroundings. The resulting work thus becomes a document of the social and environmental conditions under which marginalized participants live. Second, by engaging young people in art making and providing them with tools to express themselves, there is an act of democratization involving a redistribution of the sensible, in which marginalized young people make their voices and perspectives on their territories heard. And third, works like the publishing project by Editorial El Parador and the cultural center of Colectivo Cielo Abierto are examples of design practices in which specific mechanisms of cultural production (in the first case) and practices of territorialization (in the second) are put forward; in other words, these art projects not only facilitate cultural participation, but also design new ways of being and making.

Similar dynamics of documentation, democratization, and design take place through the collective mapping of Iconoclasistas, which blends design work with community activism to produce visual tools that are useful to ecoterritorial struggles. What we see in all these practices is site-specific artistic work that is embedded within larger dynamics of (re)territorialization and that follows the ethos of territorial work.

The work by Chandía and the music of Puel Kona, on the other hand, bring to mind an additional "D" to the five-function framework I propose in this book, namely decolonization.[89] Decolonization means challenging official histories and the erasure of indigenous and Afro cultures. It means recuperating territory and identity. And it means fighting against contemporary forms of colonization embodied in extractive projects. Decolonization aims to denaturalize accepted truths underpinning extractivism and the ontologies from which they originate, and to dismantle the coloniality of knowledge and of power with a view to other ways of living. Because of this, in the works discussed here, decolonization builds on the artistic function of deconstruction. Chandía's installation in particular exposes and maps out the different players of extractivism and the colonization of the region in situ, opening up in this way the official history for it to be critiqued and rewritten. It de-normalizes the ingrained colonial hierarchies of value that support widespread racism, the negation of indigenous cultures, and the view of territory as resource for endless extraction.

By activating different functions, these artistic practices contribute to transforming the way those involved in the making engage with their own territory and develop practices of (re)territorialization, and invite audiences to reconsider their understanding of territory and its relevance in relation to socioenvironmental conflicts today. Indeed, as Castro-Sotomayor argues, "territoriality functions as a pragmatic environmental communication insofar as its visualization attempts to capture genealogies of thought, practices, and connections to a territory."[90] Visualizing, performing, and intervening the territory, in other words, allows multiple ways of confronting, challenging, and moving beyond the extractivist regime of visibility as described by Molinari, one that was imposed through coloniality.[91]

The works discussed in this chapter are the result of a range of experiences of the territory—artistic research, art in territory, art at the frontlines of extraction—that correspond to different positionalities regarding different territories. As discussed in the introduction to this book, the positions and experiences of different groups and subjects under an extractivist model vary greatly within Argentina and other countries in the region. For instance, the reflective effort to visibilize and trace the connections between territorial conflicts from across the country from within Buenos Aires is different to the urgency and interventionist nature of artistic expressions by Mapuche artists and others at the frontlines of extraction in territories marked by the constant threat of violence. Additionally, in the case of Mapuche artistic expressions, it is important to consider how these works are not only about denunciation, but are also exercises in affirming identity and political subjectivity. At the same time, all practices presented here begin *from* the territory, including artistic and other forms of research that form the basis of the performance lectures for Territorios en Conflicto. Contrary to the traditional understanding of site-specific art, the situatedness of these works is not just physical and/or conceptual: it is inherently political and ontological. What is at stake in making art in territory is the (re)making of that territory.

Finally, in this (re)making, the works discussed integrate and enact the different perspectives on the political experience of territory presented earlier: the territorialization of movements, the ecoterritorial turn, and the decolonization of territories. This results, using Svampa's term, in renewed languages of valorization of the territory:[92] new conceptions of the territory that manifest deeper conceptual and aesthetic connections between different territorial struggles and perspectives, from the decolonial to the environmental, and grow the understanding of territory as basis of political and social organizing.

In the following chapter, I return to some of the points discussed here, but I do so from the viewpoint of ecofeminism. This will allow me to analyze extractivism and the various forms of creative resistance to it from an embodied perspective, one that takes into account the gendered aspects of extractive violence.

# 2 Our Bodies, Our Territories

## *Ecofeminism and the Ethics of Care*

ON SEPTEMBER 27, 2019, two simultaneous political events took place outside the Argentine National Congress: the worldwide climate strike and the demonstration in support of a law guaranteeing the right to legal, safe, and free abortion. In the run-up to the day, the youth organization Les Jóvenes made a call for participation in both events by posting a video on social media that juxtaposed images of extractive projects and environmental disasters with joyful images of protest from past mobilizations demanding the sanctioning of the abortion law. The video stated, "our demands are different, but we are brought together by a shared desire: social justice." It ended with an invitation: "let's invent the future." The physical and symbolic merger of these two protests created an opportunity for strengthening the links between two movements, feminism and environmentalism, which until recently had remained separate—at least in their mainstream manifestations. It was the younger generation that pushed for such connections, turning this day in September into a "double green tide" consisting of "green" activists and the green scarfs in support of women's reproductive rights.[1]

The connections between feminist and environmental movements, however, are far from new. Whether we look at ecofeminist traditions in the Global North, or at popular and indigenous feminist and antipatriarchal organizing in the South, women for long have been at the forefront of environmental justice struggles, highlighting the connections between the oppression of women, feminized bodies and racialized groups and the plundering of the Earth in search for profit and endless growth. Due to long-standing issues such as the division of labor, as Federici argues,[2] women are often those who "put their bodies on the line" in defense of the territory and to safeguard their communities from the hazardous effects of extractive activities and other forms of pollution.[3]

Following the discussion on territory in Chapter 1, this chapter looks at the relationship between territory, extraction, and gender, considering that, as Diana Ojeda puts it, "gender roles, stereotypes, values, and expectations are fundamental in the constitution of subjects and their relationship to their environment." Furthermore, "by looking at the way that dynamics rooted in sexism, machismo, and patriarchal logics give shape to the environment, it is possible to unveil fundamental aspects of the way that the environment is inescapably political."[4]

This chapter discusses (eco)feminisms and antipatriarchal movements in Argentina and Latin America and engages with their cultural and artistic manifestations. It first considers debates surrounding ecofeminism and the different strands of feminism in Latin America. This is followed by a discussion of the surge of the Ni Una Menos feminist movement in Argentina and the Movimiento de Mujeres Indígenas por el Buen Vivir, highlighting how the latter has engaged with mainstream feminism in an effort to call out the ingrained coloniality of Argentine society and to put forward a feminism that is decolonial and antiextractivist. The chapter then considers how different forms of ecofeminism underpin the work of artists Claudia Tula and Pao Lunch in Argentina, and the collectives Mujeres Creando in Bolivia and Miradas Críticas del Territorio desde el Feminismo in Ecuador. The analysis of these practices draws out such issues as the violence of extractivism exerted on bodies and territories and the relationship between feminism and the Catholic Church and reveals the ways artistic practices can contribute to denouncing violence and deconstructing ingrained ideas about gender and the nature/culture divide at a conjuncture marked by an ecological crisis and the expansion of feminism across the region. I conclude the chapter with a reflection on the potential of ecofeminism for tackling the multiple crises we are currently facing, and make the case for the care for territories and communities as "the fundamental political task of our times."[5]

## *On Ecofeminism*

Ecofeminism is an environmental and feminist ethic and social movement that brings to light the ways the oppression of women and the domination of what is perceived as an external nature are linked symbolically, historically, and experientially.[6] Ecofeminists argue that both of these dynamics are rooted in Western dualist ideas and hierarchies of value that separate nature and culture, valuing the latter over the former, and that position women and Black, indigenous, and people of color closer to "nature" and further from civilization than the white man.[7] Indeed this value system underpins different forms of oppression against anyone who deviates from the white, male, able, cis, heterosexual standard.

Ecofeminism includes a broad range of practices and approaches from different parts of the world and is not a homogenous movement or theory: while some strands sit close to Marxist ideas and call for material and institutional change, others focus on spiritual and cultural transformations.[8] Similarly, we can link ecofeminism to scholarly fields like feminist political ecology, and to the everyday practices of women at sites of extraction. In all cases, however, we could argue that ecofeminism tends to be defined by an ethic of care that guides the relationships to other human and nonhuman forms of life.[9] This ethic of care should not be regarded as something exclusive to women and those who have been historically portrayed as being "closer to nature", but rather is proposed as an approach to our relation with other beings and with our environment that needs to be embraced by all.

Critiques of ecofeminism have mostly focused on its apparent essentialism and Western dualism (i.e., arguing that women are biologically "closer to nature" instead of challenging this construct).

These concerns are valid and important, however, there are two points we must consider. In the first place, as stated earlier, ecofeminism is not a homogenous field. While some proponents have displayed essentialist and dualistic perspectives, others have challenged such ideas, adopting intersectional approaches instead and framing the oppressions of women and nature as linked historically, materially, and conceptually, but not essentially.[10] And second, it is paramount to take into account the differing world(view)s or ontologies from which different strands of (eco)feminism emerge, given that in some contexts, as I explain later, the Western category of essentialism does not apply.

In Latin America-*Abya Yala*, we can identify what Maristella Svampa has termed a parallel "feminization" and "environmentalization" of social struggles, as conflicts resulting from the expansion of extractivism multiply and women become more present and visible in such conflicts.[11] However, and especially so when talking about indigenous and community movements, the identities of "environmentalist" and "feminist" are not always assumed. This is because, contrary to Global North contexts, in Latin America women often organize against the patriarchal, extractivist model not as a political stance or out of choice, but due to a more extreme and immediate threat to life. Feminisms in Latin America-Abya Yala often exist in contexts heavily marked by the interconnected violences of ingrained patriarchal structures and extractivism, as highlighted by anthropologist Rita Segato.[12]

While a broad range of (eco)feminisms exist in Latin America-Abya Yala, including some that are more akin to Western versions (especially in large urban centers), in general they tend to manifest in the form of popular, community, and indigenous feminisms. Contrary to liberal feminism, these forms are more deeply concerned with the links between land, territory, and bodies as a result of lived experiences of violence, and they engage in situated forms of knowledge production.[13] Furthermore, these feminisms "connect the struggle against the patriarchy with the struggle to overcome capitalism, ethnocentrism, and anthropocentrism,"[14] and they recognize the role of global economic dynamics and agents—for example, multilateral organizations such as the International Monetary Fund and the World Trade Organization—in the threats and violence experienced in their territories. Indigenous, popular, and community (eco)feminisms are rooted in the idea of interdependence between the different elements of an ecosystem, and they tend to approach their organizing from a decolonial perspective that challenges imposed models of development and modern understandings of the "human-nature divide."[15]

Decolonial Latin American feminisms argue that indigenous women are yet another territory under the domination of invaders.[16] Scholar and activist Silvia Rivera Cusicanqui has examined, for instance, how the processes of Westernization and patriarchalization in the Andes developed in parallel.[17] At the same time, the body is understood as a site of lived emotions and experiences, and therefore it is also a site of resistance from which women can devise strategies for collective liberation. Certain forms of Latin American feminisms calling for decolonization have cosmogonies and conceptions of nature and of gender that differ from Western traditions. Because of this, they see the label of "essentialism" often imposed upon them by Western feminists as a misguided category.[18] This is an important consideration, and one that calls for the recognition of different worlds and perspectives where plural ecofeminisms coexist.[19]

Finally, among the other strands of ecofeminism present in the region, there are grassroots feminist groups, academics, and artists that put forward a queer ecology approach, weaving US and European perspectives with local theories and experiences on queerness and environmental conflicts. Broadly, queer ecology views nature as strange, varied in its forms, and under the constant discipline of human intervention. It thus stands against essentialism and binarism from this perspective, and instead positions itself for multiple differences.[20] Queer ecology seeks to reconcile postmodern theorization with material approaches to gender and ecology. As Bauhardt puts it, "the aim is to overcome the epistemological deadlock of postmodern theorization in favour of a feminist theory of action which recognizes language and materiality as being of equal value."[21] It shares the critique of the natural/unnatural divide of ecofeminism, but it goes deeper into challenging normative, essentialist concepts of women, femininities, and nature.[22] Furthermore, it focuses on "how heteropatriarchy disciplines sexuality in ways that also denaturalize particular gender identities (e.g., childfree heterosexual women, butch-lesbian masculine femininities, non-cisgender and genderqueer identities)."[23]

Having discussed some of the different ecofeminist and ecofeminist movements and strands of thought in Latin America, in the next section I focus on Argentina specifically to show how, in the face of expanding and increasingly violent extractivism, barriers between different kinds of feminisms can be challenged to give place to new, intersectional movements for social change.

## *Feminist and Antipatriarchal Movements in Argentina*

The Ni Una Menos movement emerged in Argentina in 2015, when women and *disidencias* (dissident gender identities) said "enough!" to an endless series of femicides and took to the streets to demand *¡ni una menos!* (not one less woman)—no more lives lost as a result of gender-based violence.[24] The movement rapidly gained size and visibility, placing feminism and gender-based violence at the center of the public agenda in a way that had never occurred before. Since then, feminism has swiftly turned Argentine society on its head. As the primal scream of "*ni una menos*" traveled across the continent and compounded with local movements in each country, feminism has arguably become the strongest revolutionary force in much of Latin America, already permeating all spheres of the social—from education to work and the economy more broadly.

Only a few years after Ni Una Menos first emerged, the new wave of feminism in Argentina consolidated around the campaign for the right to free and legal abortion, giving this decades-long issue a massive push and eventually achieving that goal when the senate passed a new abortion bill in December 2020. This new wave thus took the baton from previous waves of feminists who had long organized around the matter of abortion and other issues concerning women's rights. In addition, the new wave builds on the legacy of other local social movements where women were the main political actors; such was the case of the Mothers of Plaza de Mayo, demanding the safe return of their children during the military dictatorship of 1976 to 1983. It was also the case with the *piquetera* women, who organized to demand work during times of economic crisis in the 1990s and early 2000s.[25]

At the beginning, the new wave of feminism did not openly express a position on environmental issues, but concerns about unhindered extraction and environmental damage soon gained weight within the movement. This has been in great part due to the contributions of indigenous women and their experiences organizing to defend their ancestral land from extractive exploitation, upholding the right to autonomy over their bodies and territories.[26] It is indigenous women across Latin America who have long led resistance against the exploitation of territories and bodies and who were the first to draw connections between colonialism, extractivism, and the patriarchy. However, the merger between mainstream feminism and indigenous antipatriarchal struggles was not easy. Argentina, as other Latin American countries, is strongly marked by the ideological and cultural legacies of settler colonialism, and this includes ingrained yet invisibilized racism in both everyday and institutional contexts. In response to this, sectors from within and at the margins of the feminist movement including indigenous, afro-descendent, and migrant women, but also *disidencias*, have been leading the way toward deconstructing these legacies, and have made it clear that the movement needs to be intersectional and antiracist if it is bound to make the profound social transformations it set out to make. Indeed, brown women, afro women, and indigenous women have been at the forefront of a movement to make Argentina confront its ingrained racism, and to challenge the myth of Argentines as a people that "came off the boats," one that was purposefully constructed in order to artificially create a white national identity.[27] A landmark occurrence in terms of making the movement more intersectional and inclusive has been the struggle to change the name of the annual Encuentro Nacional de Mujeres (National Gathering of Women) to Encuentro Plurinacional de Mujeres, Lesbianas, Trans, Travestis, Bisexuales, Intersex y No Binaries (Plurinational Gathering of Women, Lesbians, Trans, *Travestis*, Bisexuals, Intersex and Non-Binary), a win that was celebrated by popular majority in 2019, despite resistance from sectors of the organizing committee.[28]

While indigenous women in Argentina have taken upon themselves the arduous task of fighting for the decolonization of mainstream feminist spaces, they also continue to organize from within their communities. October 2019 saw an unprecedented action by indigenous women from across Argentina who, supported by the federal organization Movimiento de Mujeres Indígenas por el Buen Vivir, convened at the Ministry of the Interior in Buenos Aires to demand an end to the terricide taking place in their territories. By terricide, they referred to the reckless advance of the extractive industries and to the killing of land, people, and spirits resulting from it. The action was titled *La rebelión de las flores nativas* (The rebellion of native flowers), and it materialized as a self-organized occupation of the Ministry with a tent set right outside the building. Next to the tent, a banner read "*Sembraron terricidio. Cosecharon rebellion*" (They sowed terricide. They harvested rebellion). Participants represented a range of indigenous peoples and nations, including Qom, Mbya Guaraní, Tapiete, Mapuche, and Tehuelche. Their action involved meetings with different government officials to demand immediate responses to urgent problems such as the lack of drinking water in certain localities, as well as solutions to wider issues including the multiplication of extractive projects, instances of institutional racism and violence, and the right to exercise their cultural identities. While their larger demands did not receive concrete responses, and they recognized that these would entail an ongoing struggle, the organized women achieved some commitments to addressing the issues of access to water and instances of state violence, and hence decided to end the occupation after its tenth day. During the time of the occupation and before their departure, the women organized a festival and several cultural activities. As one newspaper reported, inside the halls of the Ministry the chant of twenty-three indigenous women bounced off the walls: "Indigenous women, women without time, the struggle for the earth is flourishing."[29]

Indigenous women's fight for decolonization, for an end to patriarchal, extractive violence, and for the free exercise of their culture, is ongoing. On March 8, 2020, women from the Lofce Newen Mapu community in Neuquén, north Patagonia, issued a public statement that made the rounds on social media and mailing lists. The statement denounced the erosion of their culture and practices and the imposition of a Western health system, which prevents them from practicing their traditional, holistic health practices. It spoke about the views on gender and gender roles of the Mapuche cosmology and asserted that it is necessary to eradicate the patriarchy in order to be able to recuperate and enact these traditional views. The statement denounced the crisis of femicides in the country and noted as well that while society has become jaded to the daily deaths of women, it is more so toward the lives of Mapuche women lost to extractivist violence. The statement concluded with the following words:

> It is not possible to move forward in the decolonization process without destroying the racist and patriarchal life system that states impose on us through their political, judicial, economic, evangelizing, and extractivist system. Hence, the emancipation of people and women will only be possible when the knots of patriarchy come undone through the construction of a new model of plurinational state that guarantees the political and cultural leadership of women from within their own identities, particularities, and knowledges, such as the strength needed to overcome this patriarchal model.[30]

In addition to the struggles of indigenous women in defense of territory and for autonomy and decolonization, there are multiple other cases of women in Argentina and across Latin America leading territorial struggles for the defense of life, and their role in such movements has become more visible as the extractive frontier expands and the stakes become higher.[31] Already in the 1990s Argentina saw the Movimiento de Mujeres Agropecuarias en Lucha (Movement of Farming Women in Struggle), the first women-led, formalized agricultural movement in the country, made up of women working in the sector as well as the partners of small and mid-scale farmers.[32] More recent examples of such struggles include the case of the mothers of Ituzaingó Anexo in the province of Córdoba, who stood against the use of industrial herbicides and pesticides in their neighborhood after noticing a spike in severe illnesses. In regions affected by mining, such as the town of Andalgalá, women have also organized and spoken truth to power, in this case through powerful performances challenging government officials and mining companies.[33] And in Chubut, Patagonia, where territorial conflicts and the threat of open-pit mining are ever present, indigenous women like Moira Millán have become icons not only of indigenous struggles, but also of the regional antiextractivism movement, as they fiercely lead the fight against corporate power and the colonial state. To these expressions, we must also add feminisms that fight for a system that is ecologically sustainable from an ecosocialist perspective, and those adhering to a critical queer perspective on gender and environment, as discussed earlier and developed further in the following section.

## *Art and Ecofeminism*

In studying the forms of ecofeminist action that have become increasingly central to movements against extractivism in Argentina and Latin America, considering artistic manifestations that emerge from or alongside collective action is an important task. In the first place, these creative expressions are crucial to the way actors express their experiences, construct alternative narratives, and begin to design alternative ways of being in the world. But also, these expressions are important interventions in public discourse, and as such they contribute to disrupting ingrained understandings of nature, environment, gender, and development based on androcentric and anthropocentric worldviews, which continue to "subject women and nature to mutually constitutive oppressions."[34] In the following pages, I engage with the work and processes of artists and collectives from Argentina, Bolivia and Ecuador to explore the ways that art can disrupt such hegemonic perspectives by activating different functions, particularly, in these cases, those of denunciation, democratization, deconstruction and design.

## MURAL ART IN DEFENSE OF LIFE

Claudia Tula is an artist from the province of Catamarca in the Argentine Northwest, a region marked by conflicts surrounding open-pit mining. Her medium is mural painting, but when presenting herself she notes that she is not a muralist but a *muralera*, a term that embodies her alignment with a strand of non-academic street art as opposed to the fine art mural tradition. Her work addresses such issues as women's rights, mining, water, and extractivism. She has an identifiable aesthetic that incorporates geometricized forms from local indigenous traditions and the combination of often contrasting, bold colors. She travels across the Argentine Northwest and across the country to paint, and most of her work is not commissioned or funded but rather self-organized and supported by local environmental assemblies (see figs. 2.1 and 2.2).

I met Claudia in San Fernando del Valle de Catamarca, the capital of the province of Catamarca, in March 2018. I had just returned to the city from Andalgalá, a town fighting open-pit mining and adorned by several of her murals, and one of the people I met in my trip insisted I talked to her. Claudia received me in her home, where we shared a few *mates* and spoke for hours.[35]

Claudia told me about one of the first works she did on the subject of extractivism. It was 2007, and she had invited artists from a collective in Buenos Aires to come and paint together in the town of Belén, also in Catamarca. During their trip, they painted murals on the streets, which were received with violence and threats from pro-mining groups. In addition, they had traveled to Belén for the

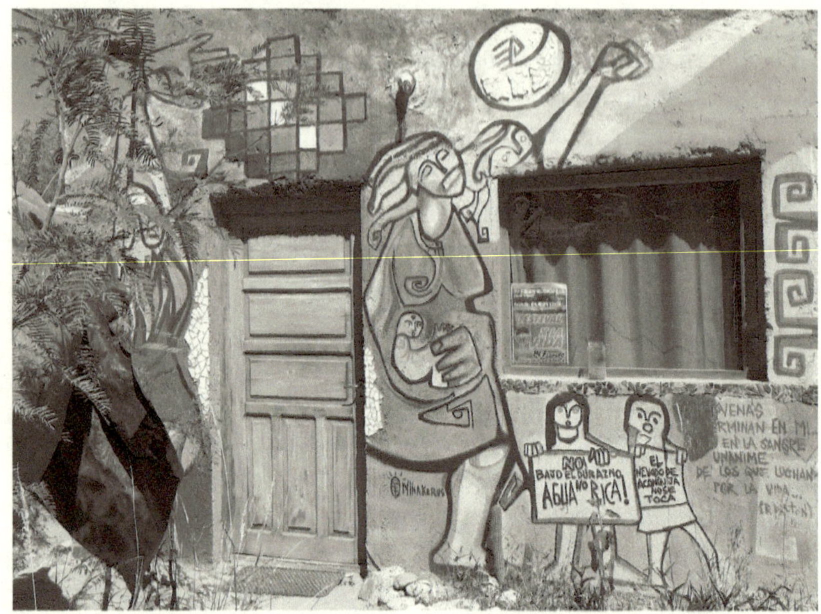


FIGURE 2.1. Mural by Claudia Tula outside a radio station in Catamarca. Photo by the author.

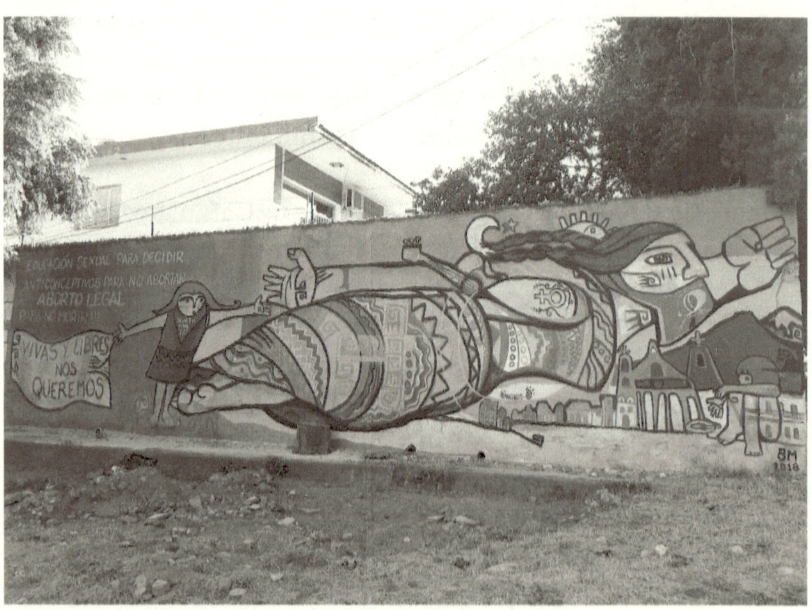


FIGURE 2.2. Mural by Claudia Tula in the city of Catamarca. Photo by the author.

occasion of the alternative music festival Belicho Metal, sponsored by the mining company La Alumbrera.[36] Claudia had been asked to do the set design for the festival stage, and she offered to do it free of charge. When the set was unveiled, it featured large signs that read "*La megaminería mata*" (open-pit mining kills), Claudia's way of voicing her opposition to the festival's sponsor. As she told it, moments after, the police swiftly removed both her and her friend from the premises. Following the incident, they decided to leave the town immediately, having realized the kind of powers they were up against.

After this episode, Claudia realized it was safer to work with the support of locals when visiting new towns. That is when she began making connections with environmental assemblies across the country and going to places where people would receive her, provide her with materials, food, and a place to stay, and make sure she had a support network when painting her murals denouncing the powerful. In return, Claudia would provide an opportunity for people to come together and express their views on their situation with the purpose of agreeing on a theme for the mural. With her skills, she would materialize those views and make a symbolic intervention in the public space.

One of the towns Claudia visited in her trips was Santa María, also in the province of Catamarca. There, she explained, the same mining company that was in Belén had covered the costs for painting all of the facades across town, making any attempts at mural art especially conflictive. She explained:

> We couldn't paint the walls. So we stretched a piece of canvas and started to paint just there. And well, each time we did this people would come to us and tell us tremendous stories about the death of their animals, of their land. The anguish of having a town that is neatly painted but inside there are millions of things going on, of social ruptures. This solidified my belief that I had to use art to do something.[37]

By painting in different cities and inserting herself within the struggles of communities, Claudia has been able to witness the power of art as a vehicle of denunciation, of democratization of the public conversations on what kind of economic model people want, and ultimately, of intervention. Indeed, as other cases around the world have shown, such as Chicanx murals in the USA and the murals that emerged in Belfast during the Troubles, murals can be powerful territorial interventions, as they enact transformations in the shared landscape and everyday life of communities.[38]

Mural art that emerges from community settings is a form of popular art, and as such, it is process-oriented.[39] It has potential for transformation because of the type of agency it provides people in how to make an intervention into their everyday space, and how to visualize and represent their situation of conflict, their struggle, and/or their shared identity. Because of its public nature, the impact of mural art extends beyond those directly or willingly engaged with it. In the case of Andalgalá, Claudia explained for instance that she had painted a mural about water, one that spoke about freedom and people's right to water. According to her friends there, once the mural was up, so called "pro-miners" would deliberately avoid that street. She added, "they were afraid of what it said."

After we were done with the *mate*, Claudia took me on a tour of the city so I could see some of her work, as well as some of the murals painted by religious groups crusading against the right for legal and safe abortion. Around that time, the movement for a new law guaranteeing safe and free abortion was gaining momentum, and as a response, groups opposing the law were organizing countermarches and making their voices heard on social media. Claudia showed me a mural she had painted about women's sovereignty over their bodies and their territories. Then she pointed to a mural commissioned by an anti-abortion group. This mural covered half a block and featured a row of headless, pregnant bodies with see-through wombs, which looked more like artificial incubators than pregnant humans. It also featured an image of the Virgin of the Valley (the local appearance of the Virgin Mary venerated by locals), with an aura of fetuses crowning her head. The image was produced by a teacher at a local art Institute, Claudia explained.

Opposition to the right to safe abortion in Argentina is in great part powered by conservative branches of religious sectors. The Catholic Church is particularly powerful in the northwest of Argentina, which was the area of the country first colonized by the Spanish. In Claudia's words, the ones who govern in Catamarca are "the Church, the police, and then the state." Such distribution of power, in addition to the corporate power of mining companies, has served to sustain certain attitudes in the region. More specifically, the constraint of women's freedoms advocated by certain strands of the Church compounded with the violence of extractivism are understood by the women I met in Catamarca as conducive to a situation of exacerbated gender-based violence. Claudia explained for instance, that when painting in the streets she is constantly exposed to sexual harassment from the police, which often turns violent. We also discussed the epidemic of abductions of young girls in Catamarca, who according to locals are trafficked for forced sexual labor to serve workers in the mines. Indeed the matter of gender and sexual violence is an issue that is widespread in other mining regions of the country, as well as in other centers of extractive activities such as those linked to the oil industry.[40] In response to these circumstances, there is a growing feminist movement in Catamarca, one that stands up to the patriarchy, to the Church, and to extractivism at once.

Many of the experiences and visions shared by Claudia were echoed by other artists and activists such as Laura. She shared that the emergence of Ni Una Menos has helped consolidate the incipient forms of feminism that existed within other spaces of political and environmental militancy in the province. While assuming the label of feminism is new for many activists in Catamarca, Laura said she has faith that feminism is the force that can bring together all other struggles such as environmental issues and against different forms of oppression and inequality: "In unifying all of these struggles through feminism we are working to achieve a cultural transformation, a social transformation that allows us to understand that the only way to achieve *buen vivir* is through the collective, the organizational, the social, the community, in a way that

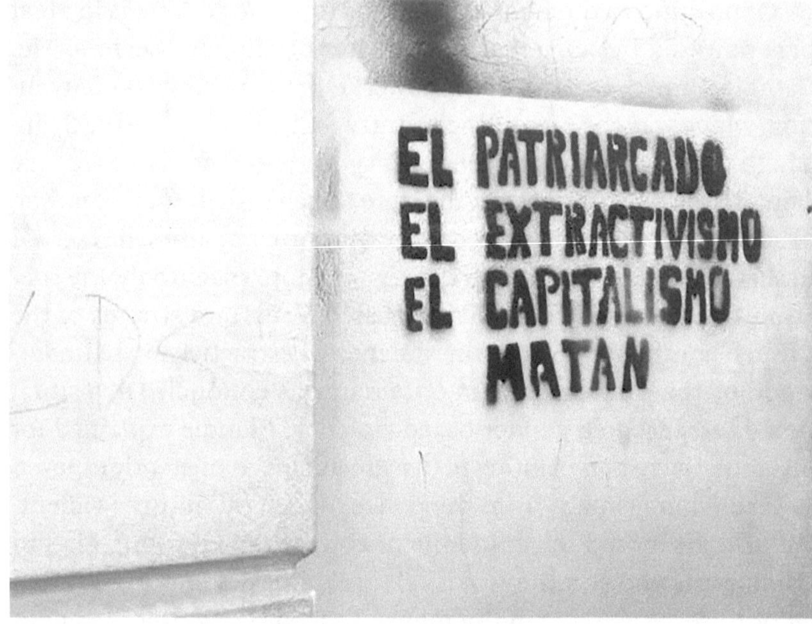


FIGURE 2.3. Ecofeminist graffiti in the streets of Catamarca: "The patriarchy. Extractivism. Capitalism. Kill." Photo by the author.

can break the most perverse and patriarchal structures of capitalism."[41] Indeed, this coming together of struggles was already visible in my visit to Catamarca in 2018 (see fig. 2.3). As I walked through the city center, graffiti on the wall read

> The patriarchy
> Extractivism
> Capitalism
> Kill

## PORNOPETROL: PETROSEXUAL VIOLENCE AND QUEER BIOPOLITICS

Pao Lunch is a visual artist from Neuquén, North Patagonia, a region that has been marked by an extractivist "petroculture" for decades and in recent years has experienced the arrival of the fracking technique for extraction of nonconventional fossil fuels.[42] Pao Lunch's work deals with gender, oil, and territory, it is research-based and autobiographical, and it is concerned with technology and subjectivity as mechanisms that regulate bodies. Key concepts underlying Lunch's work are biopolitics, the type of governmentality that is built around the control of life and its reproduction, and biopower, the mechanisms through which biopolitics is enacted in society and a potential location of resistance.[43] Lunch approaches the politics of control over bodies and territories by working with the materiality of three fluids: oil, blood, and saliva, and generating a "picket" or blockade to biopower—in other words, an intervention in the daily flows of such fluids, which are governed and ascribed specific values by patriarchal, extractivist capitalism.

Lunch explains:

> I realized that the main picket had to do with petrol and blood, so I said "this petrol is not going to give you energy because I am going to steal it; this blood won't give you work, I am picketing, I am stealing it." So I steal from a multinational or find people to steal petrol for me, and I find people to come to my house and . . . draw blood. [And then there's] saliva, the act of speech, and everything that saliva means to dykes: lubrication, words, everything you need to know to survive in this world being different.[44]

Lunch's picketing as a strategy of resistance, interruption and empowerment follows a similar logic to that of the International Women's Strike, a form of collective action that emerged in 2017 organized by Argentinian and Polish activists and other feminists from around the world. As Gago explains, "the strike is a way of blocking the continuity of the production of capital, understood as a social relation. The strike is also a disobedience to the continuous expropriation of our vital energies . . ."[45]

The works that Pao Lunch composes through the use of fluids include images of bodies and body parts, as well as images of oil workers. Her series Pornopetroleo: Transcripciones y Traducciones Desobedientes (Pornopetrol: Disobedient transcriptions and

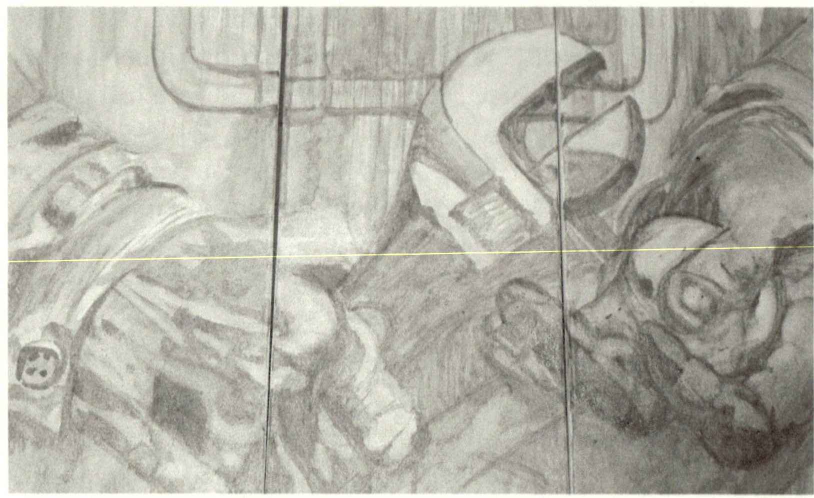

FIGURE 2.4. Pao Lunch, *Triptich*. From the series Pornopetroleo (2004–2016).

translations) is composed of five paintings and one triptych made out of petrol, saliva, and blood, one installation of lab objects, and three video pieces (see figs. 2.4, 2.5, and 2.6). In the words of the artist, the work "recirculates the fluids that sustain work (blood), and energy (petrol), cushioned by saliva." It "exposes the reality of the province of Neuquén in relation to these liquids, the masculine hegemony that surrounds them . . . and the machinery of the construction of desire."[46] Pao Lunch's work seeks to uncover the biopolitics of the oil industry, particularly in relation to gender, pointing to the hypermasculinity of the oil industry and a society that is heavily marked by it. It simultaneously challenges the oil industry's overtaking of bodies and territories and the violence exerted upon them. Furthermore, Lunch adopts a queer perspective to the analysis of the control over, and visual consumption of, oil and flesh, framing such consumption as pornographic, in what could be read as a nod to Paul B. Preciado's "pharmacopornographic era."[47]

Work from the Pornopetroleo series was displayed as part of the exhibition *Cuatro escenas artepolítica en la Argentina del modelo* (Four scenes "artpolitic" in the Argentina of the "model") in Buenos Aires in 2015.[48] In a sterilized and delicate manner, as if

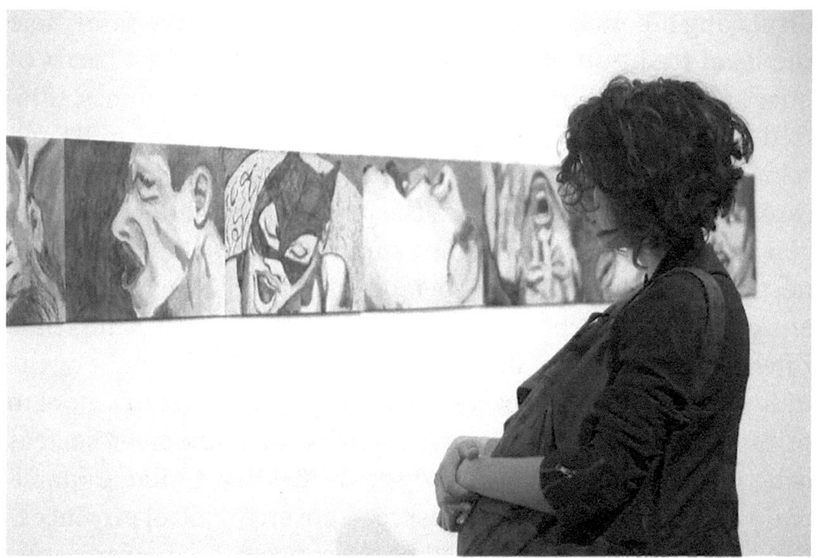

FIGURE 2.5. Pao Lunch, *Artistas Contempo*. From the series Pornopetroleo (2004–2016).

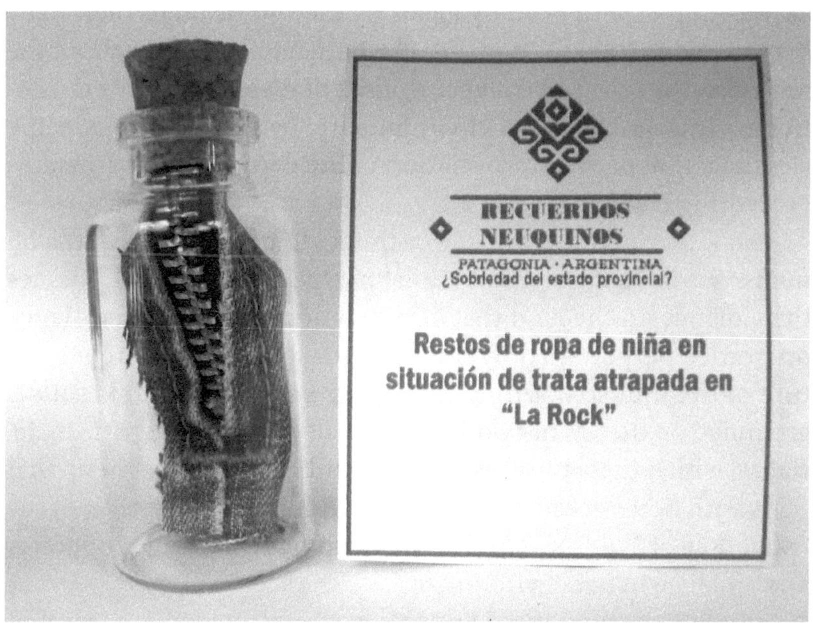


FIGURE 2.6. Pao Lunch, *Objetos Laboratorizables*. The sign says "Remains of the clothes of a young girl who has been trafficked and is trapped in 'La Rock.'" From the series Pornopetroleo (2004–2016).

displaying laboratory samples and referencing at the same time the local tradition of souvenirs, the artist showcased "tears of queer petrol industry worker," "vaginal discharge of a masculinized petrol industry admin worker," "sample from oil spill" and "clothing of a girl, victim of sex trafficking," among others. As she explained in our conversation, the provocative exhibits aimed at generating images in the viewer's mind, images that create connections between different social dynamics that cannot later be erased. With this, she pointed to the way that life in Neuquén is ruled by the fossil fuel industry. The power relations built by the industry are felt in all spaces, from the supermarket to school to private relationships, and made manifest in phenomena such as drug use, gender violence, and sex trafficking. Unlike Catamarca, a province marked by widespread poverty, "petrol provinces" like Neuquén are characterized by the concentration of excessive wealth in and around the industry. However, while some forms of power and violence are highly visible, others are not, and manifest as a feeling experienced by locals as they go through their daily lives. Same as Claudia Tula did, Pao Lunch talked to me about the ways that the forms of violence against bodies and against territories are interlinked in her environment. She said, "It is a palpable violence, that of the expropriation of the earth, which permeates everything else."[49]

Pao Lunch's work invites us to think about the effects of the oil industry from a queer, ecofeminist perspective. Her work equates the violence on the land that oil extraction delivers with violence on bodies perpetuated by the hypermasculine, patriarchal culture of the industry. While developing a narrative that is solidly grounded on theory, her work engages the viewer through its materiality, which displays a provocative and dissident aesthetic that plays with both pleasure and disgust. In this way, her picket of the usual flow of fluids symbolically disrupts the dynamics of power and violence in her environment.

Finally, we can situate Lunch's work within a wider trend of queer art and criticism on the relation between extractivism and the oppression of women and *disidencias*. Such perspective is shared in an essay by Johana Kunin and Patricio Simonetto which analyzes the experiences of *disidencias* in rural areas of Argentina where agribusiness is king:

> The agro sector in the Pampa and its cities have been narrated as masculine, heterosexual landscapes. Highlighted as moral reserves of a fatherland under threat by the dissolving elements of urban modernity, or, on the contrary, signaled as conservative sources of backward culture, they were valued as hostile spaces for sexual *disidencias*. The presence of lesbians, *travestis*, gays, bisexuals, nonbinary people in these territories problematizes the political and cultural construction of a (hetero)sexuality that takes to the extreme the binary character of gender and that has as its main protagonist the *macho pampeano*. This figure is presented as the carrier of a bestial masculinity that stands up to the "difficulties of nature." The *macho gaucho* that sleeps in the outdoors is a hyper-icon of national tradition. The rest, "are all fags."[50]

Having discussed ecofeminist art practices in different parts of Argentina, and how they respond to the violence resulting from different kinds of extractive activities and contexts, I now move on to discuss two examples from Bolivia and Ecuador respectively, which have been widely influential across the region: Mujeres Creando and Miradas Críticas del Territorio desde el Feminismo.

## ANDEAN ECOFEMINISMS

Mujeres Creando (Women Creating) is a feminist, anarchist, and decolonial movement and artist collective founded in La Paz, Bolivia, in 1992. Its founding members were María Galindo, Julieta Paredes, and Mónica Mendoza. In 2001, due to political disagreements, the group split into two organizations: Mujeres Creando and Mujeres Creando Comunidad, the latter emphasizing their community focus.[51] When Mujeres Creando first emerged, Bolivia was suffering the effects of neoliberal austerity policies on every aspect of everyday life. In this context, explains Julieta Paredes, "Feminist communalisms offered economic and social alternatives, as well as a critical stance during the failure of the Washington Consensus."[52]

Mujeres Creando carries out political actions, organizes community events, makes art, and produces publications that seek to challenge the oppression of women, particularly queer (and) indigenous women, who are some of the most oppressed groups in Bolivian society. Their approach is intersectional, and they aim to deconstruct the multiple axes of oppression experienced by women, looking at the role of the state and the pervasive effects of colonialism in contemporary social structures and gender relations.[53]

The art of Mujeres Creando spans across genres, including performances in public spaces and performance videos, as well as graffiti and murals. Some of their performances are symbolically powerful but subtle, such as a lesbian kiss in front of a police line visibilizing queer identities and defying homophobia. Others might have a communal character, like inviting people to share food in a square as a way of reclaiming public space. Yet others are more directly interventionist and fit within the realm of performance actions, or "political actions that have been heavily influenced by processes from performance art."[54] An example of the latter is *No Woman Is Born to Be a Whore* (2007), an action that took place in Buenos Aires, Argentina, as part of an international arts event. For the action, women met outside the National Congress and headed to the streets carrying spray cans and marking out areas of the city where sexual exploitation of girls and women takes place with the complicity of the police.[55]

In her analysis of Mujeres Creando's work, Macarena Gómez-Barris argues that the collective puts forward "a composite consideration of the intertwining of race and gender within the stratified public sphere, and a confrontation to expectations about traditionalism," and that their work "articulates local vernaculars with respect to sexuality."[56] In other words, Mujeres Creando visibilizes queer identities from within an anarchist, decolonial position, rather than adopting queer discourses from the Global North. Mujeres Creando is also concerned with the advance of the extractive frontier and has been critical of the government of Evo Morales, which maintained a discourse of respect for nature and indigenous peoples but in practice broke the social contract on multiple occasions. They also criticize Morales for excluding the emancipation of women and sexual *disidencias* in his decolonial project, which Mujeres Creando argues is a manifestation of his patriarchal position.[57] This critique can be seen, for instance, in the mural *Somos ingobernables* (We are ungovernable) from 2016. The mural offered a modified version of the Bolivian coat of arms that now reads "Bolivia under destruction," over a naked male body carrying "the weight of machismo" attached to his genitals. It also includes the phrase "neither the land nor women are territory of conquest." The mural, which was part of the International Art Biennale SIART, generated much controversy, and the artists were the target of insults and aggressions.[58] Indeed, the work was painted over soon after its unveiling.

Another collective that contributes to a region-wide ecofeminist body of work is Miradas Críticas del Territorio desde el Feminismo (MCTF; the name can be translated as Critical Approaches to Territory from a Feminist Perspective). MCTF is a Quito-based collective of activists and thinkers from Ecuador, Mexico, Brazil, Spain, and Uruguay. In their words, "we locate ourselves in Latin American and Caribbean feminism as a place of struggle, invention, creation, transformation, and thinking. Our perspectives knit the link between diverse bodies and their territories."[59] MCTF sees the body as the first territory and argues for a recognition of the territory in our own bodies, employing the concept of *cuerpo-territorio* or body-territory. When violence is exerted upon the places we inhabit, they argue, our bodies are affected as well. When violence is exerted upon our bodies, in turn, it is also exerted upon the places we inhabit.

Through its work, MCTF develops a critique of the extractivist model and its members work toward creating worlds otherwise, generating methodologies for communal organizing and ways of living beyond extractivism. Their work areas and methodologies cover a wide range of genres and ways of collaborative knowledge creation and sharing, including sensorial theatre, radio theatre, and storytelling. Acknowledging the deep connection between body and territory, much of their work tends to adopt embodied methodologies that focus on the sensorial and the wisdom of lived experience. Such is the case of "corporeal cartographies" or mappings of the body-territory, a methodology employed as part of group work with people experiencing territorial conflicts. Corporeal cartographies are drawings of one's own body that develop into maps. They aim to make visible the violence exerted upon territories and how this is experienced in participants' bodies, bringing to light the different urgencies for defending the places we inhabit. This technique is also a powerful instrument in gatherings that bring together land defenders from different territories, as it allows them to exchange their personal experiences of extractivism and reflect on the similarities in their affective responses.[60]

MCTF puts forward a feminist, ecologist, and community-oriented *sentipensar* (or feeling-thinking), which is a kind of collective, affective, knowledge creation process.[61] Its work, in other words, deconstructs the dominant colonial and patriarchal understandings of body, gender, and territory, and challenges the primacy of technocratic structures of knowledge creation, proposing others that are appropriate to the needs of communities in the defense of territory. They also rethink the meaning and location of violence, breaking it down and locating it at the multiple levels on which it operates (body-community-territory). Finally, MCTF utilizes methods rooted in a popular pedagogy ethos to co-design new ways of *sentipensar* together, which in turn allows the design of strategies for collective liberation.

The mapping work of MCTF can be understood—alongside the collective mappings of Iconoclasistas discussed in Chapter 1—as an example of "heretic cartography."[62] In other words, the very foundations of mapping are put into question, as embodied, creative, collective methodologies take over the scientific approach to produce knowledge that is democratic and situated. The practice of mapping is thus both democratized and redesigned and put to the service of those committed to community-led transformations away from extractivism.[63]

## OUR BODIES AS TERRITORIES

What the artists and collectives discussed above have in common is that through their work they jointly address the violence exerted upon bodies and upon territories—the *cuerpo-territorio* or body territory, exposing the common ontological roots and the mechanisms of such forms of violence. For instance, the participatory, site-specific murals of Claudia Tula denounce the effects of an extractivist model, and they also democratize the public narrative on mining and other extractive activities by providing a space for discussion and a format of expression for affected communities. Pao Lunch's work, on the other hand, denounces the relationships of power and oppression in a province where life is marked by the presence of the oil industry. Furthermore, it deconstructs and challenges the heteronormativity of the industry by picketing the flows of fluids and exposing the different kinds of sexualities, gender identities, and sexual dynamics that exist within the industry, as well as the various forms of sexual violence. Instead of a collective, constructive approach, Lunch resorts to a dissident "aesthetic of disgust" that does not solicit enjoyment or contemplation and aims directly at disrupting our naturalized ideas on gender, sexuality, nature, and progress.[64]

Mujeres Creando also aims to deconstruct strongly held hierarchies of gender and sexuality, in this case in Bolivian society, and it does so by disrupting patriarchal imaginaries through performances and graffiti that celebrate queer indigenous identities and link the country's ingrained machismo to its extractivist model. As for Claudia Tula, much of their work is in the public space and seeks to generate and strengthen human bonds, as well as make a spatial intervention. Finally, Miradas Críticas del Territorio desde el Feminismo engages in a deep deconstruction of our relationship to our bodies and territories, challenging Cartesian ideas of mind as separate from the body and humans as separate from nature and proposing instead a relationship to the territory that is deeply embodied. Like Pao Lunch, MCTF turns focus to the body as territory of struggle, but it approaches this from a collective perspective and with specific transformative objectives in mind: MCTF's mapping practice is an example of the methodologies they design for generating communal spaces of transformation. In a way, these methodologies become blueprints for ways of living and collective organizing that are more democratic, that value local forms of knowledge, and that treasure a relationship of interdependence with the territory.

If we situate the works discussed in this chapter in the current context of increased ecological destruction and gender-based violence, we can see how in their own way, each artist and collective discussed here counteracts the mainstream media pattern in which, as described by Gago, "feminized voices are only heard when they narrate an episode of pure horror and violence." Instead, these works turn denunciations of violence into "a political enunciation that also deconstructs the causes of those events."[65] Furthermore, by activating in different ways the concept of *cuerpo-territorio* or body-territory, they make a statement on the impossibility of "cutting up and isolating the individual body from the collective body, the human body from the territory," and "'deliberalize' the notion of body as individual property,"[66] highlighting instead the interdependence that allows the reproduction of life. In this way, these works address one of the main challenges of ecofeminism, which is "the mediation between a deconstructivist understanding of gender and a materialist understanding of nature."[67]

We could therefore say that the notion of *cuerpo-territorio* not only constitutes a site of enunciation for deconstructing patriarchal and anthropocentric ideas, but also becomes the starting point for the construction of a distinct political subjectivity. When body and territory are one, this gives place to holistic narratives, and actions and demands, even when specific, become integrated to a wider vision for profound social transformation, as we have seen in the case of the occupation and symbolic action *La rebelión de las flores* discussed earlier. In addition, the integration of body and territory in these struggles serves to confront a rationalist understanding of resource and territorial struggles. The centering of the body and overlapping experiences of violence, but also of joy, pleasure, and collective care, opens up possibilities for new and deeper understandings of extractivism: if we factor in affect and emotion, we can see how these "influence the very ways that resources are imagined, accessed, used and controlled on a daily basis," as Farhana Sultana argues.[68]

Indeed, by exposing and challenging forms of gendered, extractivist violence, the above works and actions pose important questions regarding care. How can we build a world where these forms of violence are no longer the norm? How can we build a world that properly cares for communities and territories? What does an ecofeminist ethic of care look like, and what is its potential on a global scale?

### *Transnational (Eco)feminisms and an Ecofeminist Ethic of Care*

The last few years have seen a sudden surge of feminist movements and mobilizations around the globe. Since the birth of Ni Una Menos in 2015 the world has witnessed the Polish women's strike opposing the ban on abortion in 2016, the women's march against Donald Trump and the surge of the #MeToo movement in 2017, the Repeal of the Eighth Amendment in Ireland expanding abortion rights and the Brazilian Ele Não movement against Jair Bolsonaro in 2018, and the viralization of the performance *Un violador en tu camino* (A rapist in your path) by the Chilean collective Las Tesis in 2019. These movements are very different from one other, responding on different levels to local and global issues and aligning themselves with different kinds of feminisms, from liberal to intersectional, antifascist, and anticapitalist. However, there are two unifying factors among them all: first, they are all reacting to forms of violence exerted upon women—in many cases minoritized and oppressed groups in general—and second, in their response it is often their bodies that stand at the frontlines, vulnerable to police repression and harassment from conservative and reactive sectors of society.

Alongside such mobilizations, we have also seen women leading the way in movements for climate action, from established figures like Vandana Shiva and Naomi Klein to new icons like Greta Thunberg and Vanessa Nakate. And, as evidenced in the example in the introduction to this chapter and in the discussion of the Ni Una Menos movement, we are beginning to see stronger connections between environmental and feminist movements, as the current state of the world makes the interconnectedness of the roots of violence, oppression, and the destruction of ecosystems increasingly evident. For instance, as Gago describes, for women across Latin America, the international women's strike emerging in 2017 has served as an opportunity to highlight how women's struggles are connected to environmental issues like struggles over land and the use of agrochemicals.[69] What we can see more and more clearly in feminist movements is the display of an ethic of care, one that goes beyond the fight against gender violence and oppression and applies a feminist perspective to rethinking the basis of our existence in this world.

At the time of writing, we find ourselves facing an ecological crisis, a rise of the far right, and the threat of new pandemics in a post-COVID-19 world. We are in urgent need of a movement that can respond to the curtailing of rights of minoritized and oppressed groups and at the same time address the global environmental, economic, and social crises. Ecofeminism can help us in this task if we adopt it as a grounding theory and as an ethic of care that guides our approach to practice.

As a theoretical approach, ecofeminism can help us deconstruct the paradigms that sustain systems of oppression, inequality, and environmental degradation, moving away from an anthropocentric perspective of nature as resource and the modern-colonial hierarchal binaries that continue to underpin the oppression of women, *disidencias,* Black, indigenous, and people of color, disabled people, and other minoritized groups. As an ethic of care, ecofeminism can provide a holistic response to the multiple crises that characterize this moment because it involves acknowledging our interdependence with the environment and other organisms and centering care for communities and for ecosystems in our individual and collective actions. In practice, this includes placing people before profit, reinforcing networks of mutual aid, and rethinking what well-being means and how we can shift our modes of production and our institutions and services to ensure well-being for all.[70] Such responses need to occur at local, regional, and global levels. Local actions need to be situated in each context, while also building strong connections at different scales.

The creative and collective practices discussed in this chapter act as examples of how we can begin to do this, activating mechanisms of democratization, deconstruction, and design that allow us to creatively reconstruct our relationships to each other and to our ecosystems. Importantly, root ideas such as *cuerpo-territorio* and interdependence directly counteract the neoliberal ideology that perpetuates self-interest and individualized solutions to social problems. An expansion of these ideas across geographies and movements and their daily experience through art, collective organizing, and other forms of *sentipensar* open up possibilities for new transnational ecofeminist horizons.

# 3 Human Rights and the Rights of Nature

## *Generating Public Narratives*

THE IMPACTS THAT extractivism has on ecosystems, human health, sovereignty, and political participation, among other issues, are often framed by frontline communities and campaigners alike as matters of human rights. Not only this, but the legal framework of rights is often one of the most powerful tools that frontline communities and campaigners have in their fight against the advance of extractive projects. It is for these reasons that looking at the ways that different social actors develop human rights narratives—and increasingly, the rights of nature—and represent and mobilize them through creative practice is paramount to understanding the cultural politics of anti- and postextractivist movements.

There are broadly two main approaches to thinking about the nature of human rights. The first considers human rights as rights that are granted by the state. The second argues that the state can only recognize and guarantee those rights, as they are natural and rooted in (universal) ideas of human dignity.[1] While different conceptions of human rights go back centuries, the human rights movement as we know it emerged in the aftermath of the Second World War, culminating in the Universal Declaration of Human Rights in 1948. Since then, human rights have been the focus of criticism from different sectors. One of the main criticisms points to the universalist nature and imperialist tendency of human rights through the erasure of diverse moral systems, arguing that international human rights impose a hegemony of Western moral values on less powerful groups.[2] Another related critique points specifically to the fact that "the colonialist-authoritative *status* of International Human Rights" derives from its "formally impositive foundation of Law."[3] Therefore, there is the question of equating rights to the legitimacy of the institutions that guarantee them, which in the case of indigenous territorial conflicts involves claimants legitimizing the authority of settler colonial states.[4]

Human rights remain a contested territory to this day. While some defend the universal and individualist character of human rights as necessary for the protection of individuals against oppression at different scales,[5] others argue that in the current state of globalization, human rights and their emancipatory potential have been co-opted, and human rights discourse "has become . . . the most (necessarily) axiomatic of (neo)liberalism's global discourse."[6] In other words, human rights serve the justification and implementation of processes of dispossession (e.g., in the name of development), while at the same time can be a powerful tool for protection and for social change.[7]

In Latin America, while many adhere to the universality and imperialism critiques, human rights have been valuable instruments in the defense against transnational corporate power and in the struggles for justice in the aftermath of dictatorships, as is the case in Argentina. Indeed, across the region, different countries adopted and championed international human rights early on, even before the founding of the United Nations.[8] In fact, judicial processes and human rights movements in Latin America have contributed to developing international human rights vocabulary, law-making, and advocacy—for example, the introduction of the figure of the *disappeared*.[9]

At the same time, the discourse and implementation of human rights have been transformed and adapted to the local context in response to social and environmental developments in the region. The right to a healthy environment and the right to water, for instance, have become more prominent within human rights discourse as the expansion of the extractive frontier in Latin America threatens the lives of communities and climate change endangers the survival of whole ecosystems.[10] A great concern regarding the limitations of human rights, however, is that in many countries the language of rights has permeated the governmental sphere, but the upholding of rights has not yet been embedded into public institutions and remains mostly on a rhetorical level.[11] Furthermore, the expansion of the extractive frontier in the name of development has opened up a new face of criminalization and violation of human rights, including the neglect of available institutional mechanisms for guaranteeing such rights, such as the right to consultation prior to the development of new extractive projects.[12]

In Argentina, the strong tradition of human rights activism that erupted as a response to the country's last civic-military dictatorship (1976 through 1983) has become a pillar of social justice mobilizations, as well as the cradle of different forms of cultural and artistic expression that have defined aesthetic-political practices for generations. With this in mind, this chapter explores how antiextractivist struggles connect with the human rights movement, building on, borrowing from, and contributing to this tradition. Specifically, the chapter looks at the way that public interventions, artworks, and performances that emerge from or respond to extractive conflicts in Argentina draw from narratives, tropes, and aesthetics that are linked to the local tradition of human rights activism, offering in this way a situated perspective on the cultural politics of antiextractivist movements. In this exploration, I examine the role of creative acts as practices of denunciation and documentation, and interrogate as well the relationship between human rights and the rights of nature. I discuss how different terms and perspectives are mobilized, and finally reflect on the role of human rights and the rights of nature in the midst of cultural transformations regarding humans' perceived position in nature.

## *Human Rights Activism in Argentina*

Argentina has a strong tradition of human rights activism. As in other Latin American countries, the human rights movement had a crucial role in denouncing violence and assisting victims during the last dictatorship, a period of violent repression and persecution that resulted in the disappearance of thirty thousand people. Once the dictatorship ended, the movement continued its role in the defense of human rights and consolidated around demands for truth, justice, identity, and memory.

In his work on Argentina, sociologist Emilio Crenzel builds on Halbwachs and explains how public memory is not only collective but also plural, corresponding to the multiplicity of groups in society.[13] The past, he argues, is not an immutable thing subject to personal interpretations, but the outcome of cultural and political dynamics, and of struggles for providing it with meaning.[14] Indeed, the social actors that have taken on the task of constructing a collective memory during and in the aftermath of the dictatorship have adopted a variety of strategies and have done so on different fronts. This includes the search for truth (and for the whereabouts or remains in the case of the disappeared), attempts to take perpetrators to trial, the creation of spaces for assistance and support to victims, and initiatives for increasing social awareness on the issues.[15]

In this context, different forms of official intervention in public spaces, like plaques and monuments, contribute to the act of memorialization, a public and political act that builds the conditions for future histories.[16] In Latin America, acts of commemoration carry a sense of urgency, as they not only look back on the past but also serve to inform the present and the near future, as a form of warning. At the same time, the monuments erected to memorialize events in the past often have a fluid quality in recognition of the truth yet to be uncovered, as is the case for monuments with names of the disappeared that include empty spaces for further names to be added.

In addition to official commemorations, toward the end of the dictatorship in Argentina a variety of examples of grassroots denunciation and memory making developed that began in the streets. Art historian Ana Longoni analyzes the various forms of action that emerged from the fields of activism and artistic practice and describes three matrices or forms of representation. In her proposal, she centers specifically on the figure of the disappeared.

The first matrix is the photograph. During the first marches demanding information on the whereabouts of the disappeared, family members brought with them photos of their own children. Toward the end of the dictatorship, these images were reproduced, archives were created, and people would carry images of the disappeared during marches even when family members where not there. Through these processes, the image as a resource of denunciation became collectivized.[17] The second matrix of representation is the silhouette, which allowed the overlapping of the disappeared and of citizens out on the streets. Silhouettes emerged as a response to the need to quantify and make "present" the absence of the disappeared. The repetition of the life-size figures created by tracing the outlines of bodies on the ground made the absence of the disappeared manifest in the public space, as artists filled the streets with anonymous and/or named silhouettes.[18] Public events in which hundreds or thousands of silhouettes were either traced or produced as posters and put up in public spaces became known as *siluetazos* and were rapidly appropriated and reproduced in different parts of the country.

A third matrix emerging later on in the mid-1990s was the performance. This matrix was first developed by artist collectives linked to the human rights organization H.I.J.O.S. (Sons and Daughters of the Disappeared for Identity and Justice and against Forgetting and Silence), namely Grupo de Arte Callejero (GAC) and Grupo Etcétera.[19] They developed the tactic of the *escrache*, which Longoni argues should not be thought of as an artistic genre but rather as a poetic manifestation of the politics of the time.[20] *Escraches* consisted of identifying the residences of officials who had been implicated in the dictatorship but had not been imprisoned and publicly exposing them to their neighbors. Etcétera brought with them the element of carnivalesque performance to *escraches*, depicting the military and members of the clergy in a grotesque manner. GAC contributed the street signs pointing to the presence of former members of the military implicated in crimes against humanity. *Escraches* were key in installing the idea that protest and political action were not confined to the space of the public square but instead could happen anywhere, any time. Importantly, they also shifted the focus away from the victims and toward the perpetrators.[21]

In these kinds of practices, memory is manifested in the actions of social actors rather than in the construction of physical spaces or artefacts such as monuments. However, while being embodied acts, they also inscribe memory in the urban landscape. These practices entail forms of physical and/or symbolic appropriation of public space, and often involve a renewal of aesthetic and political languages. Memory, in these instances, is an embodied, collective act, as argued by sociologist Estela Schindel, in a comparable way to the *rondas* (circular marches) of the Mothers of Plaza de Mayo, the landmark embodied act of defiance of the human rights movement.[22]

When dealing with public monuments and artworks that visibilize the past, also argues Schindel, there is the question of how to bring to light other aspects of the dictatorship, such as state policies introduced during that time, or the political economy of infrastructure projects, which were part of "everyday life" during a time of horror.[23] It is equally challenging to represent the complicity of certain sectors of society sustaining the situation such as economic actors, and indeed the aforementioned *escraches* are good examples of practices that engage with those multiple layers and actors. Generating narratives that shed light on the different forms of complicity in human rights violations is challenging but also necessary. As we will see later on, it is a task also taken up by artists denouncing the extractivist model.

## *Extractivism, Human Rights, and the Rights of Nature*

Human rights discourse is elemental to the framing of many anti- and postextractivist struggles. For instance, representatives from a range of Latin American countries convened at a session of the Inter-American Commission on Human Rights in October 2018 to present evidence on the impacts of fracking, framing the extraction of nonconventional fossil fuels as a threat to human rights and urging governments to adopt appropriate measures to prevent human rights violations.[24] In cases such as this, the narrative centers on how a certain activity constitutes a threat and points to the power of the implicated industry. Other narratives that oppose the advance of extractivism instead center on the object to be defended (e.g., water), adopting on occasion a more positive tone. An example of this, also from 2018, was the first International Forum for the Right to Water, which took place in the Argentine city of Catamarca in the northwest of the country and brought together artists, campaigners, and community representatives from a range of countries in order to discuss strategies for the defense of water as a human right.[25]

We can also recognize this focus on the object to be defended in the work of campaigners advocating for food production and nutrition as human rights issues. The right to food has been acknowledged in the Universal Declaration of Human Rights, and it involves the access to sufficient amounts of food that is sustainable, of satisfactory quality, and acceptable according to a person's culture.[26] The narrative of food as a human rights issue is embodied in the movement for food sovereignty and the sovereign use of seeds,[27] although, as I will now show based on my ethnographic work, there are markedly different understandings and approaches to thinking about food as a matter of human rights.

Marcos Filardi is a lawyer, human rights activist, and champion of food sovereignty. When I met Marcos, he told me about the struggles surrounding food production in Argentina and the link to human rights activism.[28] Marcos explained that there are five pillars of food sovereignty: peasant agro-ecology, holistic agrarian reform, food as a human right, seeds as patrimony of the peoples in the service of humanity, and local production for local consumption. He explained that so far the international human rights paradigm has followed the line of individual rights and the right to nourishment when it comes to talking about food as a right. The movement for food sovereignty, on the other hand, takes a wider approach that includes food in all its dimensions, as well as water, and also involves collective rights and the people's right to define their own policies and practices surrounding food production.[29] Marcos explained as well that incorporating human rights discourse in the movement for food sovereignty is a necessary, strategic choice. By applying the human rights angle—which brings with it a strong, local tradition of activism—to an issue that is simultaneously taken on by antiextractivist and environmental groups, it is possible to unite actors from different sectors and work on common causes and joint projects.

There is yet another way antiextractivist movements frame their struggles in terms of human rights, and this is by applying the perspective of state violence. As the extractive frontier expands and conflicts over territorial autonomy, the right to prior consultation, and the right to a healthy environment intensify, so does the repression of protest, in ways that human rights and other social organizations see as a reproduction of repression and persecution during the times of the last dictatorship.

In 2017 Argentina saw two high profile cases of death and of disappearance followed by death following police and military repression in the context of territorial conflicts in Patagonia. These were the disappearance of Santiago Maldonado in August, whose body was found in October, and the death of Rafael Nahuel in November. Maldonado was a white activist from the province of Buenos Aires who was protesting in solidarity alongside a Mapuche community. Nahuel was a young Mapuche man who had recently become involved in territorial struggles. Maldonado's disappearance and death took place following a protest by a community claiming back ancestral territory from Italian magnate Luciano Benetton in the province of Chubut. Nahuel's death took place when a special squad of the Navy Prefecture was evicting a Mapuche community that was reclaiming land near a tourist town in the province of Río Negro; he was shot in the back and killed. Both deaths occurred in the context of repression of protests for the recognition of ancestral territories and against the advance of extractive and tourism projects.

Despite the fact that deaths of land defenders are unfortunately not a new phenomenon, the deaths of Maldonado and Nahuel were the first high-profile media cases of the sort in Argentina, as they took place in a moment of heightened conflict concerning territorial rights. These cases contributed to generating links between human rights narratives against state violence and antiextractivist ones, both among activists and in the left-leaning media. These connections were expressed for instance at the twenty-fourth of March demonstration in 2018, a yearly march that commemorates the last Argentine dictatorship and is a landmark event in human rights activism. Rally speakers including the Mothers of Plaza de Mayo and other social justice activists framed the recent deaths of Maldonado and Nahuel within a context of state violence and extractivism.[30]

But these kinds of connections between movements are relatively new. While human rights have an important space in the national imaginary and the identity of Argentinians, the view of human rights held by most people until recently, including movements on the left, was one tied to a particular period in time and to particular kinds of rights. Even though the national constitution recognizes the right to nourishment and the right to a clean environment as belonging to all citizens, most people are not aware of this. As Marcos argued during our conversation, human rights in Argentina are

> closely tied to the agenda of memory, truth, and justice. What has been an incredible struggle, which has made us proud on an international level, also generated a very narrow agenda in the collective imaginary, and this needs to be deconstructed. When we talk about the right to food this has a very low level of social recognition, despite having a high level of normative recognition; it is part of the National Constitution, and still people do not know that there is a right to food . . . it is the water you drink every day, the food you eat, the air you breathe; it is health, life, integrity, dignity, all of those issues.[31]

It is important to consider as well how movements against extractivism and movements for the rights of indigenous peoples have problematized the way the recent progressive governments of Nestor Kirchner (2003–2007) and Cristina Fernández de Kirchner (2007–2015) adopted the human rights narrative. Human rights lawyer Mariana Katz, who works for the SERPAJ (Servicio Paz y Justicia, or Service for Peace and Justice), argues that

> *Kirchnerismo* used [human rights] in a partisan manner and some organizations got caught up in that, and unfortunately did not see that the defense of human rights is the defense of integrity. Human rights are . . . about protecting the dignity of the person against the arbitrary exercise of power . . . , so if human dignity is threatened by the model of economic development that a country wants to promote, it is [also] a violation of human dignity.[32]

Mariana's words are representative of a strand of the human rights movement that fights for, but also goes beyond, the preservation of memory and the continued search for justice for victims of the dictatorship and goes on to develop a radical critique of systemic violence. This kind of critique does not only focus on the most extreme forms of violence as executed by the military junta, but also denounces the sustained violence of neoliberalism and extractivism, one that is systemic, classed, and racialized.[33] As the extractive frontier expands and the connections between different forms of violence become more evident, this understanding of human rights becomes more widespread.

## GENOCIDE, ECOCIDE, AND TERRICIDE

Following the end of the last dictatorship, the persecution and murder of anyone perceived as a political dissident or left-wing—which resulted in the forced disappearance of 30,000 people—was denounced by human rights activists as a genocide.[34] Indeed, tribunals in Argentina and Spain used the same term to label the crimes of the military junta. There were several reasons behind such qualification, including the similarities in reasoning and practice between the Nazi holocaust and the crimes committed by the Argentine dictatorship; as pointed out by Feierstein, in both cases genocide functioned as a technology of power.[35] While the use of the term *genocide* in the Argentine context has not gone unchallenged,[36] it remains a crucial concept in the human rights movement to this day and has been incorporated by different antiextractivist struggles. The term *genocide* has, for instance, been employed by groups of mothers, teachers, and doctors in the province of Entre Ríos, where locals claim the extensive use of glyphosate (an herbicide traded by Monsanto under the name Roundup) has led to hikes in birth defects, cancer, respiratory problems, and other health conditions. The inaction of the state, the silencing of victims, and politicians' siding with large-scale farmers and corporations is regarded by those in the struggle as a death sentence resulting from placing profits before people. *Genocide* is not used here to signal targeted persecution but rather to highlight the value that is denied to certain lives, deemed disposable for the sake of an extractivist development model.

In addition to defending the rights of humans, those at the frontlines of environmental conflicts have also began to speak about the rights of nature, a key concept in postdevelopment discourse as argued for instance by Arturo Escobar.[37] The concept of the rights of nature recognizes nature as an independent subject of rights, with intrinsic value independent of the use that humans might have for it. For this reason, explain Martínez and Acosta, the rights of nature are different from environmental rights—the latter sustaining an anthropocentric logic—though upholding these rights is necessary in order to properly guarantee the environmental rights of humans. Human rights and the rights of nature can be said to follow different logics, but in practice, they can complement each other as tools in the defense of life.[38]

The leading legal examples on the matter of rights of nature are the cases of Bolivia and Ecuador, where the rights of nature were incorporated into the countries' constitutions—even if in practice, they are upheld in a selective manner.[39] In reality, the rights of nature are still in a process of becoming; in order for them to be upheld, it does not suffice to incorporate them into constitutions, but what is needed rather is to break with the long-held perception of nature as resource and humans as separate from nature. In other words, as proposed by Mario Blaser, there is need for an ontological shift in the way we understand the different elements and beings on Earth and our relation to them.[40]

One of the terms often employed in attempts to reconcile human rights and the rights of nature is *ecocide*, a concept that describes devastating ecological damage, often implying the annihilation of species and the degradation of whole ecosystems. In 2021, an independent panel of experts put forward a definition of the term with the intention of amending the Rome Statute of the International Criminal Court, which stated that ecocide involves "unlawful or wanton acts committed with knowledge that there is a substantial likelihood of severe and either widespread or long-term damage to the environment being caused by those acts."[41] "*Ecocidas* . . ." (an approximate translation is "Perpetrators of ecocide . . .") was also the title of an exhibition in Buenos Aires in 2018, featuring artists Laura Luciani, Santiago Fredes, Eduardo Molinari, and Nicolás Rodríguez.[42] In a text for the exhibition, Molinari wrote,

> The struggle of the people and the communities that defend themselves from fumigation and deforestation moves forward every day. The struggle of those of us who believe that there is another way for the production of food beyond the transgenic model moves forward as well. . . . The battle is fought meter by meter, and those who defend the agribusiness model, the politicians, scientists, academics, and producers of course, must face up and provide explanations. . . .
>
> Extractivism, in its contemporary version of biotechnology and finance, presents a singular quality: it pretends to construct a regime of visibility based—paradoxically—on everything that it does not allow us to see, that it conceals. From the world of images, we propose to use our counter-power strength. This exhibition is our humble contribution to try to visibilize some of the social, sanitary,

> environmental, urban, and cultural consequences of a kind of thinking that is ecocidal, annihilating, and exterminating of life, sadly related to genocidal thinking. With the conviction that there is another path, and that many of us are already on it.[43]

Molinari's text emphasizes the importance of strategies of visibilization within a regime based on concealing the consequences of an extractivist production model. It also points to the links between ecocide and genocide, suggesting not only that the disregard for human life is linked to a disregard for nature, but also that the perpetrators of such crimes are often the same.

In addition to the term *ecocide*, which signals the grave damage done to ecosystems, different groups and movements employ other terms that better describe their experiences and positioning. In Chapter 2 I described how in October 2019, a self-organized group of indigenous women occupied the Ministry of Interior in Buenos Aires under the banner "they sowed terricide, they will harvest rebellion," calling on the state to respect their rights as indigenous women, and demanding an end to the *terricidio* (terricide) carried out by the extractive industries. In 2020, the same group called for the recognition of terricide as a crime against humanity and nature, defining it as "the murder of not only tangible ecosystems and of the peoples that inhabit them, but also the murder of all the forces that regulate life on Earth, what we call a perceptible ecosystem."[44] And in 2021, their claim was taken from the northernmost and southernmost points of the country to the National Congress in Buenos Aires by means of a months-long walk that culminated with the global day of action *Basta de terricidio* (Stop terricide). In this way, their call highlights the ongoing genocide of indigenous people and integrates the fight against extractivism with the defense of the territory and of human rights.

Finally, in Andalgalá, where the local assembly El Algarrobo is fighting against open-pit mining, members of the assembly speak of the effects of open-pit mining as crimes of *lesa naturaleza*, referencing the legal expression *crímenes de lesa humanidad* (crimes against humanity), but placing nature at the center.

The use of different terms and the inclination for highlighting either human rights or the rights of nature brings up questions around framing and how to reconcile a historically and culturally significant and useful yet anthropocentric category (human rights) with still-evolving frameworks for respecting and safeguarding non-human entities. Indeed, we can see how in the field of law, the complexity of the climate crisis has translated into calls for new epistemic parameters.[45] Biocultural rights thus emerge as a new paradigm for safeguarding the human rights of indigenous communities and, acknowledging their knowledge of the land and understanding of ecosystems, following their stewardship in protecting the environment.[46] Such an approach opens up many opportunities for valuing and enacting indigenous ontologies and knowledges—though it is important to recognize the dangers of essentializing indigenous subjects and of placing inequitable responsibilities to protect nature upon them.[47]

Having considered some of the terminology and perspectives employed in framing extractivism as a matter of human rights and the rights of nature, the next section will take a closer look at performative and artistic public interventions. This will provide insight into the ways that narratives about rights, power, and the defense of life are materialized and manifested in the public sphere, and to what effects.

## *Extractivism and Human Rights in Artistic Interventions*

Both human rights as an issue and the aesthetic tropes of human rights struggles have become central to contemporary Argentine art as well as to social movements. Numerous contemporary artists in the last four decades have built on this tradition to address a range of social issues and conflicts, as was the case in the aftermath of the economic crisis of 2001.[48] Indeed, several artists whose work currently engages with issues surrounding extractivism have a background in human rights activism. The list includes artists like Susana Palomas, who collaborated with the human rights organization H.I.J.O.S. for the project *Silo siniestro* depicting environmental and health effects of the GMO model of soya production. It also includes Diana Dowek, who after decades of engaging with and supporting human rights causes received the 2015 Grand National Painting Award for a harrowing landscape depicting the open-pit mine Bajo La Alumbrera in the aforementioned town of Andalgalá.

Political and aesthetic interventions borrowing from the tradition of human rights activism in the fight against extractivism take different forms, from exhibitions to ritualistic marches and performances in the public space. In what follows, I consider the local history of art and political action discussed at the beginning of this chapter and reflect on some of the actions and artworks that adopt a human rights perspective in their response to extractivism, focusing on three types of practices: demonstrations and performance actions, visual arts, and documentary photography. After analyzing the processes and approaches of the different practices and their roles within local and wider struggles, I move on to discuss how they activate the functions of denunciation and documentation in the movement against extractivism.

## BODIES IN THE STREETS

The case of Ituzaingó Anexo, a neighborhood on the edges of the city of Córdoba, is one that has gathered significant international attention. In 2002, a few women in the neighborhood, who would later be known as the "Mothers of Ituzaingó," began to notice a hike in diseases, including several cases of cancer, affecting their families and loved ones. They reported this to the local authorities but their concern was dismissed, and so they decided to take matters into their own hands. After initial exercises in popular epidemiology and community mobilization, followed by scientific testing from allied scientists and eventually media attention, their struggle resulted in the conviction of a soya bean producer and an air fumigator for spreading toxic substances in farming. Now, almost two decades after the beginning of their struggle, the Mothers of Ituzaingó still march around the central square in the city of Córdoba each month, demanding the prosecution of other responsible actors who remain to be held accountable. In their marches, they wear surgical masks as a unifying element that points to the health hazard caused by the use of "agrotoxics."[49] Sometimes these masks are worn as headscarves, a nod to the *rondas* of the Mothers of Plaza de Mayo.

The practice of ritualistic marches taking place in a cyclical manner was also adopted by the community of Andalgalá in Catamarca. The local assembly organizes walks against open-pit mining around the main square, which they call "walks for life," every Saturday, and they had hundreds of walks under their belt at the time of my visit in 2018. These marches have had a significant impact in the local habits and culture, as explained by local artist Eliana: "Every routine or custom in Andalgalá has been modified as a result of the Saturday marches. The municipality no longer holds events on those days, and if they try to, people make a fuss."[50] Andalgalá's protest repertoire also includes the performances of Mujeres del Silencio (Women of Silence), who would meet outside the local court house, the police station, and the premises of the Canadian mining company Yamana Gold with their hands tied and wearing gags in their mouths. They would stand in silence, for an hour, facing the entrance of the building, confronting the company's staff with their silent stare. In the words of Silvina, an activist from Andalgalá, their ritualistic action was "a symbol of the lack of justice, the lack of freedom, lack of everything." Their strategy was one of "deafening silence," which generated a very particular atmosphere: "you could cut the tension with a knife."[51]

In Andalgalá there is also another medium that has been crucial to the struggle, and that is mural painting. Murals in Andalgalá have depicted several themes, from the need to safeguard nature to explicit opposition to specific mining companies. But the most controversial murals have been those that portray instances of police repression. In 2010, Andalgalá was the site of a siege and violent police repression of protest that led to mass arrests and several injured. This episode of extreme violence left a deep wound in the social fabric of the town, and most remember it as the darkest moment in the fight against mining. Local artists captured the episode in murals as a way of conserving that memory and, as Schindel would argue, as a warning for the future, a past of state violence never to return to. Worth noting is that while other murals and graffiti against the mine are not usually covered up by the council, those depicting police repression were.

Another example of embodied interventions in the public realm is Fuerza Artística de Choque Comunicativo (Artistic Force of Communication Shock) or FACC, a collective that emerged in 2017 with a series of performance actions in public spaces that are often livestreamed as well. The collective consists of artists that link up with each other in a networked manner in order to plan actions in different parts of the country. The identities of participants, however, are kept anonymous to the press. FACC performances address social and political issues, and they tend to follow particular aesthetics: while some of their actions use naked bodies as building blocks for public installations, on other occasions performers wear black clothes and masks with bird-like beaks and stand in a formation resembling a murder of crows (or "birds of ill omen"). Their performances range from the interventionist and shocking to the largely static and contemplative and sometimes involve live music as well.[52] One of the main slogans that FACC has used in their performances is "*Quién elige?*" (Whose choice is it?), a reference to the lack of democratic participation in matters related to development and the management of resources, among other issues (see fig. 3.1). FACC have often targeted sites of symbolic significance in the fight against extractivism, such as the Ministry of Energy and Mining in Buenos Aires.

One of their performance actions, which took place on 20 October 2017, consisted of four interventions in four cities across the country. The action involved five hundred people in total and presented a narrative frame that connected issues of extractivism with workers' rights, state repression, and corporate power. The performances were captured in a five-minute video that brought together images from all four sites and stated the relevance of each location. The first performance action took place in Comodoro Rivadavia, in the province of Chubut. The action was carried out

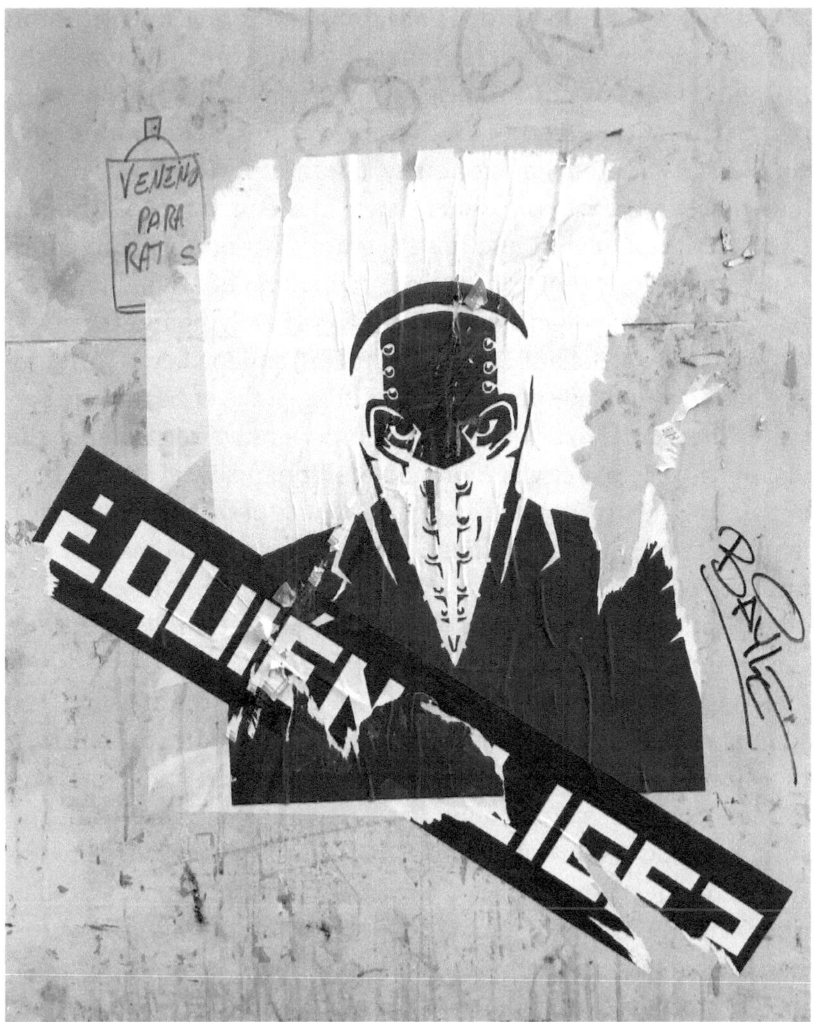


FIGURE 3.1. Poster by FACC reading "Whose choice is it?" Photo by the author.

outside the petrol tanks of YPF, the national fossil fuel company, and the video described the city as "Land of Fracking." Above the images of the still, black figures, on the video we can also see the hashtag *#EstoEsDictaduraCorporativa* (this is corporate dictatorship). The second performance action, some hours later, happened in Ledesma, province of Jujuy. The place is defined in the film as

"Land of sugar exploitation, pollution, and repression of union organizing." The performers gathered outside the mansion of the Blaquier family, owners of the sugar company Ledesma. They carried a banner that read "This is murderous exploitation. Whose choice is it?" Later that same day, another performance action took place in the city of Esquel, again in the province of Chubut. The description read "Land of struggle against mining companies and corporations that concentrate ownership of Mapuche land," referencing the indigenous land conflicts involving international billionaires like Luciano Benetton (Italian) and Joe Lewis (British). The action took place outside the building of the gendarmerie battalion that took part in the repression operative resulting in the disappearance of activist Santiago Maldonado. They held a banner stating, "This is state terrorism. Whose choice is it?" Finally, in the early evening of the same day, the group held their last performance action outside the National Congress in Buenos Aires. They used stencils to record the phrase "Whose choice is it?" on the pavement, and then stood quietly in place.[53]

FACC's performance actions look to denounce the abuses of the state and of extractive corporations and to speak truth to power. In a similar manner to the Mujeres del Silencio in Andalgalá, performers stand in silence outside places that symbolize state and corporate power in a defiant manner that asserts their right to territory and their noncompliance with a system that abuses human rights and the rights of nature. Their focus is not on the effects of extractivism but rather on the role of specific agents, and through their performance actions, they expose connections between powerful sectors and question the corrosion of democracy under an extractivist model. By referencing the dictatorship, these actions made explicit the connections between the economic and political processes of the last dictatorship and those under the current phase of extractivism, and took the opportunity as well to denounce the banalization of history and memory espoused by the national government of Mauricio Macri at the time.[54]

## MEMORIALIZING EXTRACTIVISM

Also looking at memory and the act of memorializing is the *Museo del neoextractivismo* (Museum of neoextractivism) by Grupo Etcétera. Etcétera is one of the artist collectives that worked with H.I.J.O.S. during the *escraches* that began in the 1990s, and, alongside Grupo de Arte Callejero (GAC), they are part of the more radical strand of the human rights movement previously mentioned. As described by Jennifer Ponce de León, in their work Etcétera connect the political to the economic, a matter often missing from mainstream human rights narratives.[55] Furthermore, much of their work highlights the perpetuity of state violence beyond the extreme period of the dictatorship.

As they continue to work on human rights issues, over the years Etcétera's practice has developed a related focus on extractivism. The *Museo del neoextractivismo* is an itinerating exhibition/project that brings together work by Etcétera (including curated displays of found objects) and pieces by other artists and researchers with the objective of deconstructing the workings of the extractivist model for a general audience. At the museum one can find a wooden, mobile recreation of a pumpjack under the title *Trampa neoextractiva* (Neoextractive trap), which exhibition goers are invited to play with (see fig. 3.2). Alongside the installation, there are texts that explain in plain language how oil is extracted, the difference between conventional oil extraction and fracking, and basic facts about the fossil fuel industry in Argentina. Each enactment of the museum includes open talks and workshops with experts such as land defenders, sociologists, and environmental lawyers, and in one instance, it also included the artists' participation in a radio show.

The choice of the museum format serves specific purposes, responding to the contemporary nature of extractivism and the different extractive conflicts in Argentina. In the first place, the museum format provides an opportunity for curating a multimedia narrative that reflects the complex nature of the extractivist model, one that a single artwork or perspective might not be able

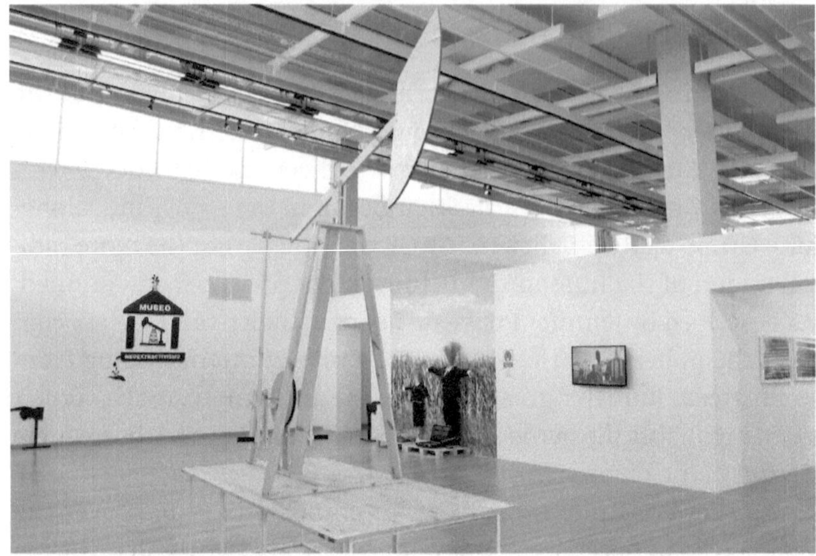


FIGURE 3.2. Etcétera, *Museo del neoextractivismo*. Part of the exhibition *Futuro de la memoria*, Parque de la Memoria, Buenos Aires, Argentina, 2018. Image: Archivo Etcétera.

to produce. Also, with each edition of the museum, new work is added and other content is updated, thus allowing the museum to respond to evolving conflicts and developments at the local and global level. At the same time, the museum format serves the purpose of legitimization. By curating a selection of content, the artists provide a certain status to specific works, people, and stories. In this sense, we can locate *Museo del neoextractivismo* alongside other initiatives of recent years such as The Natural History Museum (NHM), a project by the US-based collective Not An Alternative. By adopting the institutional discourse of the museum, but maintaining an agile, responsive, and continuously evolving practice, NHM is able to smoothly move between the spheres of cultural institutions and art activism, engaging with different stakeholders in order to advance an environmental and social justice agenda from the grassroots and at the same time carve their own space to speak with and from within the cultural establishment, in the process challenging the idea of a museum and demonstrating

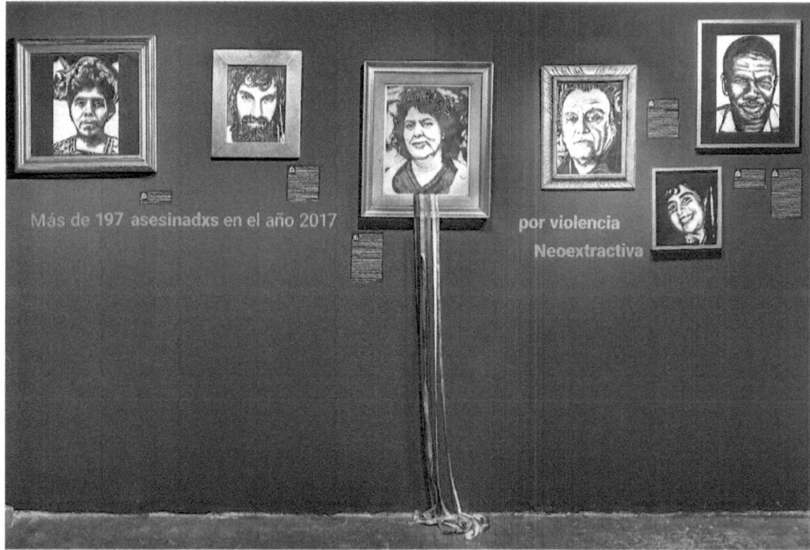


FIGURE 3.3. Etcétera, *Museo del neoextractivismo*, exhibition at Radio FM La Tribu. Buenos Aires, Argentina, 2018. Image: Archivo Etcétera.

how cultural institutions could be otherwise.[56] In the case of *Museo del neoextractivismo*, we can see how engaging with the codes of the museum space allows the artists to support and enhance certain narratives. For instance, a wall displaying the framed portraits of activists, researchers, and environmental defenders who have recently passed away (some murdered in the context of resource conflicts) gives the deceased the status of martyr or hero for the cause (see fig. 3.3).

For an edition of the museum in October and November 2018, the exhibition was set up at a radio station in Buenos Aires. This time it included displays by artists and researchers working on such issues as agribusiness, open-pit mining, and fossil fuel extraction, and it served as an opportunity to organize screenings of relevant films and talks. In this way, the exhibition not only deconstructed the dynamics of different aspects of the extractivist model—from the financial to the social—but also generated a democratization of information and gave place to instances of exchange and debate.

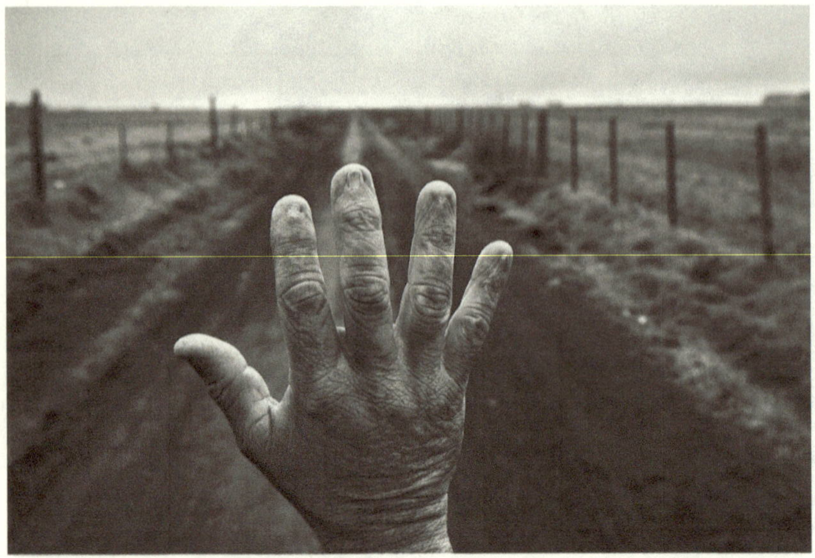

FIGURE 3.4. From the series El Costo Humano de los Agrotóxicos, 2014–2019, by Pablo E. Piovano.

## DENOUNCING GENOCIDE

The arts have become hugely valuable tools for documenting and visibilizing the effects of extractivism on human rights where mainstream media is conspicuously absent. Such is the case of the visual essay El Costo Humano de los Agrotóxicos (The human cost of agrotoxics) by environment and human rights photojournalist Pablo Piovano, which documents the lives of people suffering the effects of agrochemicals in their bodies and territories (figs. 3.4, 3.5 and 3.6).

Piovano began this line of work as an independent project in 2014, when he came across some alarming statistics about the health conditions suffered by people living within and near fields of genetically modified monocultures, where the use of chemicals like glyphosate is rampant. He began his research by traveling to provinces in Argentina including Entre Ríos, Misiones and Chaco and talking to local workers and doctors, as well as to journalists and scientists. I met Pablo in a café in Buenos Aires in 2017. He shared that the kinds of health consequences he had learned about and seen first-hand during these trips were shocking, and that he

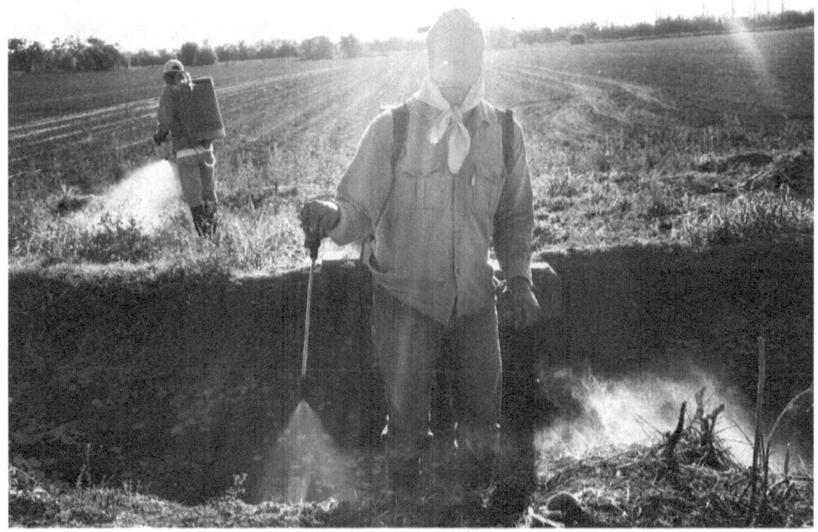

FIGURE 3.5. From the series El Costo Humano de los Agrotóxicos, 2014–2019, by Pablo E. Piovano.

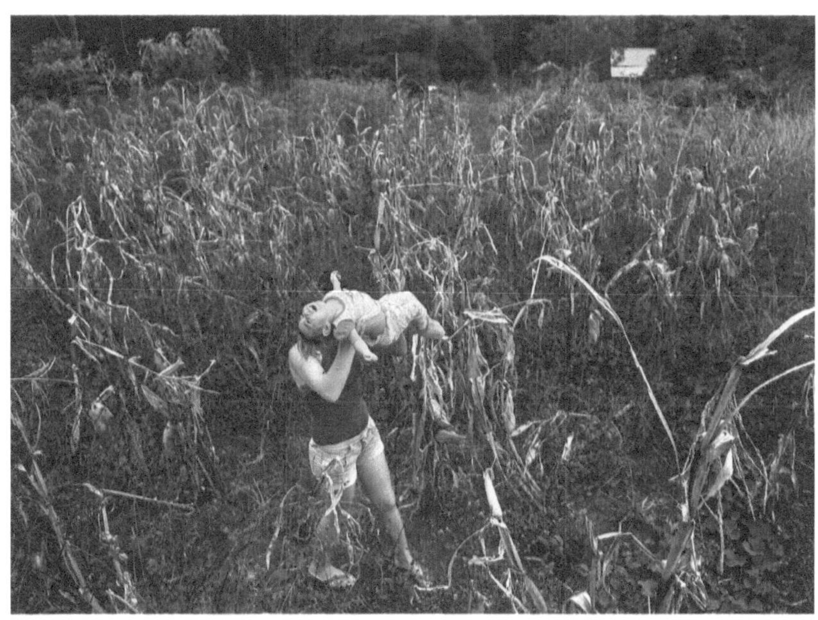

FIGURE 3.6. From the series El Costo Humano de los Agrotóxicos, 2014–2019, by Pablo E. Piovano.

knew there was no way this material would be published by the mainstream media outlets he usually worked with. He realized that a possible alternative channel for sharing these images was photography and photojournalism awards, so he began sending his work abroad to various awards, and his images started to gain recognition. Pablo won his first award at an image and photography festival in Mexico in 2015. That same year he had his first exhibition abroad in Italy, and in 2016 he had his first solo show in Buenos Aires at the prestigious art venue Palais de Glace. I asked Pablo whether the exhibition had featured in the media. He said,

> No, barely. Usually, if an artist has as few as two pictures at the Palais de Glace, they could be featured on any media platform. I had a solo exhibition that was packed [and it was not covered]. The director of the venue could not figure out how [despite the lack of mainstream media coverage] there were so many people at a photography exhibition. It was a political gesture because people came along without me promoting it much, I just posted on Facebook that this was happening and the alternative media picked it up. It was quite something.

Pablo connects this lack of mainstream media coverage of his exhibition to a deliberate obfuscation of the subject:

> Here there is an evident case of complicit silence of the mainstream media; this is an issue that should have been on the front cover of newspapers more than once and it never has been. So there is a clear complicity that responds, on the one hand, to the fact that often the owners of the land are the owners of the papers, and the politicians are landowners as well, the famous aristocracy . . . and then you have the advertising of corporations [in the media], so there is complicity there.[57]

Pablo's images consist of single and group portraits of people who are suffering the consequences of the use of agrochemicals in their environment. In this sense, his work is a testimony of the lives sacrificed to an agricultural model detached from its local context and neglectful of the effects on local populations and ecosystems. Much of Pablo's work centers on the figure of Fabián Tomasi, a former worker at a fumigation company whose health was heavily damaged due to exposure to glyphosate. Fabián became an advocate against the factory agricultural model and the use of glyphosate, and he and Pablo established a close friendship that lasted until Fabián passed away in 2018.

El Costo Humano de los Agrotóxicos was shot in black and white so as to focus on what is essential, explained Pablo, to evade the distraction of the eye. Black and white, he proposed, also allows a relationship with poetry. A more recent series of images focusing on Fabián, however, was shot in color. This carried the intention of honoring the vibrancy of Fabian's fight, and his defiance of death.

Interested in the circulation and reception of his work and how it interlinked with antiextractivist movements, I asked Pablo about his own perception of his photographs: are they journalism, are they art, maybe something else? He said that this work aims to communicate through every possible platform, and therefore he sees it operating on different levels. However, he confessed, he is still surprised by the way that the art world has embraced his photographs: "I cannot see as art a group of photographs that have ceased to be just that, to become the embodiment of a cause, a testimony that denounces what we could call—when it comes down to it—a slow, silent genocide."[58] Pablo said he wanted his photographs to enact real change. And indeed, in 2015 the Red de Médicos de Pueblos Fumigados (Network of Doctors from Fumigated Towns) included a selection of his photographs as evidence in an application for provisional remedies against the Argentine state submitted to the Inter-American Commission on Human Rights, to protect the right to health of children exposed to toxic pesticides and herbicides.[59] While Pablo's photographs portray the lives of specific people, his work is not only about the struggle of his subjects. Instead, his photographs put into question a whole model of food production that is unsustainable and undemocratic. In his own words, "what is at stake here is food sovereignty."

## *Art as Denunciation and Documentation*

The artworks, performances, and interventions discussed in the previous pages reflect the two main narrative axes through which extractivism is framed as a human rights issue presented earlier in this chapter. The first focuses on the objects and subjects of rights. It emphasizes people's right to clean water, high quality food, and health. These are presented as basic human rights, and therefore as human rights issues, in addition to being positioned within wider struggles against extractivism. The second narrative focuses on power and its role in the threatening and violation of rights, specifically the power of the state as the enforcer of repression and a development model that causes ecological wreckage, and the power of corporations in the deployment and expansion of extractivism. This second narrative axis takes on a local-global dimension, pointing both to local actors and transnational ones, and to present dynamics that are the result of economic relations of dependency that go back to the colonization of the continent.[60]

In addition to these two narrative axes, we can also identify two main and overlapping modes of action or functions under which to place these different interventions, works, and manifestations of dissent, namely denunciation and documentation.

In order to understand contemporary practices of denunciation, it is useful first to look back to the early days of the human rights movement in Argentina. Since the beginning, argues Longoni, the Mothers of Plaza de Mayo looked for symbols to make themselves visible to the state and to international press. Such was the case of the *pañuelo* or headscarf worn during *rondas* and marches, which identified them as a group and became an emblem of their struggle. Wearing the headscarf was an act that countered the official position that the disappeared did not exist, an act of denunciation that made what was happening visible. With the photographs of their missing children, and the scarves on their heads, the mothers said, "We are here, we exist."[61] The same could be said of contemporary struggles against extractivism: the negation on behalf of the state and of the hegemonic media calls for strategies of denunciation that bring attention to those issues, such as the ritualistic walks and marches, performance actions in public spaces, and the use of unifying symbols. Taking to the streets in embodied acts of protest and performance indeed continues to be the main strategy of denunciation and visibilization used by social struggles in Argentina. Furthermore, in a context in which the land beneath people's feet is being privatized at an increasing speed—both in big cities and in rural areas—taking to the streets is also an act of spatial demarcation, of asserting one's presence and right to the territory.[62] Finally, denunciation through visualization also takes place through the creation of images that counter the obfuscation of certain topics in the mainstream media and in state narratives. Exhibitions like *Ecocidas . . .* , for instance, are an embodiment of this aim: to make visible that which is deliberately invisibilized.

In addition to denouncing the often-unknown effects of extractivism, the human rights violations that take place as a result of it, and the power dynamics in place between local and transnational actors, many of these creative practices are valuable as forms of documentation. Pablo Piovano's images make for a raw denunciation of the effects of agrochemicals, but they are also important documents of a crisis that is not being properly recorded by the relevant authorities. *Museo del neoextractivism* is another project that involves ongoing documentation of events related to extractivism—including the deaths of land defenders—through images, text, and objects. In this way, acts of documentation give place to memorialization, and a public memory of extractivism begins to emerge. Furthermore, in addition to denunciation and documentation, certain works and exhibitions like the *Museo del neoextractivismo* also serve the purpose of deconstructing the dynamics of the extractivist model and democratizing information, with the aim of generating awareness and mobilizing publics.

Lastly, it is important to consider how, by highlighting connections and continuities between the present and the past, these practices make interventions in local human rights imaginaries as well, creating narratives that shape the formation of contemporary memory and the frames of human rights activism. As Ponce de León has argued in reference to the work of Etcétera, this kind of work "participates in the fashioning of counternarratives that enable a more comprehensive accounting of ongoing state violence, as well as the apprehension of its relation to other forms of violence—such as labor exploitation and environmental destruction."[63] And by drawing connections with the past, these practices also look into the future; they act as warnings, as evidence of that which should not be happening and which should be remedied in order to move into postextractivist worlds where the rights of nature and of those at the frontlines are not sacrificed in the name of development, worlds in which our basic needs like food and water are not seen as individual rights but as collective rights, and where our well-being is not perceived as separate from that of the Earth's ecosystems.

## *Changing Paradigms?*

In 2014, the Argentine judicial system issued a ruling that would challenge the foundations of both human rights and the rights of nature. In response to a habeas corpus filed by the Association of Officials and Lawyers for the Rights of Animals (AFADA), a judge in the city of Buenos Aires granted Sandra, an orangutan in the Buenos Aires zoo, the status of "non-human person." This meant that the ape was recognized as a person with feelings, the right to freedom, and the right to legal representation. As a result of the ruling, AFADA's request to relocate Sandra to a sanctuary was granted and took place in 2019, when Sandra travelled to an ape sanctuary in Florida in the US.[64]

Sandra's case went on to feature as part of the project *Ape Law* by the research agency Forensic Architecture. Based at Goldsmiths, University of London, Forensic Architecture undertakes spatial and media research into human rights and environmental violations in collaboration with affected communities, activist groups, and human rights organizations, and their work has both served as evidence in legal cases and gained recognition in the international art circuit. Forensic Architecture's *Ape Law* investigates the legal standing in the killing of orangutans. It specifically considers three "limit conditions" and how these relate to one another: "the threshold of the human species; the threshold of the forest; and the threshold of the law. What can we accept as a 'human being'? How does this question interact with shifting environmental thresholds, and the political limits of territory and sovereignty?"[65]

Sandra's case thus invites us to reflect on the preconceptions that underpin our use of the human rights discourse as a frame for denouncing the effects of extractivism, including our relationship to nonhuman beings. It prompts us to ask whether an anthropocentric human rights narrative is the right approach, when defending the rights of affected communities necessitates a defense of nonhuman beings and whole ecosystems in the first place. And it asks us to consider: are human rights compatible with the much-needed deconstruction of the still hegemonic human/nature divide? Should we be expanding their remit, or getting rid of anthropocentric frameworks all together?

In the context of conflicts surrounding extractivism in Latin America, human rights continue to be an important force, given the strong tradition of the human rights movement, as is the case in Argentina, and the possibilities that human rights provide for the internationalization of conflicts. Furthermore, the tradition of human rights offers valuable creative resources as well as a network of organizations that support environmental struggles and contribute to drawing links between human rights abuses and ecological destruction. Existing legal frameworks hold possibilities for change and for the expansion of rights, as was the case for Sandra and the constitutional reforms in Ecuador and Bolivia.

However, as societies face the task of rethinking the place of humans in relation to other beings, it might just be that centering human rights and expanding those rights to other beings and elements is no longer the way toward the holistic protection of ecosystems. Indeed, indigenous and grassroots organizations as well as artists are putting forward other terms and paradigms such as *ecocide* and *terricide* that, while appealing to the framework of rights, emerge from and reflect a different ontology that extends beyond legal claims. What remains to be seen is how developments in legal frameworks, in social movements, and in artistic production will interact with each other to further much-needed epistemological and ontological changes, popularize these new perceptions in everyday culture and practice, and make sure advances in the law are not mere gestures, but rather an effective avenue for the protection of communities and ecosystems in the now, while we continue to work toward a needed change of paradigm, toward one that no longer places humans at the center.

# 4 Reclaiming the City

## *Urban Extractivism and Contested Cultures*

There seems to be consensus among campaigners that people in Buenos Aires are not aware of what is happening in the rest of the country, and/or they see these conflicts as alien, happening "over there." There were marks on the city, however, that seemed to be telling a different story.

It was a sunny afternoon little over a week ago, and I had two hours to kill in between interviews. I decided to walk from the neighborhood of Chacarita to Palermo and wander around streets I hadn't walked in years. In my stroll, which had a final destination as well as the purpose of re-experiencing and relearning the streets, I began to notice certain signs of resistance to the extractivist model among the rich tapestry of street art and urban interventions of Buenos Aires.

My first clue was a street sign intervened with the word *agrotóxicos* (agrotoxics) which featured a skull in place of the second "o." With this small intervention, the issues of health and food contamination caused by industrial chemicals were inserted into the urban environment.

[. . .]

Once in Palermo, I stopped to look at a wall covered in graffiti and stencils, and my eye was caught by a figure at the center of the wall: a fist holding a carrot. The fist, a universal icon of resistance, was on this occasion bringing food to the forefront: food production as a contested issue, and food as a place of resistance. While the skull in *agrotóxicos* highlighted the dangers of the current agricultural model by representing the threat of death, the fist and the carrot pointed to the importance of defending food and food sovereignty as the right to life.

While these interventions could easily go unseen in a sea of street art and urban interventions, their presence made me wonder whether the city is indeed so isolated from the effects of the extractive industries and the struggles of frontline communities, or whether we just need to look closer.

– Notes from the field, August 2017

THE ABOVE PARAGRAPHS, excerpts of reflective field notes from my research in Buenos Aires in 2017, shed light on two themes that are central to this chapter: in the first place, the relationship between extractivism in rural areas and in urban centers—How are such processes related? And how are they visibilized?—and second, the city as a site where culture is contested, both spatially/materially and symbolically.

This chapter explores such themes and questions by bringing forward two perspectives on extractivism that continue to be underrepresented in the literature. First, it looks at the concept of "urban extractivism" recently developed and employed by academics, activist networks and local communities fighting processes of dispossession in urban settings. After discussing the concept of urban extractivism and how it is connected—theoretically and materially—

to other forms of extractivism, I propose a second category, that of cultural extractivism. With this, I aim to provide a perspective from which to consider the connections between the field of cultural production and models of extractive development in the Latin American context, in this way expanding critiques of development and extractivism that fail to fully consider the role of cultural dynamics. I adhere to a perspective that understands extractivism as a phenomenon affecting different spheres of life, in addition to a kind of economic model and type of economic activity.[1]

In order to illustrate how these concepts can help us better understand urban dynamics of inequality, dispossession, and displacement in the context of extractivism, I present the case of the housing crisis in the neighborhood of La Boca in the city of Buenos Aires and the process of culture-led and state-sponsored gentrification that it is currently undergoing, two phenomena that are countered through the mural art of local artists and activists. The case of La Boca thus provides an opportunity to problematize the role of cultural production within extractive economies as both a driver of inequality and dispossession and a possible space of resistance. I also examine other cases of urban cultural resistance, such as the "subvertizing" collective Proyecto Squatters in Buenos Aires—which deconstructs the chain of production of food and extractive industries in their interventions of advertisements in the street—and the political print interventions of activists against state violence in Córdoba, who reconfigure urban spaces as sites of popular resistance. Finally, I frame these cases as instances of democratization of the arts and of urban spaces and consider them in relation to global processes of gentrification and displacement.

## *Urban Extractivism*

Extractivism is often associated with the extraction of "natural resources" from the land. The imaginary of activities like open-pit mining and oil extraction tells us that extraction takes place in desolated rural areas, although in reality, these activities often take place in proximity to people's homes, and this is increasingly the case as the extractive frontier expands. In addition to the matter of proximity, there are two other aspects of extractivism we must take into account in order to understand the concept of urban extractivism: the ubiquity of the logic of extraction, and the direct effect of rural dynamics of extraction on urban centers.

In the first place, we must consider the fact that the logic of extraction is also reproduced in urban spaces, be that through the direct extraction of nature and the elimination of green spaces, or through other forms of extraction of value from the land, such as the privatization of public spaces and real estate speculation. Indeed, in cities, the intense appropriation of natural goods is directly linked to the speculative use of urban land and the commodification of collective services: the city occupies a strategic place in the capitalist process of accumulation precisely because of the possibility of extracting profit from production, services, housing, and even public space.[2] According to this logic, the potential of land as a source of revenue trumps all its other forms of value and potential uses. As such, a key factor here is the tendency toward increased financialization across different spheres: monocrops such as soybean became commodities, and so did housing.[3]

The second aspect to consider is that extractive dynamics in urban and rural settings are not just taking place in parallel, but rather are interrelated. For instance, the expansion of industrial agriculture across various rural regions of Argentina and other Latin American countries has led to the loss of work for many small-scale farmers and peasants, which in turn led to mass migration toward large urban centers. Here, there is lack of suitable employment for former land workers, and the financialization of housing means that construction is on the rise, yet affordable housing is not available, leading to an increasingly dispossessed population settling in informal and unsuitable housing.[4]

Julián, an activist with the collective Todos los 25 hasta que se Vaya Monsanto (Every 25th of the Month until Monsanto Goes), which organizes regular protests against Monsanto in Buenos Aires, describes from his experience how the connection between the rural and the urban unfolds under an extractivist model:

> The Argentine Pampas, one of the most fertile regions in the world, ideal for agriculture, is sowed with transgenic corn and soy and this is only profitable for a few. We have seen how the shantytowns in Buenos Aires have filled with people that have been excluded from their sources of income, which is working the land, by the agribusiness. Now the countryside only has work for fumigators, poisoners, speculators, those who sell "agropoison," and actual rural activity has been lost. We even see this in the cities, people no longer have a lemon tree in their house, instead they have an exotic plant. We don't have a rosemary plant or oregano, we have an orchid or some weird thing. This is also part of what has been installed through the current agricultural model.[5]

Another activist, Alejandra, from the group Tierra para Vivir (Land for Living), adds that these dynamics should not only be read as forms of territorial dispossession but also as forms of cultural dispossession, given that people who migrate tend to lose the possibility of continuing to grow their own food, and thus whole sets of knowledge are lost for future generations. In this way, Alejandra highlights the ubiquity of the logic of extraction, under which certain forms of knowledge are neglected and left to perish because they are not regarded as instrumental to the generation of profit in an increasingly industrialized agricultural sector (or in the urban centers).[6]

In order to grasp more fully the notion of urban extractivism, it might be useful to consider a few further concrete examples. In the city of Buenos Aires, for instance, there are multiple cases of pollution and environmental risk, a notable case being the contamination of the Matanza-Riachuelo basin that has caused significant health problems for local populations for years; due to a lawsuit against the government and against polluting businesses, it became a landmark of environmental justice struggles in 2006.[7] Cases like this one have led citizens in urban areas to organize and demand environmental justice in what we can also understand as a claim for the "right to the city."[8] Another crucial matter of urban extractivism in large Latin American cities is the way the financialization of land and the concentration of housing capital tend to have irreversible consequences in protected areas and natural reserves while also displacing local populations. This is observable, for instance, in the case of gated communities disrupting suburban ecosystems in the area surrounding the city of Buenos Aires.[9]

Another important issue is the use of green spaces and unequal access to them, a line of inquiry that artist Azul Blaseotto has developed, for instance, in relation to extractive real estate development in the south of the city of Buenos Aires.[10] Indeed, inequalities surrounding access to green space became an issue of public debate in many cities around the world during the lockdown periods introduced as a response to the COVID-19 pandemic beginning in 2020. The lack of a garden or nearby accessible greenspace for parts of the population was quickly linked to class and race and indeed highlighted as an intersectional issue, with significant effects on well-being and mental health.[11] In Buenos Aires, 2020 also saw a major conflict regarding the city government's plans to sell land bordering the river in the north part of the city for the construction of luxury housing, in a context of housing crisis and when green and riverside spaces are increasingly transferred from public to private hands.[12] Another issue that became prominent as a result of COVID-19 was the lack of access to running water, a matter that particularly affects shantytowns and informal settlements in cities of the Global South. While this problem is far from new, and advocates of hydric justice have been highlighting this issue for a long time, the COVID-19 crisis exposed the ways environmental injustices faced by some in the city, and largely neglected by governments who favor other kinds of infrastructural projects, could quickly become a matter of public health for all.[13]

Taking into account these interrelated dynamics, scholars, artists, and activists in Argentina have begun to develop the concept of urban extractivism to signal the connections between extractive dynamics in rural and urban spaces and highlight the forms of socioenvironmental injustice experienced in cities. While the term is not as widespread as others that are often used in order to frame the wider dynamics of the city (e.g., exclusion, inequality) or more specific processes (e.g., privatization, displacement, gentrification), urban extractivism has been gaining traction in recent years, and, as I will demonstrate in this chapter, can provide us with a useful framework for understanding the problems and inequalities of Latin American cities as the result of a development model that is based on a constant expansion of extraction.[14] Furthermore, even in other cases across the world where the connections to the extractive industries seem distant, the framework of extractivism can still make useful contributions to social, political, cultural, and economic analysis, given that in addition to being a localized phenomenon with devastating consequences for those at the frontlines, extractivism is also the logic behind the global economy, meaning that all countries are imbricated in a web of extractivism in one way or another, be that as extractors of nature or as centers of accumulation and mass consumption of resources (and sometimes both). The frameworks of extractivism and urban extractivism thus can be useful in other ways beyond the Latin American and Global South contexts. Indeed, despite the fact that urban extractivism might not yet be applied in the Global North, we can see comparable conceptual connections with longstanding urban environmental movements in places like the US, and more recently, with initiatives like the Green New Deal that frame issues such as the right to adequate housing as a matter of environmental justice.[15]

While urban extractivism offers a perspective from which to consider how extractive dynamics unravel in the urban context, in the next section I propose the term cultural extractivism as a way of framing and understanding the ways the logic of extraction permeates the cultural sphere, and in turn, how cultural production and cultural policy serve to perpetuate the hegemony of extractivism. In the urban context, as I will demonstrate later, cultural extractivism can be imbricated in urban extractive dynamics in multiple ways, as culture is increasingly deployed by governments and developers as an agent of urban transformation.

## *Cultural Extractivism*

In the same way the framework of extractivism gave way to the concept of urban extractivism, which serves to understand a series of interrelated processes and dynamics affecting cities, in recent years some artists, activists, researchers, and frontline communities have also begun to use other terms like "epistemic extractivism" and "cultural extractivism." Writer and professor of literature and aesthetics Susana Romero Sued speaks for instance of an "extractivism of knowledges" that occurs when Global North researchers and companies develop patents and products based on the extraction and dissection of nature from the Global South.[16] Mapuche leader and writer Moira Millán has described cultural extractivism as "the subtraction of a form of knowledge or ancestral art form with the aim of destroying it," in reference to processes of appropriation which are inherently violent and damaging to indigenous cultures.[17] Here I propose a broader understanding of cultural extractivism, one that considers this type of dynamic as well as other ways culture reproduces the logic of extraction and supports the expansion of extractivism. I offer an attempt to theorize the term, with the aim of providing a concept that can be useful in analyzing the different ways cultural production and extraction intersect.

From this perspective, cultural extractivism can be defined as the mobilization of a logic of extraction through cultural policy and production. Cultural extractivism can manifest in different ways and at different levels, from the symbolic to the material. The construction of meaning in certain forms of cultural production can lead to the perpetuation of the ideological underpinnings of extractivism—for example, discourses of development and modernization and an anthropocentric standpoint. In addition, the economic and political powers behind much cultural activity are often the same ones behind the extractive economy, and so they have the means to instrumentalize culture in acts of greenwashing and the power to censor and marginalize dissident voices in the sector. We can see this for instance in the relationship between museums and galleries and extractive companies, who act as sponsors to different cultural activities, or directly as curators of exhibitions and public programs about topics like climate change and the history of mining, having in this way complete control over narratives.[18] We can also see it in what artist Eduardo Molinari refers to as a "pact of mutual legitimacy" between the economic and political elites and a sector of the art world, which in the Argentina of the 1990s served to sustain a violently neoliberal status quo, introducing the policies and technologies of the current stage of extractivism.[19] Another form of cultural extractivism is the way these same powers activate the extraction of value from non-commodified art forms for the creation of economic value. All of the above can lead to the dispossession of people and to dynamics of expulsion, whether in direct or indirect ways.[20]

The concept of cultural extractivism can be related to the idea of the expediency of culture developed by George Yúdice. Yúdice argues that "culture as an expedient gained legitimacy and displaced or absorbed other understandings of culture," and that "culture-as-resource can be compared with nature-as-resource."[21] The author proposes that both capital and the political establishment in the postmodern era have begun to approach culture as a resource upon the realization of its various potential forms of value. But at the same time, the demise of state support for culture—he refers to the US context specifically but it applies at a larger scale—has led to cultural practitioners themselves seeking legitimation for their work in the potential social and economic effects of culture, and to marginalized groups organizing around cultural rights as a way of securing other rights and material gains. Here I propose a parallel perspective on the expediency of culture, focusing on its instrumentalization under extractivism. However, while I acknowledge the strategic role of culture as a tool in subaltern struggles, I choose to examine cultural practices in their transformative potential, rather than their instrumental use, in an approach that focuses on the constructive role of culture in subaltern contexts in addition to its political role.

In order to understand the notion of cultural extractivism, we must first ask, Where lie the roots of cultural extractivism? And in what kinds of local and global processes can we locate it today? In developing this concept I build on the theories on development, extractivism, and decoloniality that make up the theoretical grounding of this book, and also on critiques of the "culture industry" that go back to the critical theory of the Frankfurt School.[22]

Cultural extractivism in Latin America has its roots in the colonization of the region, a process through which the knowledges and worldviews of indigenous peoples were suppressed in order to impose a Eurocentric paradigm of modernity—one that would be formed and transformed through coloniality itself—and eventually the Enlightenment.[23] This suppression and annihilation of indigenous worldviews has been termed epistemicide, and it was (and continues to be) carried out through violent means, but also through other processes of assimilation through which world(view)s, beliefs, and traditions were integrated into Christian practices so as to facilitate a process of domination.[24]

In Argentina, the colonial legacy in its epistemic and cultural dimensions shaped the formation of the cultural field in the early days of the republic. This period was marked by a binary and hierarchical understanding of culture captured in the slogan "Civilization or barbarity," which remains influential to this day.[25] From this perspective, the cultural production of popular and indigenous sectors are left outside the modern ideal and considered lesser in value.[26] This implication was and still is key to justifying a development model based on the expulsion and extermination of indigenous people for the appropriation of territory and the development of extractive activities, despite the current valuing of vernacular culture on a rhetorical level.

Indeed, until not too long ago, cultural expressions and differences were seen as grossly idiosyncratic and as barriers to development by governments and multilateral organizations;[27] however, current development discourse celebrates culture as a pillar of sustainable development.[28] The issue that arises still is that local culture and "authenticity" become selectively co-opted into the market logic, and the economic potential of culture begins to gain importance over culture's other capacities and its intrinsic value.[29] In Latin America, development through the cultural and creative industries has been championed, for instance, through approaches such as the "Orange

Economy," which is based on notions of entrepreneurship and intellectual property.[30] This has led to contentious debates on whether culture should be promoted as an engine of economic development or if such an approach will endanger forms of arts and culture that fall outside the market logic.[31] Furthermore, as expressed by Saifer and particularly relevant in the Latin American context, "creative economy discourse sanitizes and depoliticizes histories of uneven development, and the power relations and structures that continue to shape it."[32] To this day culture is a crucial agent in maintaining the hegemony of so-called "central" countries over the peripheries, and the cultural industries are means for sustaining that order.[33] Finally, and of significance to the themes of this book, in contemporary cultural economy discourse the cultural and creative industries are often presented as inherently green, when in fact many of these industries are highly polluting and imbricated in violent processes of resource extraction.[34]

Nevertheless, conflicting visions of culture and its role in society and development coexist. In Latin America, on the one hand, there is a longstanding tradition of community arts, of forms of cultural production and experience that are collective, democratic, and noncommodified, that are embedded within territories, contributing in this way to the social cohesion and well-being of communities. Over the last two decades, this approach to culture has even become institutionalized, as was the case of the Pontos de Cultura (Culture points) program for supporting community culture in Brazil, later taken up by other countries, including the progressive government of Cristina Fernández de Kirchner in Argentina in 2011.[35] On the other hand, there is a vision of culture that is detached from the democratic and territorial ethos and centers on culture's potential to contribute to modernization and generation of economic revenue. We can identify such an understanding of culture in the city of Buenos Aires, governed since 2007 by the market-oriented Pro Party, which has replicated the creative industries approach of the United Kingdom.[36] While the city government invests significantly in culture, investments are mostly geared toward entertainment and consumption, rather than a socially inclined vision of cultural democracy and participation. As the next section will demonstrate, clashing conceptions of culture not only give way to struggles for meaning but can also have weight in battles over the right to the city, particularly in a context in which the logic of extraction is mobilized through cultural policy in the name of modernization and for the aim of increasing land value.

## *Urban and Cultural Extractivism: The Case of La Boca*

Cultural extractivism can develop in different ways and on different levels. It includes cultural policy, arts and media production processes and content, and the instrumentalization of culture to support and legitimize political and/or economic ventures. In what follows, I will discuss the ways the logic of extraction is mobilized through urban policy and state-led cultural programming.

Cultural policy, production, and programming can be key elements in processes of urban change, particularly in what is often termed the "urban regeneration" of neglected or "under-productive" areas, or, in a more critical vein, gentrification. In Latin America, Rodríguez and Di Virgilio argue that gentrification develops as "a result of neoliberal socio-spatial dynamics supported by variegated forms of symbolic and/or material displacement of low-income people, coupled with their exclusion from political decision-making."[37] Gentrification can be seen as a process of displacement parallel to the displacement taking place in rural areas due to the expansion of the extractive frontier. In this case, as I will show, what is expanded is the reach of the cultural and creative industries and the creative class,[38] and this expansion "can only be produced through the subalternization of other modes of socio-ecological reproduction."[39] Such consequences of gentrification have now been acknowledged even by early promoters of the creative class and the cultural and creative industries as vehicles for social progress.[40]

La Boca is a neighborhood in the south of the city of Buenos Aires. It was the first natural port to the city, and for long stood as a vital point for industry and immigration. La Boca is a working-class neighborhood with a strong Genovese heritage resulting from migration from Italy that began in the nineteenth century. It is also known for being the home to the football club Boca Juniors and for its colorful façades, which have their origin in the leftover ship paint people used to decorate their houses. The neighborhood has a rich cultural heritage: it was home to several famous artists and sustains to this day an important tradition of mural art. In the twentieth century, the area underwent a period of industrial development followed by the closure of factories in the 1970s. As a result, it became a neglected part of the city, with no state planning and with many people living in unfit multifamily housing and facing the risk of fires due to the prevalence of wood and plate in old buildings.[41]

While longstanding inhabitants of La Boca continued to face housing problems, in the 2010s the government of the city of Buenos Aires began a project for redeveloping the area as an arts hub. To this end, in 2012 the city government sanctioned law 4353, known as the Art District Law, which provides tax breaks, and other benefits such as access to credit, for arts organizations moving into the area. The authority for the application of the law is the Ministry of Economic Development, with the intervention of the Ministry of Culture for "matters of its competence."[42] Thus began a project for culture-led regeneration, following a universalist development logic that aimed to replicate the urban regeneration processes of leading "creative cities" of the Global North in the Argentine context.[43]

Following the classic strategies of creative cities development as put forward by champions of the creative economy like Florida, the project for regenerating La Boca has as one of its objectives attracting young creatives to the area.[44] The last few years have seen the proliferation of luxury studio apartments aimed at young professionals—which do not cater to the needs of the local population—as well as the privatization of public spaces and buildings. These processes have been met with resistance by sectors of the local community, which see such changes as mechanisms of gentrification and expulsion. One of the organizations that leads the resistance to this transformation of the neighborhood is called La Boca Resiste y Propone (LBRP; La Boca Resists and Proposes).

LBRP is a local organization that emerged in 2014 and brings together local people in La Boca around issues that concern them, such as the housing crisis and instances of police and institutional violence, particularly concerning young people in the area who are criminalized on a systematic basis. As their name suggests, the organization *resists* dynamics of violence and dispossession and *proposes* alternatives, engaging with public servants and policymakers in order to try to effect change in their local area and beyond. Natalia, an activist with the group, describes their work as threefold: there is a judicial branch, a legislative branch, and a branch concerned with territorial work, or work that responds to the social, health, and economic needs of people living and working in a specific context.[45] For instance, the organization was part of the working group that led to the modifications in the so called "rent law," benefiting renters across the city.

LBRP is currently coordinating the local working group on housing and habitat that organizes around the right to housing. LBRP claims that in service to the regeneration plans for the area, the city government is speculating with old, unsafe housing. Instead of carrying out necessary renovations to existing buildings, once fires and collapses occur, which unfortunately are frequent, the government declares these properties uninhabitable and gives green light to demolitions, which eventually opens the way for new types of housing that are not affordable to previous inhabitants. When inhabitants are evicted, there is no possibility for relocation in the neighborhood. In our conversation in La Boca, Natalia explained that at LBRP they see housing and habitat as fundamental rights, without which young people cannot fully develop as well-rounded citizens. This view on the right to housing emerged in Argentina between the late nineteenth century and beginning of the twentieth; it was championed by various civil groups, public figures, and lawmakers, and eventually consolidated and promoted by President Juan Domingo Perón in the 1940s and 50s. After this period the state abandoned this vision, but the idea of universal housing remained in the collective imaginary.[46]

In addition to tax breaks and incentives, real estate investment, and specific public works, the gentrification process of La Boca has included a cultural-programming dimension led by the Art District division of the Ministry of Culture. This instrumentalization of culture, I will argue, has at points followed a logic of extraction and appropriation for the purpose of capitalizing on the cultural and historic value of the neighborhood.[47]

A first example of such use of cultural programming is the mural art festival Color BA, which had its first edition in 2016 as part of the city-wide arts festival Ciudad Emergente. Color BA led to a conflict in La Boca, because it failed to properly engage with local artists and the local community: artists from other parts of the country or from abroad would come in to paint murals, but they would not engage with themes that are of relevance to locals or with the local tradition and aesthetic of mural art. Artists would paint surrounded by fences and guarded by the police, and their work contributed to a dynamic in which the artistic heritage of the area—its mural art tradition—was superficially referenced in order to capitalize from it as a marker of place and "authenticity," but a universal "hipster" aesthetic was introduced instead.[48] Images of these murals then became advertisements selling the luxury studio flats unattainable to local populations. In our chat, Natalia described this as "a reconfiguration of the urban space that is installed through the visual."[49]

For the second edition of the festival in 2017, described Natalia, local artists were given more space to participate, but conflicts emerged once more, as they found out that nonlocal artists were offered payment when local artists were told there would be no compensation for the work. In response, LBRP decided to organize their own series of murals around La Boca with local artists and others from the national street art scene. Their mural painting developed as participatory events in a manner that differed greatly from the dynamics of the festival, with neighbors contributing tools and paint, and schoolchildren singing songs to the artists. Also, the themes of the murals related to the history and culture of the neighborhood, from landmarks of political history to murals honoring notable members of the community. Natalia explained,

> These walls are also us. And if these walls are not going to be used for communicating our histories, and they are going to tell predecided histories of people we don't even know yet, it is going to be very difficult to save our neighborhood. And this is not a naïve matter. It is linked to the hikes in our rents, it implies many things. It not only affects those at risk of eviction. It has to do with the overpricing of the land, and the matter of who the land is for.[50]

Color BA commissioned twenty murals that year, and LBRP did thirty-two. The Color BA murals were soon covered with graffiti, while the ones coordinated by LBRP were not. Natalia suggested this was because there is no collective ownership over those works. They do not speak to local people, they speak to a different audience, and in a different language: "They try to appropriate in a coarse manner, in a clumsy and impetuous manner, all our representations, and then they end up with just the shell, you see? And they think that the shell is enough to represent a whole process, to display 170 years of conceptual, collective making, generation after generation."[51] Another difference between some of the artists that were brought in by Color BA and the artists that worked with LBRP is that in the latter case, they usually refer to themselves as *muralerxs*, not mural artists (a concept that also came up in my talk with artist Claudia Tula, in Chapter 2). This is, on the one hand, in order to differentiate themselves from a fine arts tradition that looks down on their technique and approach to murals, but it is also about adopting an ethical commitment when making mural art. In Natalia's words: "What we are trying to show is that art always fulfilled a social function, the question is, What kinds of interests does it serve?"

An additional way the local cultural heritage of La Boca was extracted and instrumentalized was the involvement of the city government in the planning and promotion of local festivities. The neighborhood of La Boca has a rich tradition of festivities, both religious and secular, that have long been organized by locals. These include the procession of the Madonna Santa and the bonfire of San Juan. Natalia explained that when the Art District was established, the city government decided they would begin to sponsor the celebrations. They invested in infrastructure, generated links with some local organizations, and invited both local and high-profile artists to perform. The events were suddenly not only local festivities, but also spectacles for tourists and other publics. The city government brought in police officers to guard the events, and members of the local community who had been involved in the organizing of those festivities for decades unexpectedly received invitations to their own events on behalf of the Art District. These local traditional and faith festivities began to be widely publicized by the city government as a cultural asset of the local area in a manner that shifted focus away from the cultural and religious value of the events and highlighted the "picturesque" quality they provide to the area for the enjoyment of "cultural omnivores."[52] Tradition became in this way, a consumable spectacle.

The examples of cultural programming discussed can be read as reproducing a dynamic in which local traditions and art forms are appropriated in order to turn cultural value into economic value, specifically the rise in property prices.[53] This dynamic is part of a process of culture-led and state-sponsored gentrification, and despite the Art District not yet completely succeeding in their attempt to create a cultural hub in the terms laid down by promoters of "creative cities," the project has already generated the conditions for the dispossession and expulsion of vulnerable, long-term inhabitants.[54] Furthermore, and as I have argued elsewhere, this appropriation of popular culture follows a logic of extraction: "culture is extracted from the local population—in some cases quite literally, as is the case of local festivities—and repackaged with the aim of serving as a tool for growth and expansion, without concern for human or environmental costs."[55] Not to be minimized is the effect that these kinds of disputes have on the social fabric of communities; while LBRP represents a section of the community that is directly opposed to the city government's appropriation of their cultural life, other neighbors and local artists welcomed changes such as investment in local festivities and certain infrastructural works. A particularly contentious situation, for instance, emerged when the city government finally offered local artists paid opportunities to paint murals, generating a dilemma for artists in need of paid work.

The case of La Boca presents us with an example of the way that culture can become a ground on which different logics are contested. On the one hand, the city government and the real estate developers incentivize cultural production and the promotion of culture so that cultural value can be extracted and turned into economic value. On the other, the local community resists processes of dispossession and expulsion by challenging the appropriation of culture through their own cultural practices, engaging with local government to make their voices heard and uphold their rights, and organizing as a community in order to move forward a vision of housing justice that puts people before profit. Their views on culture are different (economic value versus the intrinsic *and* social value of heritage), as are their views on the right to the city.

The kind of gentrification and dispossession processes taking place in La Boca are comparable to those taking place in other parts of the world. As Natalia expressed, these are global processes: "it is here, in London, in Barcelona, in Venice, . . . wherever there is a way of extracting resources it doesn't matter at what cost." Indeed, considering the case of La Boca in relation to other experiences of gentrification in Latin America and on a "planetary scale" allows us to see recurrent patterns and to identify the role of culture as engine and legitimizing agent of gentrification.[56] In addition, by looking at such processes from the perspectives of urban and cultural extractivism, we can understand how they relate to other sectors of extractive society and its economy. Such perspectives allow us "to locate these processes symbolically within the imaginary of a country and a region that is still invested in specific visions of development based on the extraction of resources, where culture risks becoming another resource for the extraction of value only to benefit those at the top."[57]

## *Taking Back the City: Art and Urban Interventions*

The case of La Boca illustrates how culture can be instrumentalized for the extraction of value leading to the dispossession and displacement of people. At the same time, culture can be a vehicle of resistance, emancipation, and reconfiguration of the urban space. For instance, Natalia from LBRP referred to the social role of murals in La Boca:

> We see the mural as an effective communication tool, and also one that we as a community are very much used to. It is a language that we practically have incorporated. We can read murals easily because here, around the corner at the preschool, there is a mural in each room. Children go to school and since that time they are used to being in conversation with mural painting.[58]

In the following pages, I will discuss other cultural and artistic practices in urban spaces where symbolic and spatial interventions aim at disrupting the extractive and violent dynamics of the city, and in turn generate relational ways of making, of being, and of sharing the urban environment.

Ciudad del Deseo is a feminist collective that emerged in Buenos Aires on the occasion of the international women's strike on March 8, 2019. It brings together architects, geographers, anthropologists, cultural workers, activists, and people from other walks of life that have an interest in exploring issues relating to the city and its political, physical, and symbolic dimensions from a feminist perspective. The collective's work is based on participatory methodologies and centering the voices of women and *disidencias* (gender and sexual dissidents), and it involves collective mapping exercises, artistic interventions in the urban space, educational events, and publications. Their work goes beyond a claim for people's right to the city and demands more: that minoritized and vulnerable groups have the right to feel joy and desire in the places they inhabit. In this sense, Ciudad del Deseo puts forward embodied ways of being in the city and of collectively constructing knowledge and making art that directly challenges cultural extractivism and the monetized, individualistic values it is based on. On their website, they offer the following words:

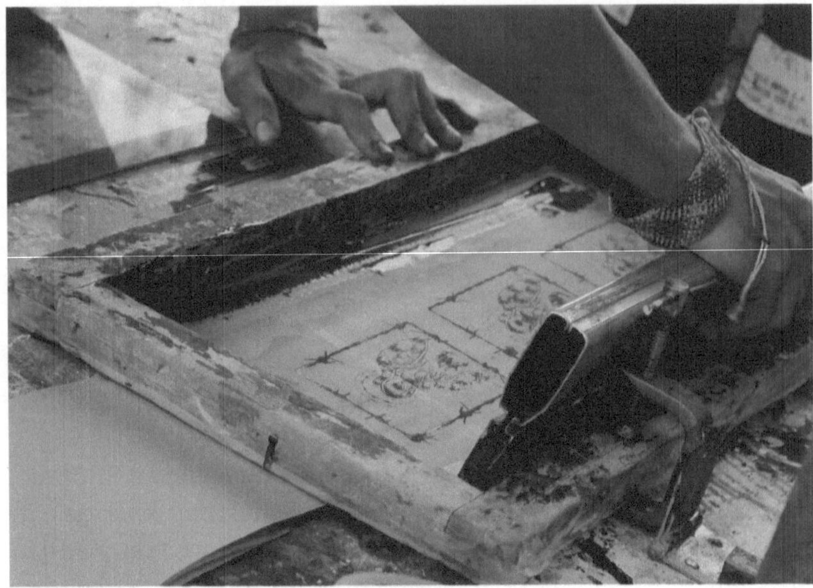

FIGURE 4.1. Silk screen. Casa 1234 Interventions Archive.

> The city is the patriarchy in the form of concrete. It promotes individualistic and commodified relationships, designed for and by men, full of walls and frontiers at the rhythm of the socio-urban segregation that worsens the unequal experience of transiting and accessing the city. However, even concrete cracks, and from within the cracks the weeds grow.[59]

Moving away from Buenos Aires and toward the center of the country, we find Casa 1234, a cultural and social center in the city of Córdoba. They do and teach silk-screen printing among other types of graphic production, and they use their skills to make interventions in the urban landscape (Fig 4.1). Córdoba is a student city with a known history of activism and political participation, and at the same time it has a famously repressive police force. I visited Córdoba in 2017 seeking to learn about the movement against deforestation, a grave issue in both urban and rural areas in the wider province of Córdoba. In my travels, I also came to learn more about other issues people faced in the city, issues concerning institutional violence that were, at the end of the day, interlinked with the wider dynamics of an extractivist model.

One of the folks at Casa 1234, Manuel, explained that at the moment, one of the main struggles they were part of was against police repression, and that they were working alongside the Coordinadora de Familiares de Víctimas de Gatillo Facil (Coordinating Group for Families of Victims of Trigger-Happy Cops).[60] Manuel explained that in their collaborative graphic work, they look to activate a particular logic, one that tears down the barrier around the figure of the artist, so that the artist disappears and people who are directly affected by a particular issue can appropriate artistic language. At the same time, he pointed out, there is a kind of reciprocal, affective relationship that is formed. Rather than seeing themselves as artists in solidarity, the crew at Casa 1234 see the people at the Coordinadora as family.

The work they do with the Coordinadora consists mostly of silkscreen posters featuring images of victims of police brutality that are put up on walls around the city. In this sense, we can relate the work of artists and printers at Casa 1234 with the landmark work of Grupo de Arte Callejero (GAC) mentioned in Chapter 3. While the groups use different tactics, in both cases we see the deployment of graphic design as a form of visual intervention in the urban landscape, with the dual aim of visibilizing and memorializing instances of state violence and appropriating the streets as a creative site.[61]

Manuel explained that all portraits are produced following the same visual language and using a common typography, a popular, Latin American *chicha* aesthetic that they borrowed from the posters used to advertise local parties and *cumbia* music events.[62] Having carried out this work for over five years at the time of our conversation, Manuel pointed to how the posters had already become part of a common landscape in the city and generated a symbolic dispute in the city center. This was a deliberate result, as their actions are conceived with multiple levels of intertextuality in mind in order to appeal to different stakeholders, from the families and friends of victims of state violence to shoppers to passersby who might be familiar with ideas around surveillance and state violence, who find

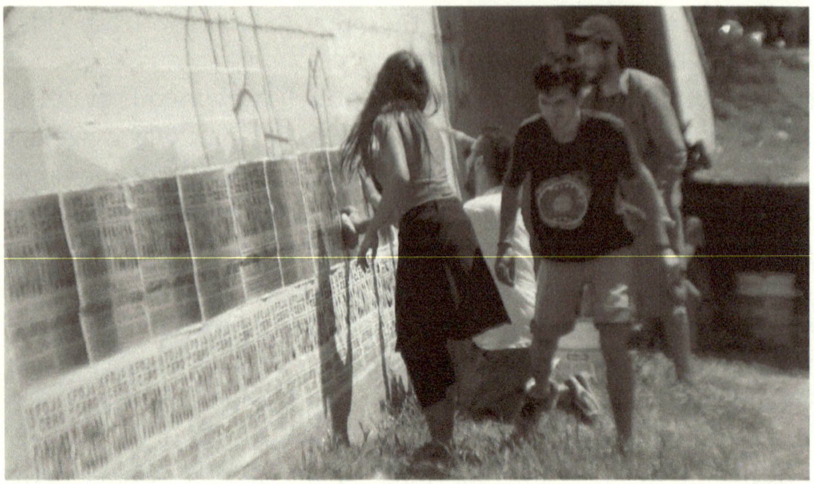

FIGURE 4.2. Intervention. Casa 1234 Interventions Archive.

in these prints an opportunity to engage further with those issues (figs 4.2, 4.3, 4.4, 4.5). In Manuel's words,

> We go for that, different degrees of intertextuality, so as not to have an empty, unidirectional discourse with a flat slogan. We know it is complex, because we are talking about death, about trigger happy, about murder. How can we avoid being unidirectional? How can you avoid saying "murder"? . . . You cannot soften it, but that's what we're trying to do, searching and generating richness in the language of graphics, and in other discursive practices.[63]

Manuel and Analía, another member of the collective, also explained that their work had opened up spaces for talking about and acting upon other issues, such as indigenous rights and the patriarchy (fig. 4.6). Analía explained that she and Manuel had met at a blockade against Monsanto as part of the antiextractivist struggle, and that it was important for them to connect the issues.[64] In Córdoba, explained Manuel, "there has been an advance of housing speculation that tears apart families, gentrifies our neighborhoods, creates ghettos, determines in which areas you can circulate and in which you cannot," and this is linked to the defense of the land.

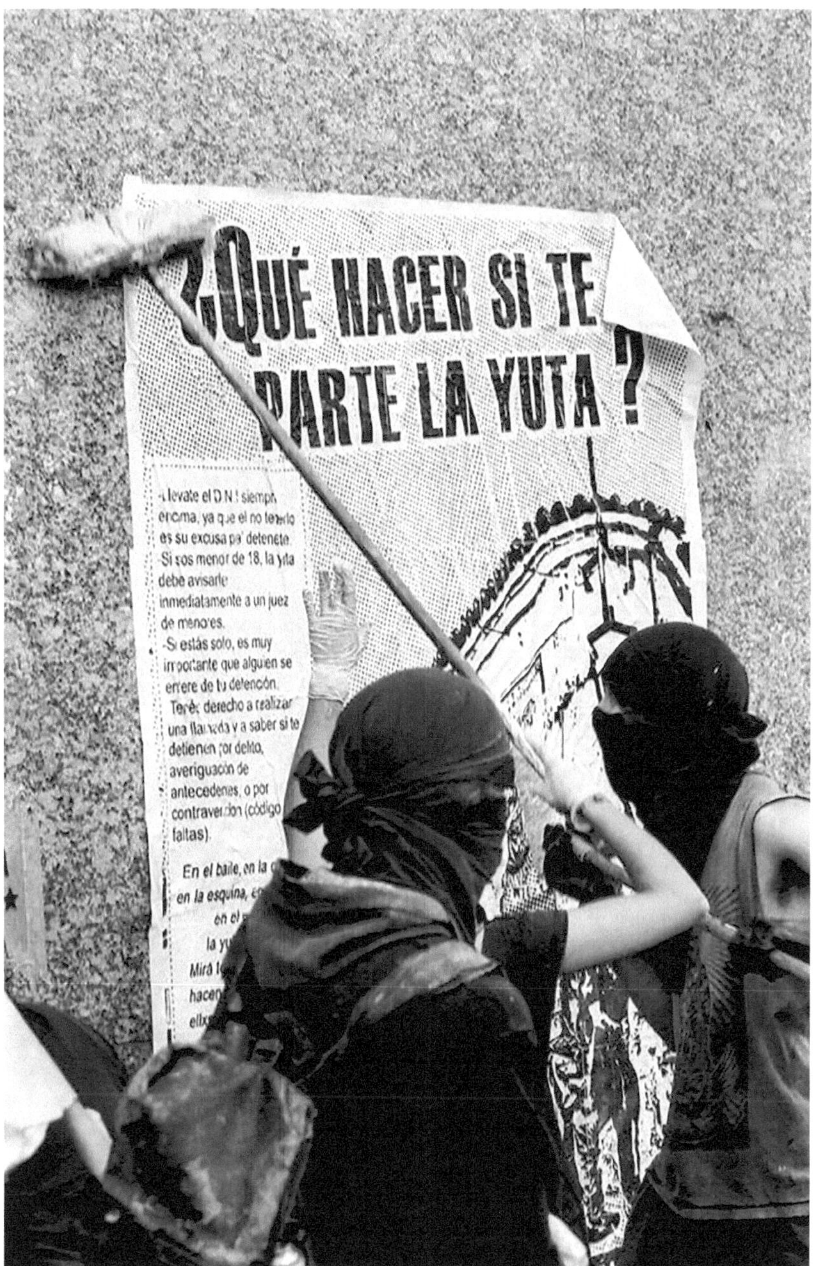


FIGURE 4.3. Intervention, "What to do if the cops stop you?" Casa 1234 Interventions Archive.

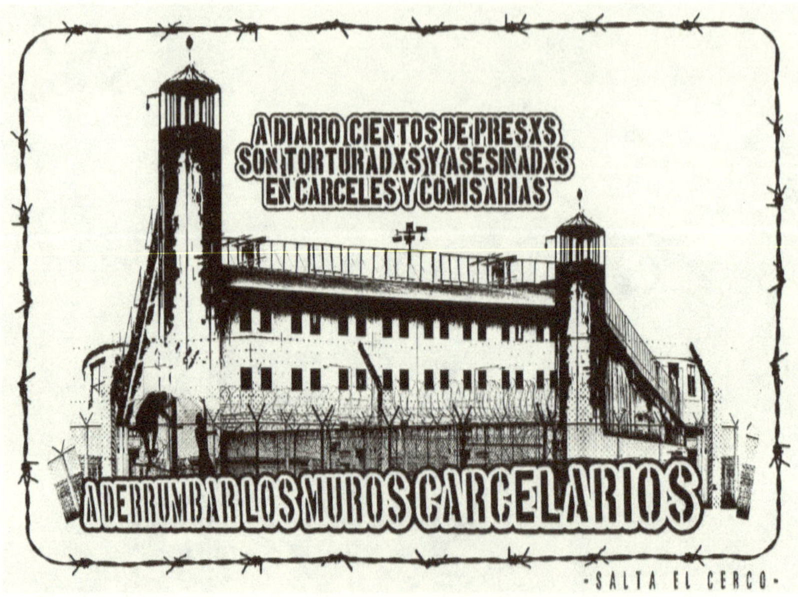


FIGURE 4.4. "Each day hundreds of prisoners are tortured and killed in prisons and jails. Let's tear down the jail walls." Casa 1234 Interventions Archive.

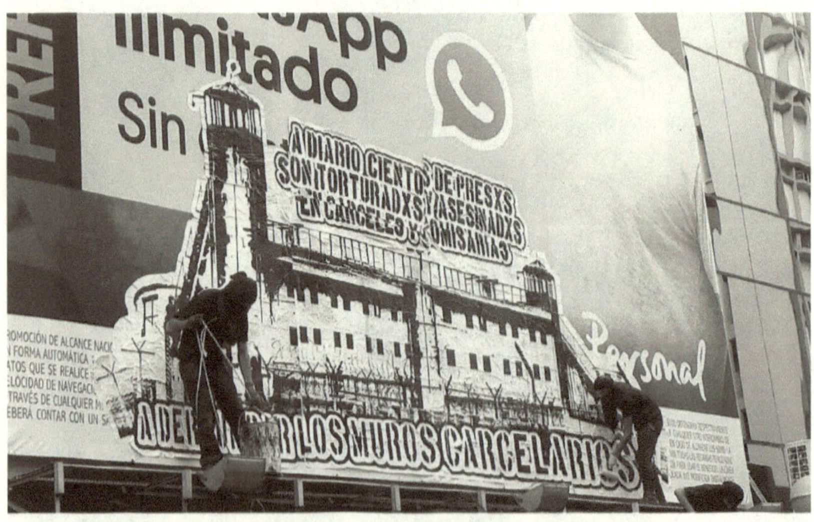


FIGURE 4.5. Intervention on billboard. Casa 1234 Interventions Archive.

FIGURE 4.6. "Neither over our territories nor over our bodies shall they pass." Casa 1234 Interventions Archive.

Violence on behalf of the state and real estate developers is widely felt among rural populations, which are forcibly displaced and violently repressed for defending their land. For this reason, Casa 1234 produced a poster of Ramona Bustamante, an elderly woman violently displaced from her farm to give way to new construction projects, and one of Heraldo Eslava, a local champion of popular agroecology. Heraldo lived in a marginal neighborhood of Córdoba that had become a site of interest for property development. He died under violent and suspicious circumstances after years of leading the fight to preserve the community vegetable garden in the precarious neighborhood of Villa La Maternidad. His poster now joins those of the victims of state violence.[65]

In the city of Córdoba, urban interventions are increasingly criminalized, and the city government makes special effort to stop things like billposting and to clean up any form of intervention swiftly. Manuel referred to the landscape of corporate advertising in the city and to the way their work responds to this:

> We see human perception as a battlefield, and we look to subvert those symbols, not destroy them, but instead find a way of

> reappropriating them, of generating something else with that same logic and that same language, from our place of *autogestión* [self-management], because we don't have the big tools to make huge signs. . . . From a place of *autogestión*, from collective, horizontal processes, we manage to challenge that logic and subvert that language.[66]

In Argentina *autogestión* refers to a form of organizing and doing that became widespread as a result of the 2001 economic crisis. It is independent from party politics, based on horizontal relationships between people and a rejection of hierarchical structures, and operates outside of the state's institutions and its structures of power.[67] *Autogestión* is also linked to a prefigurative ethos, which seeks to enact in the present time the kinds of social relations and ways of being for the society we want to build.[68] In the cultural context, *autogestión* is linked to artistic production that is not officially or consistently supported by the state and does not ascribe to the commercial logic of the cultural industries either.[69] Instead, *autogestión*, also known as "independent" culture, is based on networks of mutual aid and camaraderie and is characterized by the pursuit of aesthetic objectives independent of market trends, often explicitly rejecting the aesthetics and processes of the art market. This form of self-management does not fit with the logic of cultural entrepreneurship but is rather a strategy of resistance to an extractive logic that sees culture as a vehicle for the creation of economic value in a globalized economy. In this way, it emerges as a path for artists wanting to carry out projects outside of a commercial logic in an environment with limited state support for culture, and indeed for those deliberately wanting to disengage from state-sanctioned culture too.[70]

The work of Casa 1234 has several commonalities with another collective from Buenos Aires called Proyecto Squatters. Proyecto Squatters also carries out graphic urban interventions, and the members describe their work as "counter-advertising artivism." In their own words, "Proyecto Squatters is an Argentinian counter-advertising project created in 2008 as a nonprofit initiative, with

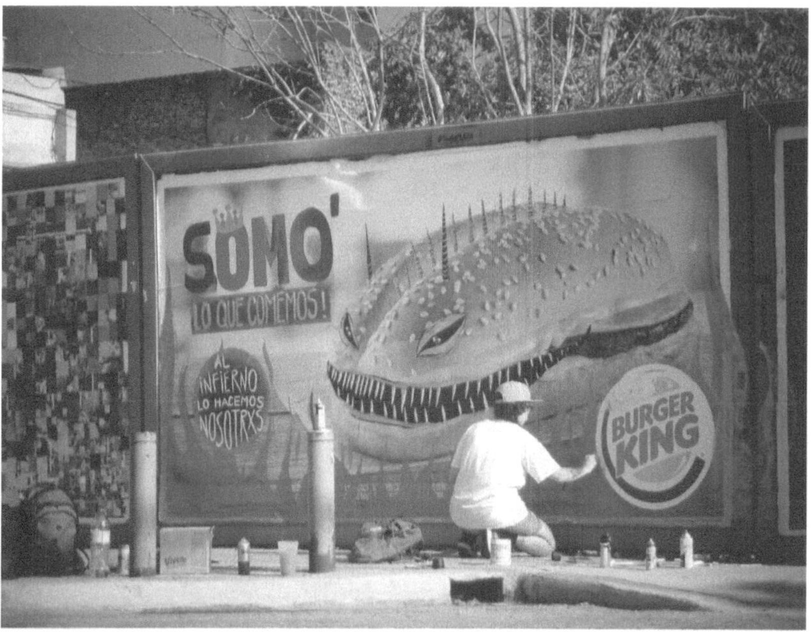


FIGURE 4.7. Intervention on Burger King ad. Proyecto Squatters (2018)

the objective of using counter-advertising techniques in order to construct a critical perspective on society and consumption, and particularly on the political, social, and subjective effects of advertising discourse."[71] Proyecto Squatters intervenes advertisements in public spaces using materials such as pens, stencils, spray paint, brushes, glue, and paper. Their work is collaborative in nature as well as territorial; there is an explicit intention to transform public space and to strengthen social bonds as well as the aim of intervening in advertisements on a discursive level (figs. 4.7, 4.8, 4.9). To this end, Proyecto Squatters sometimes organize their interventions as open events, following what can be understood as an "event modality" in community arts.[72] For these events they often collaborate with other collectives and with local neighbor organizations, as was the case for the event "The square is ours!!" in April 2018. The event description stated that "artists, urban activists, and neighbors will get together to transform the public space that has been colonized by corporate power."[73]

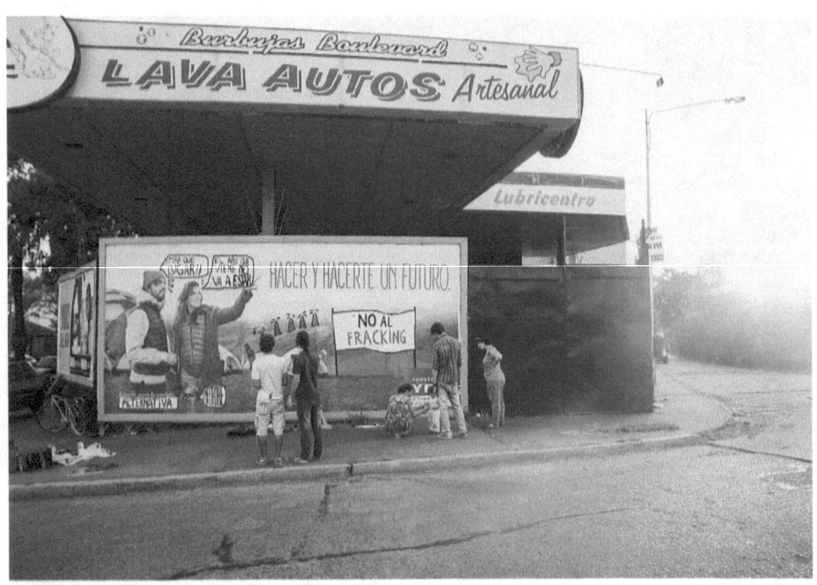


FIGURE 4.8. Intervention on YPF ad. Proyecto Squatters (2015)

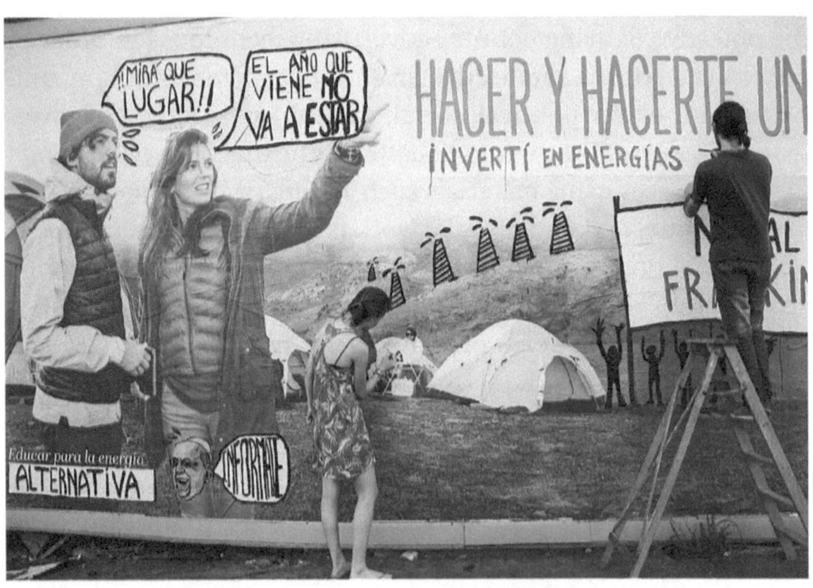


FIGURE 4.9. Intervention on YPF ad. Proyecto Squatters (2015)

I met Julián from Proyecto Squatters in August 2017. It was a winter afternoon in Buenos Aires, and we met at a bar known for its links to street art culture. Julián told me he has a background in communication and in psychology. When he was in Spain some years before, he had come across the anticonsumerist, counter-advertising group Consume Hasta Morir (Consume until Death). At that moment, he explained, there were no counteradvertising initiatives in Buenos Aires, so he decided to get one started. He proposed the name "Squatters," taking inspiration from the squatter culture he had encountered in Spain. Squatters, he said, "take over buildings or institutional spaces, much like we take over advertisements."[74]

Something else that Julián shared is that they don't consider themselves to be *anti-*, but rather *counter* advertising. They are not against the idea of communication in the public space and advertising in itself, but they are against an advertising system that promotes consumerism and an ecologically unsustainable capitalist model. They are also against the way these messages take over public discourse and public space, and counteract this by redeploying the tools of advertising against itself. By changing the content but sustaining some of the communicational devises, they aim to expose the psychological mechanisms used by the advertising industry to promote consumerism.[75]

Parallel to their urban interventions, Proyecto Squatters runs an education program for schools, in which they discuss issues like gender and environment through the lens of advertising and provide children and young people with tools for their own "subvertizing" exercises. In addition, they are regularly invited to speak at universities, mostly on the subject of art and politics. A notable occasion was an invitation by the Centre for Legal and Social Studies (CELS) to give a workshop to lawyers working on human rights issues, who had realized that they needed creative ways of communicating their research. Such activities tend to take place on a voluntary basis, as their practice is *autogestionada* in the same way as Casa 1234's.

Finally, while their interventions take place on the ground in public spaces or during talks in institutions, Proyecto Squatters reaches most of its audience through social media. Julián made reference to the contradictory use of platforms like Facebook for a project that is inherently a challenge to certain forms of interaction and consumption. However, as suggested earlier, Proyecto Squatters prioritizes content (messages) and process (collective, collaborative) over the tools and tactics employed.

## *Cultural Battles and the City*

In Argentina, and particularly in Buenos Aires where a disproportionately large part of the country's cultural industries are concentrated, we can identify three coexisting cultural logics: state-sponsored community arts, creative industries, and *autogestión*. The creative industries follow a logic of growth and a fast-paced rhythm dictated by the globalized market and the modernization imperative. The making practices of the *autogestivo* cultural field, on the other hand, are more concerned with thinking and working through the relationship between time, history, memory, and territory,[76] issues that are also important to state-sponsored community arts even if they are limited by the structures and processes of the state. The three logics are not completely separate, and they do overlap in practice: while the government of the city of Buenos Aires follows a creative-industries vision, it still funds community arts venues and programs, and while independent artists and collectives do not produce for the market and distance themselves from state-sanctioned culture, some do seek subsidies and wish for more state support, or commercialize their work, albeit outside of big distributors and platforms.[77] The interactions and clashes between these different understandings and practices of culture, however, make for cultural battles in which perceptions of culture and its place in society are disputed, but what is also disputed are the different visions of development and well-being attached to those conceptions.

In the case of La Boca, for instance, the Color BA mural festival organized by the city government turned murals into a contentious issue by instrumentalizing this art form to alter the cultural dynamics and aesthetic of the area for the purpose of increasing property value. LBRP responded by deploying their own artistic heritage and local knowledge, reinforcing in this way the historic presence of their mural art tradition and the value that this holds for the local community as a democratic art form. While the city government aimed at increasing the cultural offerings of the neighborhood with new artists and aesthetics and through the formalization and spectacularization of local festivities, LBRP sustained an idea of democracy in the arts that is situated and linked to local identities and processes of subjectivization. The value and role of culture was contested, but also what lay behind this battle for the inhabitants of La Boca was the struggle over the right to the city, to housing, and to sustain communal life.

The democratization of art is also of utmost importance to the artists and activists at Casa 1234 in the city of Córdoba. In their work with the families of victims of trigger-happy cops, they aim to blur the lines between artist and activist, so that everyone involved has agency in the representation of issues and in how these representations are then displayed in public spaces in order to denounce institutional violence. Another important aspect of their work is the *autogestión* approach, and how they sustain an ethos of autonomy.

The interventions of Proyecto Squatters are in many ways similar to those of Casa 1234 in terms of the unauthorized use of public space and the democratization of the creative act. While Casa 1234 creates its own prints following a *chicha* aesthetic that its interlocutors can relate to, Proyecto Squatters intervene on the advertisements they find in the street. In both cases, the objective is to dispute the logic of advertising using some of its own communicative tools but employing different relationalities, aesthetics, economies, and modes of organizing. In other words, activists appropriate the communicational tools of advertising and use them against itself, a mechanism that has often been termed "culture jamming." In turn, they resist the cooptation back into the capitalist system—which feeds off transgression, digests it, and repackages it for the market—by presenting a kind of critique that is "in a dialectical relationship with the public interest," meaning that their connection to antisystemic movements sustains the interventionist act and allows the practice to continue to reinvent itself in the face of possible cooptation.[78]

A question that emerges is whether reproducing the one-directional communication dynamics of advertising is not in fact contradicting the ethos of these groups. As Audre Lord would put it, can the master's tools dismantle the master's house? This question is not new, and in fact, similar issues arise for instance for activists using corporate digital platforms as part of their tactics. A way of reconciling these tensions is to consider these practices as part of an ecology of activist tactics and approaches. While other practices presented in this book place special emphasis on the design of processes that are prefigurative throughout, if we step back, we can see how different practices can be placed upon a spectrum: some design new approaches to art making, others reappropriate existing methodologies such as mapping and remake them, and others employ tools of hegemonic culture against itself in disruptive acts of denunciation. What is important to consider is how in the end, as I will develop in the conclusion, each practice activates different mechanisms to resist and dismantle extractivism, and that the different mechanisms complement each other.

The cases discussed here, both the examples of cultural extractivism and of cultural resistance, relate to urban processes in cities across the world, where gentrification is often pushed through cultural development and resisted through grassroots cultural initiatives.[79] However, the Latin American context is characterized by the expansion of the extractive frontier and its various consequences on the social, the economic, and the cultural. The combination of the frameworks of cultural and urban extractivism allows us, in this case, to reach a nuanced understanding of urban processes and how these relate to other realities of the country and the region. Making such connections is also paramount in order to understand the multiple dimensions of extractivism and devise alternatives to that model. The forms of artistic resistance discussed here display such an understanding and challenge extractive dynamics through discursive and spatial interventions based on an ethos of *autogestión* that is concerned with creation, not production, and with thinking other forms of being in the world.

Finally, the notion of cultural extractivism brings to the forefront important considerations at a time when multilateral organizations like the United Nations are promoting the cultural and creative industries as vehicles for sustainable development in the Global South.[80] What visions of development and of sustainability do these institutions uphold? Do they challenge or at all consider how the cultural and creative industries fit within extractivist projects of modernization? The perspective presented in this chapter emphasizes the need to consider such projects within the reality of extractive economies and to widen conversations about the many different ways investment in culture can take place as a way of contributing to more just and sustainable societies.

# 5 Our Place in the World

## *Autonomy, Sovereignty, and Narratives of Self-Determination*

*Fuera Monsanto, fuera Chevron, ¡fuera el modelo de saqueo y represión!*

Out with Monsanto, out with Chevron, out with the model of looting and repression!

Popular Argentine chant

POSTEXTRACTIVIST WORLDS ARE about moving beyond the hegemony of extractive capitalism, redistributing and rethinking power, and upholding communities' right to decide how to live their lives in balance with ecosystems and other communities. This is why autonomy, sovereignty, and self-determination are grounding concepts for such struggles.

In Latin America, extractivism operates by the hand of corporate, national, and supranational powers, and in response, resistance manifests in different forms, at different levels, and through different channels. We can therefore see how within these movements, narratives of autonomy and sovereignty intersect at points and operate separately at others, in response to multiple forms and levels of oppression operating in interrelated manners and with the aim of fighting for the right to self-determination. While indigenous communities lead situated struggles to assert their right to ancestral territory, nationwide networks of activists stand against international organizations and transnational corporations and their influence in the region. "Out with Monsanto! Out with Chevron!"

In this context, notions such as autonomy and sovereignty are not only ideas that help frame an oppositional stance, but they are also building blocks in a particular ethos that guides the day-to-day practices and processes of antiextractivist movements. At the same time, the fact that there are multiple interests and forces at play means that sometimes such concepts are mobilized in ways that generate contradictions. *Sovereignty* can refer to national sovereignty, but it can also apply to other issues such as food sovereignty and energy sovereignty. In turn, while food sovereignty and energy sovereignty are often framed as national issues, as per the discourse of most progressive governments, for many communities the struggle is about sovereignty at the local level. This latter position is related to struggles for self-determination, and in fact, it often clashes with governments' discourse of sovereignty, especially when it comes to the extractive industries and the state's management of the commons in ways that continue to be unequal and without democratic participation.

*Autonomy*, in turn, can be understood in the Latin American context as the creation of the conditions that allow us to change the norms of a world from the inside, and it can include the defense of certain practices, the transformation of others, and the invention of new ones.[1] Autonomy is linked intrinsically to territory. For this reason, this chapter is very much connected to, and should be considered in parallel to, Chapter 1. However, by dedicating this space to engaging with the ways autonomy, sovereignty, and self-determination are conceived and mobilized by social actors, I am able to develop other thoughts on autonomy relevant to the aims of this book. These include the perception of transnational corporate power, the forms of organizing that have emerged from social movements, including the positioning of artists, and the anti-imperialist narratives that underpin much organizing against extractivism.

I thus begin this chapter by discussing the recent history of autonomous art practice in Argentina, as a way of providing further political and aesthetic grounding for reading the practices discussed in the rest of the chapter and reflecting on others discussed throughout the book. I then look at the movement for sovereignty from transnational capital, analyzing recent political and artistic manifestations against the presence and intervention of international organizations in Argentina and in Latin America, including the 2019 exhibition *Malvenido FMI* (Unwelcome IMF), and the performance action *Procesión pagana del Plumero de La Pampa* (Pagan procession of the Plumero de La Pampa, or Pampas grass) during the 2018 G20 summit in Buenos Aires. Following from this I look at autonomy and sovereignty in the struggle of indigenous nations, and I discuss the artistic interventions United Killers of Benetton, which draw connections between colonialism, state violence, and the power of transnational capital. Finally, I consider how ideas of self-determination and autonomy have been adopted by antimining activists in Andalgalá, a town in the northwest of Argentina that has been fighting open-pit mining for over two decades and that has evolved from opposition to the negative effects of mining to a movement for autonomy and postextractivism. The case of Andalgalá is examined through the testimonies of land defenders themselves, and with reference to the murals and performances that have served to denounce the violence exerted upon nature and human communities for over twenty years.

Autonomy, sovereignty, and self-determination are preconditions for people's exercise of reworlding, or designing other worlds. This chapter therefore acts as an important grounding for Chapter 6, where I focus on design practices for worlds otherwise.

## *Art and Autonomy*

Arturo Escobar argues that Latin American autonomy is based on a radical notion of relationality; more specifically, "at its best, *autonomía is a theory and practice of interexistence and interbeing, a design for the pluriverse*."[2] On her part, political theorist Ana Cecilia Dinerstein focuses on the creative potential of autonomy as an organizing force, and speaks of autonomy as the "art of organizing hope."[3]

In the introduction, I discussed autonomous politics in Latin America. At this point, it is important to clarify the use of *autonomy* in specific reference to art theory, since the word refers to markedly different concepts in each context, and our task of understanding art in antiextractivist movements will benefit from both. In the study of the nineteenth- and twentieth-century avant-gardes, *autonomy* refers to the role of an art sphere separate from other fields where artists had freedom to create, a factor that paradoxically facilitated the conditions for artistic movements *against* that kind of autonomy or separation from the rest of society to emerge. When discussing contemporary art and activism, however, *autonomy* refers to independence from artistic institutions (both private and public) and tends to imply a closer relationship to social and political movements.[4]

In Argentina there is a long-standing tradition of praxes that connect art, politics, and the public space. However, following the 2001 crisis there was a moment of collective reaction that led to the development of new ways of engaging with the political, the aesthetic, and the ethical, drawing from the principles of a rising autonomous politics in the streets.[5] With the crisis emerged the spirit of autonomous *autogestión*, which I began to discuss in Chapter 4; as a result of the absence of the state and the absence of funds, artists (in the same manner as other workers) began to self-organize as collectives, supporting their practices by establishing social and affective bonds, networks, and new forms of exchange and support that would later consolidate into a new approach to cultural production. This approach transformed the national cultural landscape and became the precursor to many of the artistic practices in the current struggle against extractivism and for post-extractivist futures.

*Autogestión* thus emerged as a strategy of resistance and ended up becoming a repertoire of tools of action. It put forward a radical form of relationality because its potential came from these newly formed bonds. Furthermore, it was not concerned with finding ways of putting forward an individual or collective artistic practice, but rather, it was about finding ways of putting to work the resources at hand to fulfil the interests and needs of others. In this way, autonomous *autogestión* gave way to a range of modalities of micropolitics that operate within and outside the logic of contemporary art, including the development of affective economies, the resignification of public space, and the establishment of networks of collaboration.[6]

An early example of this is the collective Arde! Arte, which emerged in 2002 from the belly of the assembly Argentina Arde (Argentina in Flames), formed after the mass protests of December 19 and 20, 2001.[7] The group was conceived as a horizontal collective, collaborating with social movements and other artist collectives and staging performance actions and interventions in the public space. These included the production of prints posted in the streets during marches, performances denouncing institutional violence, and other, more ludic actions, such as *Suelta de globos* (Balloon release), a mass release of balloons carrying small gifts near the main square in Buenos Aires. The action marked the one year anniversary of the December 2001 uprising in a manner that involved political denunciation and play at the same time.[8]

Autonomous *autogestión* also gave place to new aesthetics that reflected the materialities and economies of the time.[9] This has been notably exemplified by the editorial project Eloisa Cartonera, which engaged cardboard-pickers in the production of books using recycled cardboard for making hand-painted covers.[10] Autonomy is an ethos that, when embodied in art making, permeates the aesthetic and discursive elements of the work, as well as the processes and the political economy of artistic production, as I began to argue in Chapter 4.

Politically, the notion of artistic autonomy is key for understanding the positioning of artists in antiextractivist movements, given that during the time of progressive governments in the 2000s and 2010s, most politically engaged artists became aligned with the government's cultural politics. *Kirchnerismo* (the name given to the political period between 2003 and 2015 under the administrations of Néstor Kirchner and then Cristina Fernández de Kirchner, and to the branch of the Peronist movement that aligns with their vision) made culture a pillar of their political project, and this was a political strategy as well as part of a progressive program of social inclusion.[11] It gave a central space to the work of artists dealing with social and political issues, particularly those working on human rights and the 1976 to 1983 civic-military dictatorship. Indeed, analysts see cultural policy as instrumental in constructing a Kirchnerist hegemony based on a discourse of inclusion, human rights, and opposition to neoliberalism.[12] During this time, artistic critiques of extractivism, or of the Kirchnerist "model" of development and redistribution, were very few. One exception to this was the 2015 exhibition *Cuatro escenas artepolítica en la Argentina del Modelo* (Four scenes artpolitic in the Argentina of the "model'[13]) mentioned in Chapter 2, which featured the work of artists like Pao Lunch, Etcétera, and Azul Blaseotto, artists that continue to be crucial to the artistic movement against extractivism to this day, and who, even when operating within artistic institutions, sustain a critical position of the art world and a deliberate distance from governmental agendas, as is the case with most of the artists featured in this book.

## *Sovereignty from Transnational Capital*

"Social justice, economic independence and political sovereignty" were the "three flags" waved by President Juan Domingo Perón in the Argentina of the mid-twentieth century. What, we might ask, do political sovereignty and economic independence mean now? And what place does the idea of sovereignty hold in movements against extractivism and for postextractivist futures in Argentina and Latin America?

In their 2000 book *Empire*, Hardt and Negri argued that modern perceptions of sovereignty centered on the sovereign state. By the end of the twentieth century, however, these territorial boundaries were no longer valid. At the same time, they argued, there was no longer one nation that governed over others: imperialism was dead and had given way instead to Empire as a force that regulates global exchanges. Empire does not have a center or fixed boundaries, and it is made up of three simultaneous forms of governance: the US as the weakened head of a monarchy; an aristocracy that consists of other powerful nation-states, international organizations like the International Monetary Fund (IMF) and the World Trade Organization (WTO), and transnational corporations; and a democracy that includes NGOs, the United Nations, and less powerful nation-states and capitalist firms.[14] In 2020, in an essay looking back on twenty years since the publication of *Empire*, the authors emphasized the increasingly weakened power of the US, now evidenced by its failure in "achieving the stable hegemony required of a true imperialist power" in the Middle East.[15] They also commented on the rise of China, sustaining, however, that it is not a case of one nation replacing another as hegemonic power, but rather one of constant struggles among nation-states within the mixed and multiscalar constitution of Empire.

Hardt and Negri's framework is useful for thinking through issues of sovereignty in relation to extractivism because it highlights the increasingly decentered nature of extractive capitalism. It is still necessary to adopt a decolonial position in movements against extractivism and for postextractivist futures, given that colonial geographies continue to condition Latin America's position in the global economy, and given the pervasive coloniality of cultural imaginaries that perpetuate extractive relations to other countries, other humans, other beings, and ecosystems. However, as nations like China become more powerful players in the global extractive economy,[16] and as corporations continue to accumulate political power alongside capital, we must contemplate the limitations of a decolonial framework and pay more attention to how extractive flows play out in the current geopolitical composition beyond the geographies of European colonialism in the Americas.

What we need, in other words, is a nuanced and multi-scalar understanding of extractive dynamics that is both historically situated and has a global outlook. In developing such an approach, I follow Elden in his argument that there hasn't simply been a shift from the striated spaces of modernity to the "smooth" space of Empire. Rather, they overlap, and nation-states still attempt to "cling to their sovereignty and territorial integrity in an age of globalizing markets and culture and emerging global modes of governance."[17]

Sovereignty and territorial integrity are in fact recurrent tropes in progressive governments in Argentina and other parts of Latin America and are usually employed in order to promote the national exploitation of nature (as well as being concepts recently taken up by right-wing governments across the world). Progressive governments in Latin America have co-opted and incorporated the discourse of alter-globalization and autonomous movements that stand "against the authoritarian imposition of neoliberal globalization . . . and against the new relations of imperialism it enacts," using their opposition to neoliberal globalization to justify nationalized extractivism, as was the case for instance in Bolivia.[18] In many cases, such as in Argentina, however, public spectacles of national sovereignty like the partial renationalization of the oil company YPF in 2012 took place in parallel to many other deals handing over extractive projects to foreign companies, from oil to mining, making evident the contradictions at the core of many *progresismos*.

## UNWELCOME IMF

One of the matters that has dominated narratives over sovereignty in Argentina for decades, and where Hardt and Negri's notion of Empire proves useful, is the country's relationship to the IMF. The IMF has not only acted as a major loan provider to Argentina for decades, but it has also contributed to the development of many of the economic policies that led the Argentine economy to default in 2001. Néstor Kirchner's government cancelled all debt with the IMF in 2006 in a political act framed by a discourse of national sovereignty. Since then, the figure of the IMF has become the most recognizable symbol of neoliberalism in the local imaginary, surrounded by a series of cautionary tales. Despite this, in 2018 under the government of Mauricio Macri and in the midst of a significant economic crisis, Argentina returned to the fund to request a loan for US $57 billion, the largest by far in the country's history, and indeed in the history of the fund.[19] As conversations took place between the IMF and the Argentine government, a group of artists and intellectuals from the collective Carta Abierta (Open Letter) published an open letter, reproduced in the newspaper *Página12*, arguing for the deal to be blocked by Congress.[20] The letter, published on June 11, 2018, warned that the agreement would deepen the neoliberal path of Macri's government and that the stipulated cuts to public spending as part of the loan would have devastating effects for the most vulnerable in society. The collective stated, "The return to the IMF means renouncing to the autonomy gained when the government of Néstor Kirchner decided to cancel all debt with that international entity. Now the heart of economic policy would reside outside of the decision-making of citizens, of their rulers and representatives, in order to be defined by experts of an organization that operates like the great auditor of global financial capital."[21] The letter mentioned as well the US government's support for the loan and the attached restructuring measures, and how the depreciation of the Argentine peso resulting from the implementation of the restructuring plan would end up benefiting the large exporters of natural resources. In this way, it connected the issue of national sovereignty with the complicity of local economic elites and transnational capital and with the deepening of an extractivist model. The letter concluded by arguing for the need for a different kind of program that counters the one of the IMF. Among the different elements of such a program, the signatories proposed the implementation of a media law that "ends the private censorship of expressions that do not coincide with the requirements of the economic, financial and media power,"[22] a crucial matter given the role of the mainstream media in perpetuating the current economic system, as I have argued already in this book.

The place of the IMF in the Argentine collective imaginary is also captured by the 2019 exhibition *Malvenido FMI*, curated by Cecilia Medina. It was an initiative by Fundación URBE, a nongovernmental organization that carries out policy analysis on social and economic issues and engages in territorial actions in the city of Buenos Aires, and Acción Cultural, an NGO working on socially and politically engaged art projects. *Malvenido FMI* responded to the 2018 "return to the IMF," as colloquially framed by locals. It was a project expressing opposition to the IMF's devastating policies in Argentina and other countries, and a call for national sovereignty in a context of unequal and imperialist global economic relations.

The exhibition took inspiration from an ephemeral one-day exhibition in 1969 titled *Malvenido Mister Rockefeller* (Unwelcome Mister Rockefeller), organized by the Asociación Argentina de Artistas Plásticos (Argentine Association of Visual Artists). The 1969 event marked the visit of Nelson Rockefeller, who at the time was working on the Rockefeller Report on the Americas, a study that aimed to generate information that could be of use to strengthen the United States' position and influence in the region. Rockefeller's visit was met with protests across the country and with an exhibition of political posters that brought together artists from a range of sectors, movements, and political affiliations.[23] The exhibition in 2019 marked the fiftieth anniversary of Rockefeller's visit and its response, highlighting the similarities and continuities between then and now.

In the spirit of paying homage, *Malvenido FMI* was also a one day, ephemeral event. The project put out an open call and selected twenty posters from among the submissions. The chosen posters varied in their messaging, techniques, and overall aesthetic. Some were bold, clean-cut graphics. Others were drawings, collages, and photomontages. Messages ranged from the straightforward "Out, IMF!," to the metaphoric (e.g., the "I" in IMF used as a straw for "snorting-up" the country [Fig 5.1]) and the satirical (e.g., a gleeful Mauricio Macri serving up an Argentina-shaped steak on a silver platter to Christine Lagarde, Donald Trump, and multinational corporations [Fig 5.2]). Others, in turn, were more poetic, such as an embroidered outline of Argentina sprouting veins beyond its territorial limits, a visual reference to Galeano's *Open Veins* (Fig 5.3). While some works were limited to expressing a rejection of the IMF, other posters developed connections to local issues, such as environmental destruction, unemployment, housing, and pensions. Some looked at the past and warned of the consequences of the

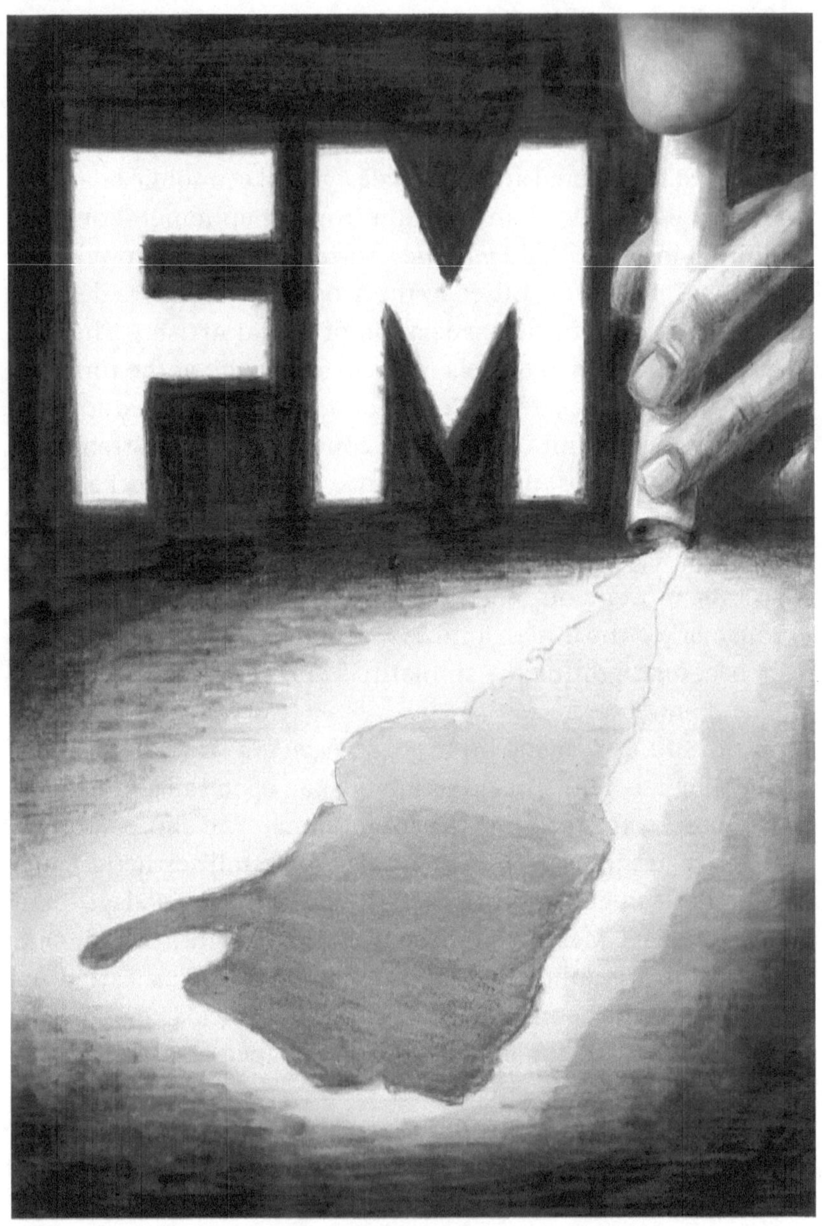


FIGURE 5.1. Filio Acosta Del Río, *Untitled*. Featured in the exhibition *Malvenido FMI*, Buenos Aires, 2019. Image courtesy of Cecilia Medina.

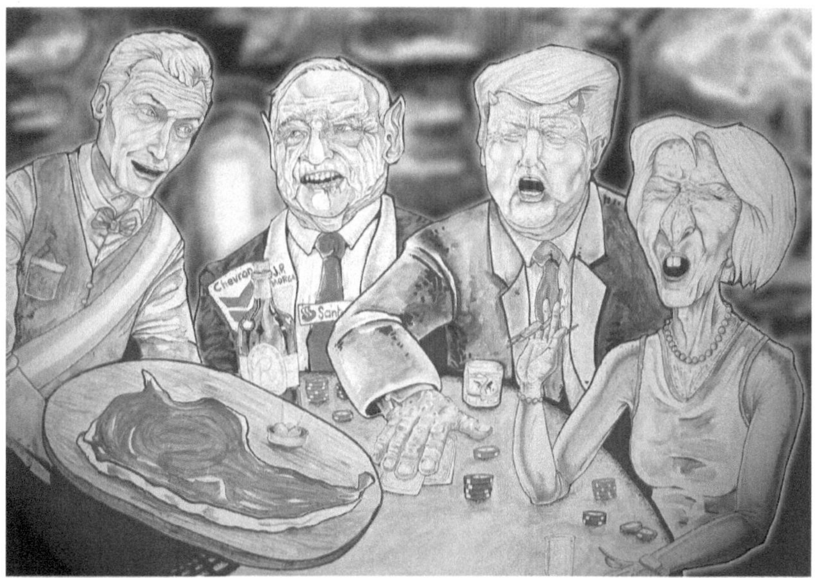


FIGURE 5.2. André Luiz Nunes Marcos, *Untitled*. Featured in the exhibition *Malvenido FMI*, Buenos Aires, 2019. Image courtesy of Cecilia Medina

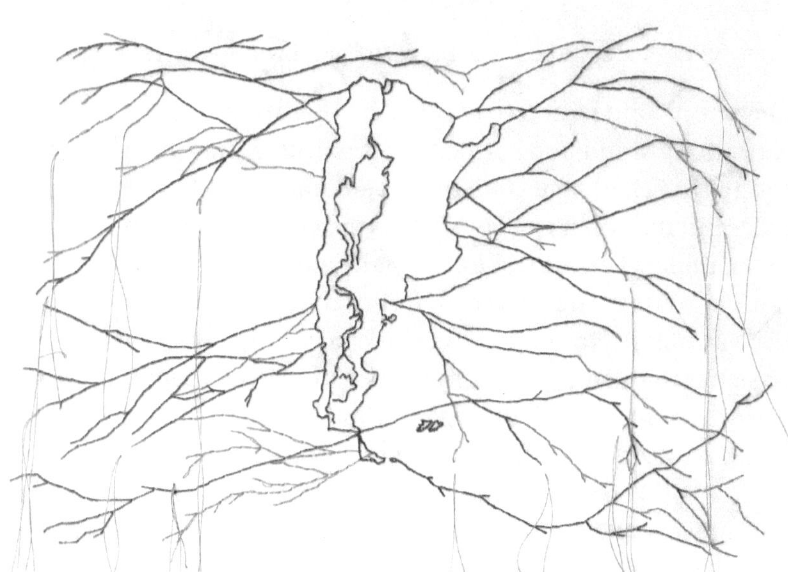

FIGURE 5.3. Lucila Amatista, *Untitled*, from the series Mapas. Embroidery on fabric, 14.7 × 19.3 in 2002. Featured in the exhibition *Malvenido FMI*, Buenos Aires, 2019. Image courtesy of Cecilia Medina.

IMF's loans and their restructuring programs, pointing for instance to the rise in unemployment after the 2001 crisis.

In this way, the exhibition served to denounce the return to the IMF as a threat to national sovereignty. The posters focused on different issues, activating the mechanism of denunciation by visibilizing the powers behind the deal or by dwelling on the threat itself, the matters at stake, and the anticipated effects, much like the works denouncing human rights violations discussed in Chapter 3. Also, by bringing together different perspectives and visual responses to the announced deal, the event served to mark and document a particular point in time. *Malvenido FMI* begs the question, Where will we be fifty years from now? When we look back, much like artists in 2019 looked back to 1969, this exhibition will act as a document of the narratives of opposition of the time, narratives that deconstruct the meaning and implications of international debt to uncover the interests behind, the consequences that lurk, and the reality of who benefits and who loses from such arrangements.

## THE WTO, THE G20, AND DARING TO ENVISION OTHERWISE

The strong opposition to the IMF in Argentina and in Latin America is not a standalone issue. It sits within a movement for sovereignty that challenges free trade agreements and the influence of other international entities such as the G20 and the WTO. In recent years, under the government of Mauricio Macri (2015–2019), Argentina was host to the WTO conference in December 2017, and to the G20 summit in November–December 2018. Argentina's hosting role was championed by Macri as part of his government's strategy to "bring Argentina back into the world," following the years of Kirchnerist *progresismo*'s discursive opposition to neoliberalism.

The WTO and G20 summits, in a manner that also refers back to the "unwelcome of Rockefeller," incited several protests and counteractivities. In 2017 Buenos Aires was host to a counter-conference in parallel to the meeting of the WTO, during which a range of social organizations, from indigenous groups to unions and environmental networks, came together to express their opposition to the WTO's vision and to co-design alternative economic and social formations. The counter-conference included talks, workshops, demonstrations, and even a festival, and featured contributions from international delegates.

In 2017 I met with Mario and Bettina from Asamblea Argentina Mejor sin TLC (Argentina Better off without Free-Trade Agreements Assembly), who were involved in organizing the counter-conference to the WTO, titled The Summit of the Peoples. They shared that a communication challenge they often face in their work is connecting free trade and the actions of organizations like the WTO to local problems. The mainstream media, they argued, does a good job of keeping things separate, and it is up to us activists to relate these global dynamics to the problems people are facing in the country right now, so that we can collectively devise other alternatives.[24] Mario talked as well about the need to generate languages that counter the paradigm of rationalism. He highlighted the importance of visibilizing and denouncing the workings of organizations like the WTO in the context of the aforementioned obfuscation on behalf of the mainstream media: "We have to visibilize what they do, they dress up as 'good guys,' and they are coming here, ministers of economy and commerce from around the world, and they look like convent girls, but those guys are going to sign an agreement on behalf of the whole world, they are going to sign agreements that will harm humanity for generations to come."[25] I asked Mario and Bettina about their communications tactics, and they said that while they produce a lot of material for online distribution, such as short videos, pamphlets, and books, they also follow an ethos of popular education. They place much emphasis on face-to-face encounters with people in order to discuss day-to-day problems and how these connect to the issue of international trade in order to deconstruct individual and collective behaviors with a view to embody the transformations we want to see in the world.

December 2018 saw international delegates gathering in Buenos Aires once again, this time for the G20 summit. And once more, a people's summit and a series of marches and protests took place in response. On December first, artist collective La Ala Accionista joined a demonstration against the G20 in the streets of Buenos Aires. Their participation took the form of a performance action, which they titled *Procesión pagana del Plumero de La Pampa*. The action consisted of a procession carrying a totem of the *Plumero de La Pampa*, or Pampas grass, a plant native to the Argentine Pampas and other parts of South America (figs. 5.4 and 5.5). Elsewhere in the world, including countries in Europe like Spain, the plant was imported due to its decorative features (tall stems and luscious plumes), but it has now been qualified as an invasive species, reproducing at a fast pace and preventing the healthy growth of native plants. La Ala Accionista brought a totem of the *Plumero de La Pampa* to the march against the G20 as a way of making a stance on national sovereignty: the *plumero*, a South American plant, represented the agency of the Latin American people in defending their sovereignty, as well as embodying the agency of nature. Alongside the procession, others from the group gave away *estampitas* (small, printed cards usually featuring saints or other religious figures and carried for protection) with the image of the *plumero*. In the words of one of the artists, "the *Plumero de La Pampa* . . . is a native plant that in European soil is included in the catalogue of invasive species. We know that this plant protects us against imperialism."[26]

Much like *Malvenido FMI*, La Ala Accionista's performance action denounced the role of international organizations in sustaining global inequality. In this case, there was also a symbolic counterattack, in which a South American plant is venerated as a savior, invading the land of the colonizers. But in addition to acting as acts of denunciation, performance actions can, as I have argued elsewhere, be a way of generating particular affects among people.[27] In their embodied nature, which in this case involved the generation of a processional ambiance as well as interaction with the protest public through humor, performance actions can reinforce collective feelings toward the issue at hand. The procession of the *plumero* embodied the notions of self-defense and self-determination and aimed at generating a sense of empowerment

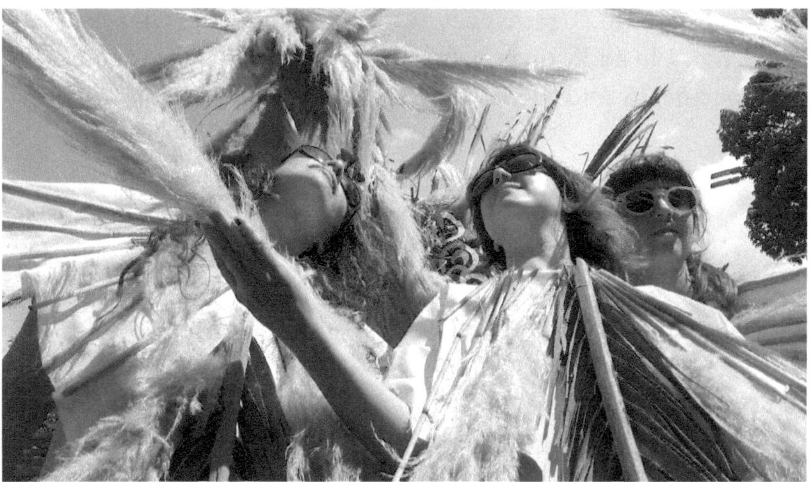

FIGURE 5.4. *Procesión pagana del Plumero de La Pampa* joins the demonstration against the G20 summit of 2018 in Buenos Aires. Photo by La Ala Accionista.

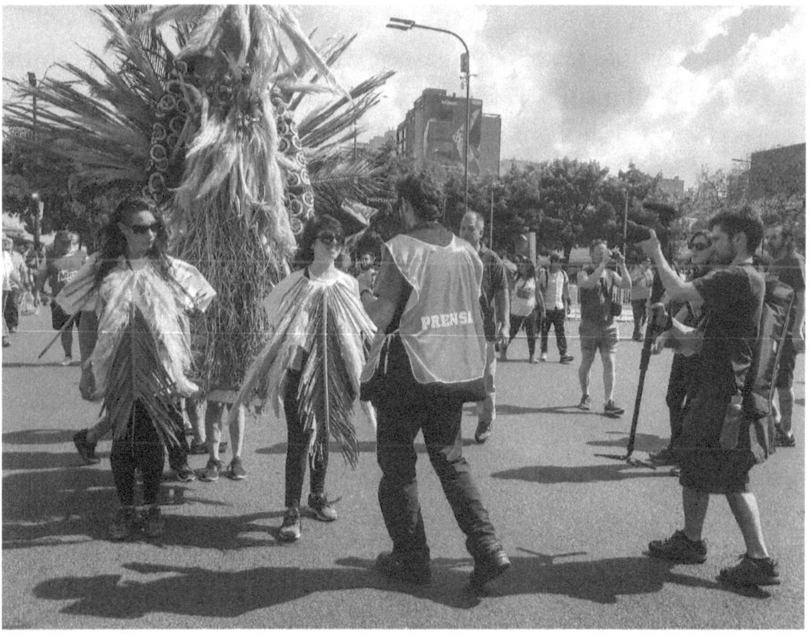

FIGURE 5.5. National and international media outlets interview La Ala Accionista during the *Procesión pagana del Plumero de La Pampa*, during the march against the G20 summit, December 1, 2018. Photo by Anna Vallverdú.

and emboldening against the international actors that threaten sovereignty, in addition to being an act of denunciation against the G20 specifically and their role in the global economy.

### *Autonomy and Sovereignty in Territorial Conflicts*

In the case of indigenous movements, autonomy often is related to "the reappearance or recuperation in the present of a longstanding alternative tradition that has been rendered invisible or unthinkable through the hegemony of Westerncentric modernity."[28] In the 1990s, across different countries, we could see the consolidation of indigenous struggles based around a kind of ethnic citizenship that became a tool of cultural recognition and a basis for struggles surrounding land and territory. This consolidation of indigenous movements was the result of a series of factors, including landmark developments such as the 169 Convention sponsored by the International Labor Organization (ILO) in 1989 and the United Nations Declaration on the Rights of Indigenous Peoples in 2007, as well as the failure of integration processes and a revalorization of ethnic and cultural identities.[29]

Territorial rights emerged originally as a defense mechanism against the occupation of the "last frontier" and the advance of extractivism, and gradually became part of a discourse of indigeneity that centers on the demand for autonomy and free determination.[30] With increased conflicts, indigenous groups in Latin America developed two avenues of response and action: the issue of autonomy and the defense of the right to prior consultation on extractive projects.[31] The right to free and informed prior consultation has been an issue of contention. It was incorporated into Latin American constitutions through the ILO 169 Convention, but different governments have purposefully minimized its standing in order to circumvent it. For instance, Argentina rectified the treaty in 2000, however, strategic laws such as the hydrocarbons law of 2014, which habilitates fracking, were approved without incorporating the right to prior consultation.[32] The matter of autonomy, on the other hand, does not refer only to the occupation and management of ancestral territories; the struggle is also one for ontological self-determination.[33] Mapuche communities in Neuquén, for instance, demand "that the state recognizes itself as plurinational," and that Mapuche people can exercise their culture, their identity, and their way of life in both their ancestral territories and outside of them, as stated by Lefxaru Nahuel, spokesperson for the Confederación Mapuche de Neuquén.[34] But most importantly, Mapuche struggles for autonomy go beyond the demand of rights to the state, which is a short-term form of action to protect communities and territories and improve living conditions. Their struggle for autonomy is an ontological and political project that sees beyond the narrow frames of a judicial system which is both imposed through violence and incompatible with their ontology.[35]

In Chapters 1, 2, and 3, I discussed and developed different aspects of indigenous struggles for ancestral land and self-determination, including forms of art and collective action. In what follows, I focus on connecting the issue of Mapuche struggles for ancestral land with the matter of transnational corporate power and sovereignty. Specifically, I look at a recent artistic intervention in Buenos Aires, one that exposes the underbelly of extractivism, the role of different actors, and the way the extractivist model is perpetuated through different forms of violence.

## UNITED KILLERS OF BENETTON

Luciano Benetton, the man behind the famous United Colors of Benetton brand, is the biggest land owner in Argentina, owning more than nine hundred thousand hectares of land in Patagonia. Benetton acquired these lands from a government enterprise at an astonishingly low price in the 1990s, and these lands overlap with Mapuche ancestral territory. Since then, Mapuche communities have been claiming back ancestral territories, but their claims have largely been ignored.

In August 2017, Argentina was shaken by the disappearance of Santiago Maldonado, a young artisan and activist from the province of Buenos Aires who was in Chubut, Patagonia, protesting in solidarity alongside a Mapuche community mobilizing for their right to occupy their ancestral territory, currently owned by Benetton. Maldonado disappeared in the context of the gendarmerie's repression of a road blockade, and his lifeless body was found in a nearby river almost three months later. The disappearance of Santiago Maldonado brought the issue of Benetton's land ownership and the Mapuche struggle to the public eye.

In early November 2017, three months after Maldonado's disappearance, and at the time when his body was being examined at the morgue in Buenos Aires, a group of academics, artists, and activists gathered at a subway station meters away from that building to carry out an intervention on a series of United Colors of Benetton ads for the company's "Purple Revolution" campaign. The group arrived carrying multiple small signs, carefully designed for placing over the original Benetton ads and transport signage at the station. The resulting intervened signs said things like "United *Killers* of Benetton" (fig. 5.6) and "60 meters from here, at the court's morgue, lies the body of Santiago Maldonado." A poster featuring the face of the Italian magnate was intervened with an image of Maldonado alongside the question "Where is Santiago Maldonado?," which had been the slogan used by thousands on marches and on social media during the two and a half months between Maldonado's disappearance and the moment his body was found (figs. 5.7 and 5.8). Another sign pointed to the nine hundred thousand hectares of land in Patagonia that were taken from the Mapuche by "blood and fire" in the 1880s and cheaply sold to Benetton a century later. The word "revolution" was changed to "devolution," demanding in this way the return (*devolución* in Spanish) of lands to Mapuche communities. The action was widely covered in the left wing and independent media and shared on social media.

Speaking from a different position from that of indigenous artists at the frontlines of extraction and state violence, United Killers of Benetton sought to make visible the connections between the case of Santiago Maldonado's disappearance and death and the land claims of Mapuche communities in Patagonia. Specifically, it wove in the issue of state violence with the rights and sovereignty

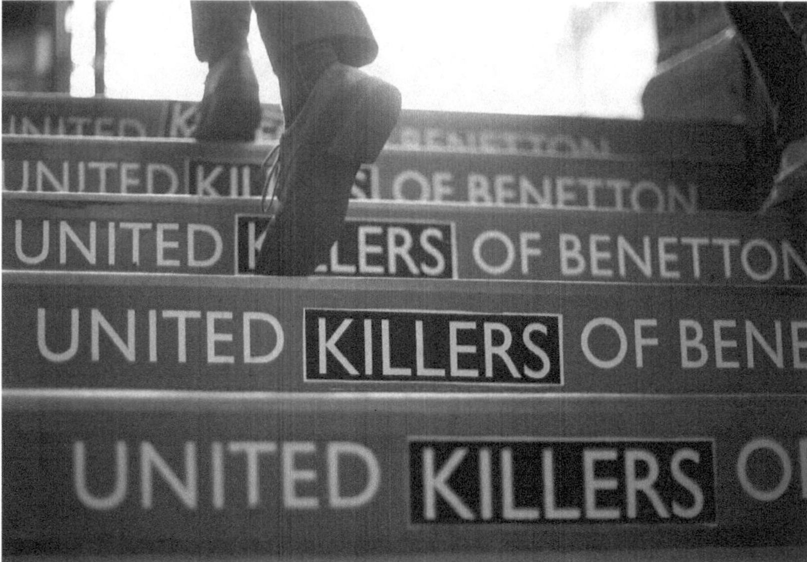


FIGURE 5.6. United Killers of Benetton intervention, November 2017. Photo by Nicolas Pousthomis / Sub.coop.

of indigenous peoples, and with the matter of sovereignty against foreign capital. By targeting Benetton ads, it offered an alternative narrative of the territorial conflict to the one being reproduced in the media, in which Mapuche protestors are framed as violent and corrupt. Instead, the interventions shed light on the longstanding injustices faced by Mapuche people, from the violent process of the "conquest" of Patagonia to the sale of indigenous lands to a foreign company. In turning the focus toward the state and the Italian company and its head, the action attempted to hold them accountable for the injustices faced by Mapuche communities, and for the death of Santiago Maldonado while supporting that struggle. Furthermore, the intervention pointed out the simultaneous dynamics of colonialism still experienced and resisted by indigenous peoples in Argentina to this day and the neocolonial practices of transnational corporations and foreign landowners, whose economic power is protected by the state in violent ways.

In addressing the different elements and scales of a complex set of interrelated conflicts, the interventions activated a series of

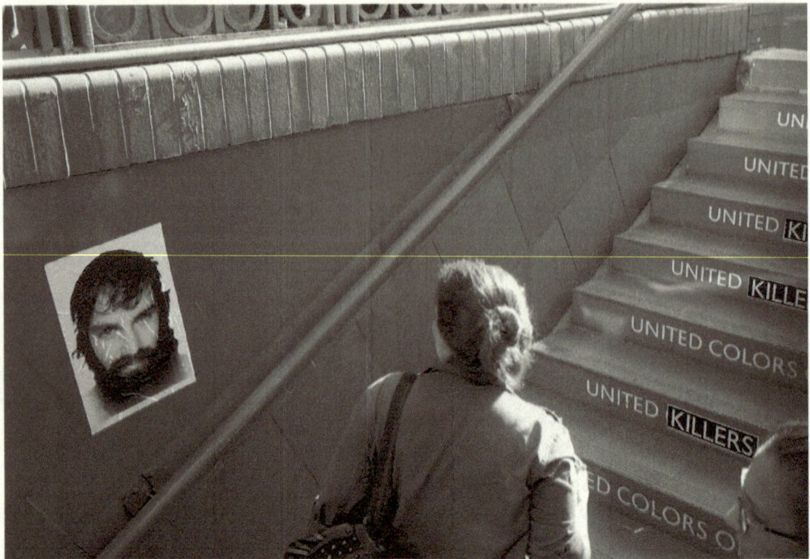


FIGURE 5.7. United Killers of Benetton intervention, November 2017. Photo by Nicolas Pousthomis / Sub.coop.

functions through the production of visual and discursive material and the reconfiguration of the urban space. In the first place, the action denounced Luciano Benetton as a responsible agent in the Mapuche territorial conflict and called out the role of the state in the disappearance and death of Maldonado in a context of repression. And second, by breaking down the different kinds of actors, forms of agency, and forms of violence that constitute the conjuncture, the action deconstructed the power relations of the overlapping conflicts, in this way exposing the wider dynamics that surround the Mapuche claim and the death of Maldonado, dynamics that lie at the core of extractivism.

### *Andalgalá Resiste*

Geographer Horacio Machado Aráoz argues that an enclave is "an *empty space in the territorial sovereignty of the state*, where the combination of its judicial ordering and its jurisdictional power are literally suspended, or directly displaced by a foreign and ad hoc

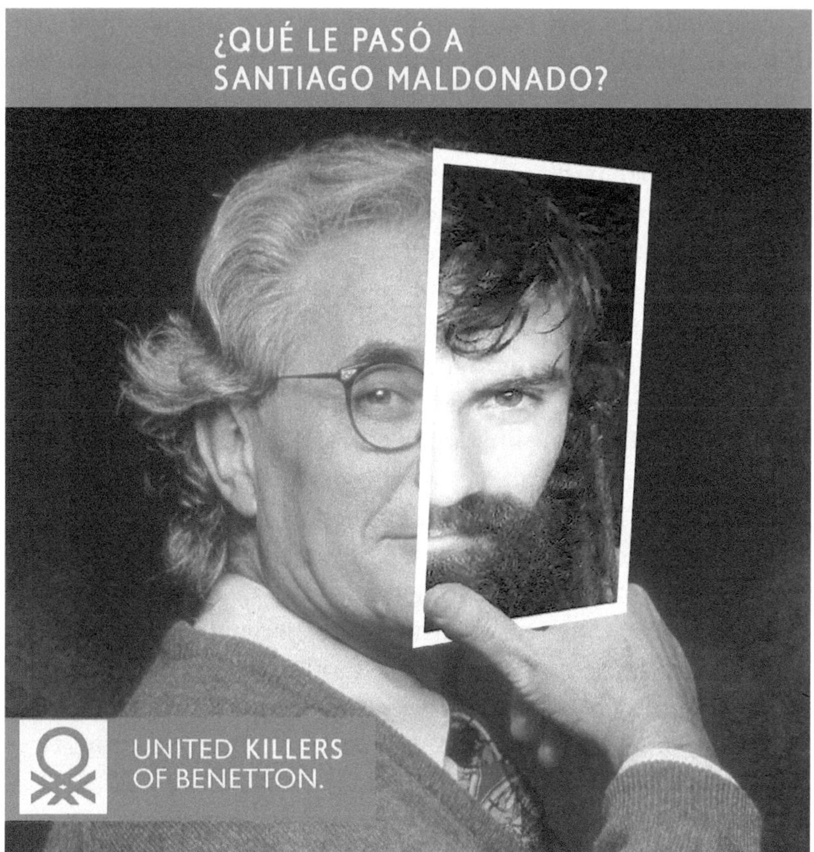


FIGURE 5.8. Poster used as part of the United Killers of Benetton intervention, November 2017. Image by Javier del Olmo.

normative, and where the fundamental political sense of that exceptional situation is to guarantee the appropriation and free transfer of capital gain to the capitals that set up there."[36]

The town of Andalgalá in the northwest of Argentina, where the first open-pit mine of the country opened in 1997, can be seen as a form of contemporary enclave. Yet in a context in which environmental and human rights are not upheld and instances of pollution and health problems are covered up, the people of Andalgalá sustain their fight for their town, the preservation of their ecosystem, access to clean water, and the right to self-determination.

Andalgalá is a case I keep coming back to at different points in this book because it has become an emblem of sustained resistance, because of the creativity that is part of their struggle, and because they dare to envision beyond the false dichotomies of the extractivist system (development through extractivism or poverty), working toward postextractivist futures that are based on different forms of valuing nature and understanding prosperity, and different ways of being in the territory.

One of the people I met when researching the case of Andalgalá was Silvina. Silvina is originally from Andalgalá and is now based in Buenos Aires, but she and her partner Ricardo are very much involved in the fight against open-pit mining. Silvina and Ricardo shared multiple stories about the struggle, including the devastating environmental effects it has had for the town, and the persecution they have faced over the years for fighting back against corporate and political powers. One of the things they told me about, something that almost everyone I met in Andalgalá referred to at one point or another, was the damage to the social fabric that the conflict around open-pit mining had caused. They referred to the town as "socially fractured," and this fracture, they explained, became stronger as time passed and the effects of the mine became more visible.[37] The social fracture in Andalgalá was deepened by an instance of police repression on February 15, 2010, when members of the Asamblea del Algarrobo (Assembly of the Carob Tree, the local assembly against the mine) tried to stop machines going into a site and were met with violent repression and mass arrests. A large mural on the side of the assembly's radio station depicts scenes of repression from that day; there used to be other murals on the theme of police violence including some depicting this same event, but they were erased by the local government (fig. 5.9). In this context of social conflict and institutional violence, art has been an important vehicle for expressing the collective emotions of those who are part of the fight against open-pit mining. Indeed, Andalgalá is known for its wealth of mural art, which not only includes images of violent repression memorializing the past, but also countless walls covered in joyful messages for the protection of water, of Mother Earth, and of life.

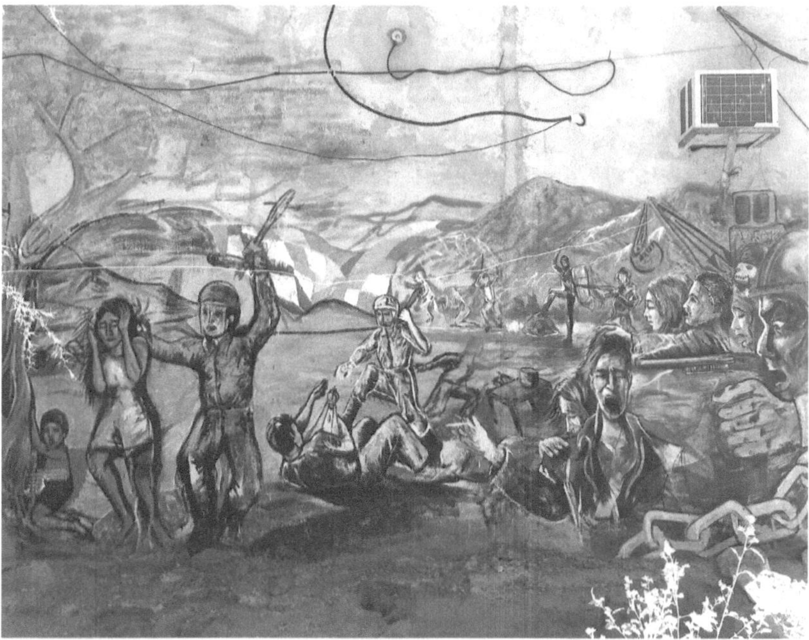

FIGURE 5.9. Image of a mural depicting an episode of police repression in Andalgalá. Photo by the author.

Over the years the movement against open-pit mining has evolved from a fringe campaign of opposition to a majoritarian autonomous movement for self-determination. Mariana Katz, who acts as the assembly's lawyer, explained to me that the movement has gone through different stages, beginning with an economicist perspective, moving onto one of preservation of the environment, and then eventually engaging with institutional matters concerning the respect for democracy.[38] Indeed, the desire for self-determination in Andalgalá seems to stem from a feeling of disappointment with the failures of the democratic system and its institutions. The democratic system failed the people of Andalgalá, for instance, by not upholding their right to informed consultation on open-pit mining projects. Silvina explained that they knew that there would never be a referendum on mining in Andalgalá, because the last time there had been a referendum of that kind in Argentina, in the Patagonian town of Esquel in 2003, the result was

82 percent against the mine. She added, "it is the self-determination of the people that is above those who govern. They never seemed to get that."

In relation to the matters of democracy and governance, it is important to note that the movement against open-pit mining in Andalgalá has remained nonaffiliated with any existing political party. In fact in 2007 members of the community started their own antimining party. They called it Alianza de los Pueblos (Alliance of the Peoples), since their initial idea was that eventually different peoples from other locations would join. They never won a seat or intendancy, but, explained assembly member Sergio, they realized that they could go for more. By 2009, the party had ceased to exist, but the assembly emerged instead. Sergio explained: "when we quit the political party . . . we started having better results, as the Radical party members would come, the Peronists, the leftists, the atheists, the faithful, everyone felt included in the assembly. So the growth was exponential."[39]

Finally, issues concerning sovereignty are also present in the narratives that emerge from the struggle, as there is a strong presence of foreign mining companies in the region, notably from Canada. In a similar manner to the territorial conflicts in Patagonia, transnational corporate power and state power operate together, and in response, the narratives constructed by communities in opposition explicitly highlight the various actors involved.

The different members of the assembly that I spoke to during my time there, and during other interviews in Buenos Aires and over the phone, shared that being part of this fight for so long has provided them with opportunities to think beyond that which they oppose and start to envision worlds otherwise. This envisioning was possible due to the fact that since the open-pit mine Bajo La Alumbrera began operating in 1997 the opposition has accomplished things that many would have thought impossible, such as halting activity at the aforementioned mine and delaying the opening of the new mine, Agua Rica, for over a decade. Such victories have enabled Andalgalá to envision beyond the limits of what the extractivist mindset deems possible.

In my conversations with several members of the assembly, the issue of water came up as a central element in the narrative of self-determination. As Sergio commented, for instance:

> Now that we started to talk about the self-determination of peoples [we realized that] there cannot be self-determination without access to water. The government should not use water as a tool of political power to freely give it to the mining companies, it should be geared toward the self-determination of the peoples to manage forms of production that are friendly to nature, be that fruits or herbs. Here in Andalgalá we have always been a town of produce.[40]

He added that even though in this region there have been small-scale forms of mining for a long time, locals do not identify with open-pit mining and the extractive industries in general.

In addition to the presence of murals and other artistic expressions like the performance actions discussed in Chapter 1, the assembly's community radio has been crucial in challenging the media blackout around open-pit mining conflicts and in allowing regular folk to be heard.[41] Ruth, a teacher from Andalgalá who was deeply involved in the radio during its early years, said, "I think that Radio El Algarrobo had this thing of communicating, of seeing things in a different light. That not everything is as those in power say. And that the power that we have was also heard."[42] Part of that envisioning has been a proposal for Andalgalá becoming an autonomous region, with the aim of enabling self-determination over the use and conservation of the local ecology and the commons. While having lunch with Ruth and with the Assembly's lawyer, Mariana, during my visit, Mariana joked about how Ruth had been driving her crazy for years now with this idea of a "Republic of Andalgalá." Ruth responded, "You laugh all you want, but it's no joke!"

Finally, the struggle for self-determination has been a force that led to connections with other communities in the region, in the country, and in other parts of the world who are facing similar situations. In September 2018, people from Andalgalá and from other towns in the province of Catamarca, under the organization

Pueblos Catamarqueños en Resistencia y Autodeterminación (Peoples from Catamarca in Resistance and for Self-Determination), organized the first autonomous Cumbre Latinoamericana del Agua para los Pueblos (Latin American Summit of Water for the Peoples) in the province's capital city. Contrary to other gatherings, such as the Foro Latinoamericano del Agua Oro Azul (Latin American Water Forum "Blue Gold"), this gathering was not organized or sponsored by any government body or government representatives and remained instead as an autonomous, grassroots gathering of and for the people. As part of the event's general assembly, Marcos Pastrana, a representative of the Diaguita indigenous people, stated, "If they kill the water they kill the culture and the life of the peoples. There are no human rights if the rights of nature are not upheld."[43] Art had a central role in the summit, in line with the ethos of the struggle for water in the region. Indeed, as reported by *Resumen Latinoamericano*, one of the official aims of the meeting was to "recognize art as a medium of expression, creation, and recreation in defense of water."[44]

The practices discussed here and in previous chapters show how in Andalgalá the arts and media production play multiple roles. Practices like performance, mural painting, and community radio have provided spaces for the local community to express their dissent in a conflict that initially felt like David fighting Goliath. Through these practices, they found vehicles for denouncing the issues that the mainstream media would not report, from pollution to instances of institutional, corporate, and police violence. Furthermore, both artistic practices and community media have been integral to generating the kind of autonomous, democratic space that enabled the longevity of the resistance, and participation in such practices democratizes the narratives that emerge around the conflict. In addition, such creative, relational, and self-sustained practices embody the ethos of autonomous *autogestión*, and as such contribute to the design of the wider autonomous space of struggle. The struggle of Andalgalá is known across the country for its creative flair, for its imaginative approach, and for its fearlessness. Embedding art in collective action allowed the community to design a space where other alternatives can be imagined and visualized; where creating worlds otherwise begins to happen in the now.

## *Rethinking the Possible*

National sovereignty and autonomy often are incompatible ideas, especially so when sovereignty discourse is utilized by national governments for deepening extractivism with disregard for communities' right to self-determination. However, given the global context, it makes sense for activists and communities to organize on different fronts, using all available tools to improve their situation in the now and create alliances between groups at different scales. Indeed, the pursuit of autonomy can rarely be a pure one, since self-organized communities exist within borders and legal frameworks that can be contrary to their principles, but which they sometimes need to draw on in order to pursue their aims. Still, this does not prevent them from enacting a particular ethos, and from showing the world that it is possible to live life differently.

A recent example of this has been the presentation of a candidate for the 2018 presidential elections by the Ejército Zapatista de Liberación Nacional (Zapatista Army of National Liberation) in Mexico. While the Zapatista *caracoles*, or communities, are governed by their own codes and reject the frameworks of the Mexican state, the candidacy of Marichuy, an indigenous woman who is a human rights activist and traditional medicine healer, was a statement on the right of indigenous women to be political actors in a context of gender and racial oppression and a way of platforming the Zapatista struggle in the national public sphere. Similarly, when anti-extractivist activists across Latin America call for sovereignty from transnational capital and denounce foreign corporations and multilateral organizations as neocolonial agents, their main goal often is not to defend the political sovereignty of the state but to fight against the forms of power fueling extractivism in their territories, alongside their objective of constructing autonomous spaces and their proposals for other ways of producing and consuming things like food and energy.

Advocating for autonomy, sovereignty, and self-determination, and enacting such ideas in practice, are therefore messy and multilayered tasks that reflect the social and political reality of Latin America and contemporary global geopolitics. Artistic practices play an important role in both the production of narratives of sovereignty and autonomy and in the practice of creating autonomous spaces, as the multiple examples in this chapter have shown.

In addition to acting as an important form of documentation, as is the case with *Malvenido FMI*, art allows us to democratize the construction of narratives, creating spaces of participation and imagination where affects are generated and shared, and where different tools of expression and construction of meaning help us navigate and communicate complex issues. This is why summits like those opposing the G20 and the WTO, and the summit for the defense of water, are always enriched by artistic practices and performances.

But art also opens up possibilities for reverting naturalized hierarchies, and both *Malvenido FMI* and the *Procesión del Plumero* demonstrate this in different ways. In the first case, artists symbolically withdraw the IMF's permission to operate in Argentina. The artists and curator of the exhibition adopt a commanding position that says "not here," in this way making possible the idea that Latin American countries do have agency, and are not forever doomed to return to the IMF and submit to its structural readjustment policies. In the case of the *Procesión del Plumero*, we also see a reversal of hierarchies. This time, hierarchies are reverted in a way that evokes the spirit of the carnivalesque, a concept famously conceptualized in the European context by Bakhtin, later considered in relation to protest culture among others by David Graeber, and retheorized, in its political dimension, in relation to the Caribbean tradition of carnival by Claire Tancons.[45] In the case of the *Plumero,* more than five centuries after the colonization of the Americas, it is now Europe that is being colonized by a South American species. This inversion of terms is celebrated in an exaggerated manner in order to revert the colonizer-colonized narrative and generate a space of emboldening. In this context, I propose that these kinds of carnivalesque experiences should not be construed as merely cathartic but rather as potentially transgressive, as they are powerful interventions in the imaginary of what is possible. Indeed, in order to better understand them, we could situate these actions in relation to a local history of artistic interventions in response to the power and effects of multilateral organizations, transnational trade deals, and increased militarization.

Notably, 2005 saw protests in Buenos Aires and the coastal city of Mar del Plata to give an "unwelcome" to President George W. Bush, who would be visiting the latter city to attend the Fourth Summit of the Americas and try to push through the Free Trade Area of the Americas (FTAA) agreement, which aimed to strengthen the economic power of the US in the region. The arrival of Bush in Mar del Plata saw the city heavily militarized, supposedly to safeguard the president from possible terrorist attacks. But this was not enough to prevent the disembarkation upon the Mar del Plata coast of the Errorists, a newly formed collective founded by artists from Etcétera (whose work I discuss in Chapter 3). With surrealist humor and a sophisticated understanding of the operations of the mainstream media, the Errorists brought their cardboard machine guns and face coverings to the site of the Summit, and they staged an action that they later shared through Indymedia. The shareable guerrilla images they constructed made an intervention into the discourses surrounding the FTAA, as they turned the lens toward the actions of the US in Afghanistan and Iraq at a time when antiterrorism laws were being adopted in Argentina. Furthermore, the surrealist mode of the action destabilized the security operation around the Summit by generating the brief illusion of an attack, subverting power dynamics by means of confusion and defying the limits of what is possible and what is not in the face of power. Importantly, as noted by Jennifer Ponce de León, "[the] Errorists intervene[d] in the aesthetic matrix that dictates the boundaries of what is seen as real and what is seen as fiction."[46] Their work is evidence of "the capacity of fiction to manipulate and make visible the machinations of ideology, revealing *it* to be a fiction that passes itself off as reality."[47]

Such an exercise in challenging what is constructed as truth falls under what I am referring to in this book as deconstruction, building on feminist uses of the concept. Works discussed in this chapter show how art allows us to deconstruct the webs of power that uphold the extractivist model, and to communicate complex structures and dynamics in engaging, striking manners. Deconstruction is important because, as argued by Hardt and Negri, "interpreting the primary structures of rule and exploitation in a global context is the key to recognizing and furthering the potential forces of revolt and liberation."[48] In the next chapter, I thus build on the ideas developed so far to engage with the way art channels those forces to generate new processes, relationalities and worlds through the function of ontological design.

# 6 Worlds in the Making

## *Postextractivism and Ontological Design*

IN RECENT YEARS we have seen a surge of scholarly work, social movements and even industry initiatives concerned with the idea of "future-making." Jeffrey and Dyson link this to the intersecting global issues of our time, including climate change, inequality, and technological transformation. In this context, the authors divide future-oriented approaches into two types: anticipatory politics, which is concerned with "preserving the present against the deprecations of hypothesised dangerous futures" and oppositional prefigurative politics, which attempt to change the present in ways that reflect wider aspirations for social change in the future.[1] This chapter looks at the latter, those kinds of practices that seek to create better worlds in the now, enacting postextractivist ways of doing and living in their push back against extractivism: practices that sustain and recuperate ancestral knowledge, that draw from popular knowledge and experiences, and that integrate the visualization and representation of postextractivist worlds with processes that directly challenge extractive and oppressive dynamics.

Throughout this book, I have adopted an anthropological approach to the study of movements against extractivism and for postextractivist futures. I have considered the big ideas that give way to narratives of opposition and to visions for other ways of being, and I have looked at how such ideas are mobilized in the day to day of collective action and artistic practice, analyzing internal processes within situated sociopolitical contexts. But I also dived into the messiness of what it is to engage in art and collective action for the creation of worlds otherwise at a time when ontological shifts are only occurring in places, in parts, and at an uneven pace. In order to understand the world we live in, the transitions we are fighting for and sometimes already part of, and the possibilities that lie ahead, we cannot focus on one level of our experience only. Instead, we must embrace the muddle and the multiple layers, and engage with the ontological and epistemological debates, the social, historical, and political context, and the daily practice too.

Considering the above, in this chapter I focus on the fifth "d" in my proposed framework of five functions, namely design, and I do so by following the perspectives of Arturo Escobar, Tony Fry, and others who have thought about design on the multiple levels on which it operates without reducing it to the technical or otherwise employing it as a metaphor. I specifically draw from Escobar's proposal of "designs for the pluriverse," which argues for the potential of design practice in thinking and creating worlds otherwise—its ontological potential.[2] At different points in the chapter, I combine Escobar's proposal with the concept of prefiguration, and propose the term *prefigurative design* as a way of describing those practices that are not only designing ways of being that oppose the colonial, extractivist development paradigm and look toward postextractivist futures but are also enacting those visions, structures, and principles in the now.

There are many practices and praxes that contribute to challenging colonial, extractivist ways of doing and being and that put forward other kinds of ethos and processes, including popular research initiatives, solidarity and feminist economies, popular education, and alternative and community media. In this chapter, I focus on three main spaces and their narrative and design practices: agroecology, environmental education, and collective cultural production. I then consider recent holistic approaches to ecosocial transformation that emerged in response to the COVID-19 pandemic, building on years of collective work with views to transitioning toward postextractivism.

Through a reflective discussion of the above praxes, I aim to illustrate the way prefigurative, ontological design can materialize in different spheres of the social. In order to do this, I integrate and sometimes oscillate between theory and practice and between symbolic and material aspects, which I believe is necessary if we want to understand certain projects and initiatives as praxes and comprehend the different elements and layers that construct them. This approach, I propose, will allow us to take away learnings that can inform thinking, feeling and doing in our move toward worlds otherwise.

## *Designing Worlds Otherwise*

We are in the midst of a civilizational crisis that is deeply philosophical and that challenges the bases of the modern episteme.[3] It therefore does not suffice to develop projects that attempt to bring about change within the material and symbolic structures of the current system. What is needed are visions and projects that engage with the ontological basis of the extractivist hegemony and work to enact other ontologies as they design alternative forms of organizing, sharing, and being.

Madina Tlostanova argues that, "understood not merely in relation to its applied and technological facets, but rather as a powerful ontological tool capable of transforming the social and cultural reality, and modeling human experience, subjectivity and life style, and environment and social events, design is clearly one of the spheres in which ontology, epistemology and axiology intersect in a dynamic and creative way."[4] In other words, in this vast task we are facing, it is useful to think of design as inherently ontological because our inventions have the potential to alter society. In turn, drawing from Illich, Escobar explains that "the project of 'reworlding' is . . . necessarily ontological in that it involves eliminating or redesigning not just structures, technologies, and institutions but our very ways of thinking and being."[5]

Because the processes of reworlding that emerge from extractive societies involve challenging the nature-culture divide and the economic and social dynamics based on this hierarchical dualism that have led to current social and ecological crises, design must be approached in a manner that deals with the ingrained coloniality of thought. As Tlostanova argues, "coloniality of design is a control and disciplining of our perception and interpretation of the world, of other human and nonhuman beings and things according to certain legitimized principles." It follows, then, that decolonizing design "requires problematizing the affective and conceptual operations that form the basis of our relations with the world, and questioning the essentialist or instrumentalist approaches that have been naturalized previously."[6] An example of this is decentering the economy in our societies and value systems, acknowledging that the economy is a construct, and that, as all constructs, it can be transformed, renewed, or even dissolved (deconstruction, one of the other functions proposed in this book, is therefore an essential prior step to ontological design).[7] This means that we can let go of a notion of the economy as something concrete, out there, that we depend on and that we, as individuals, have little control of, and begin to envision and create worlds that better integrate the management of resources, production, distribution, and consumption with other aspects of life and the sustaining and reproduction of ecosystems. Another example concerns the deconstruction of knowledge hierarchies and the rethinking of our methods for the creation of knowledge. In her work on mushrooms, Anna Tsing supports a proposal for ontologies that decenter the human by identifying practical remedies to the current state of agriculture and environmental management. She argues for models of vernacular science and citizen's engagement with forest management and environmental remediation as ways of countering "the hegemonic, extinction-oriented practice of what might be called 'plantation science.'"[8] In these kinds of practices, proposes Tsing, the question of well-being is democratized, and multispecies love acts as the basis for a different way of relating to nature.

Finally, in addition to being decolonial, I propose that in a context of multiple crises, we need our ontological design practices to be prefigurative. Jeffrey and Dyson describe prefigurative politics as "an inherently spatial and performative genre of political activism in which people enact a vision of change—through organisation, design, architecture, practices, bodies, or something as simple as a gesture or demeanour—and promote this as indicative of an imminent or more distant 'future.'"[9] Prefigurative design involves the design of objects, practices, systems, and ideas that are not only functional to specific aims (be these linked to the resistance to or the deconstruction of extractivism), but that are also transformative of current structures and dynamics, and embody and enact the ethos of worlds otherwise.

In the next sections, I engage with a series of realms and praxes and demonstrate the workings of prefigurative design as a multi-scalar and inherently ontological practice. In the first place, I look at agroecology and consider the ontological implications of its design for rethinking our relationship to the territory, to the economy, to the production of food, and to each other.

## *Agroecology and Ontological Design*

Agroecology is an approach to food production that is based on following the dynamics of natural ecosystems and often prioritizes small-scale, family-centered production. While in Latin America we are witnessing an expansion of the industrial agricultural model, the vision of food sovereignty and the project of agroecology as a way to achieve it have also become more and more widespread in the last decades.[10] In Argentina and other countries in Latin America, agroecology has a marked political dimension, as it is often linked to a particular vision of society and a political project that looks beyond the matter of food production and stands against the concentration of resources and the mechanization of certain processes.[11] Indeed, in Argentina supporters of agroecology portray it as an emerging alternative to the hegemonic development model.[12]

I begin this section by recalling an event of significance involving the Unión de Trabajadores de la Tierra (UTT; Union of Land Workers), a grassroots organization bringing together thousands of agroecological family producers from fifteen different provinces in Argentina. On February 15, 2019, in the midst of a deep economic crisis in the country, the UTT arrived at Plaza Constitución, a square in the south of the city of Buenos Aires, to carry out one of their famous *verdurazos*: a pop-up produce market with low, standardized prices and/or giveaways, which acts as a form of social protest against poverty and inequality as well as being a public statement on the importance of family farming and a call for state policies that support it. *Verdurazos* can also be read as performance actions, given that they are symbolic acts of gifting that disrupt the chains of the extractivist system to create temporary spaces underpinned by an ethos of solidarity. The UTT had been carrying out *verdurazos* for years, bringing agroecological produce to different neighborhoods in the city. But this time, the city government and the police intervened, claiming there was no authorization to set up the market, and the producers' resistance to their eviction was met with batons, tear gas, and rubber bullets.[13] The incident was reported in the news, and an image from the confrontation by photojournalist Bernardino Ávila went viral: a line of police officers in riot gear bordering the square, and next to them, an elderly woman reaching down to grab some eggplants that had fallen to the ground, most likely as part of the altercation (fig. 6.1). In response to these events, the UTT stated:

> We are those who received tear gas, bullets, and sticks on February 15 for bringing food to the people at accessible prices. We are Teresa, the grandma that kneeled down to grab an eggplant at the foot of the infantry. We are all of that. We propose food sovereignty. We choose access to the land. We propose fair trade. We chose to build together and fight, firmly, tireless, and with dignity for a better world. For all.[14]

The *verdurazo* of February 15 was a space where the extent of the economic crisis and the needs of the people were publicly displayed, and where agroecology came to a momentary rescue. *Verdurazos* are therefore as much politically charged events as they are acts of care and public manifestations of a care-full approach to production and distribution. The repression of the *verdurazo* and the iconic image

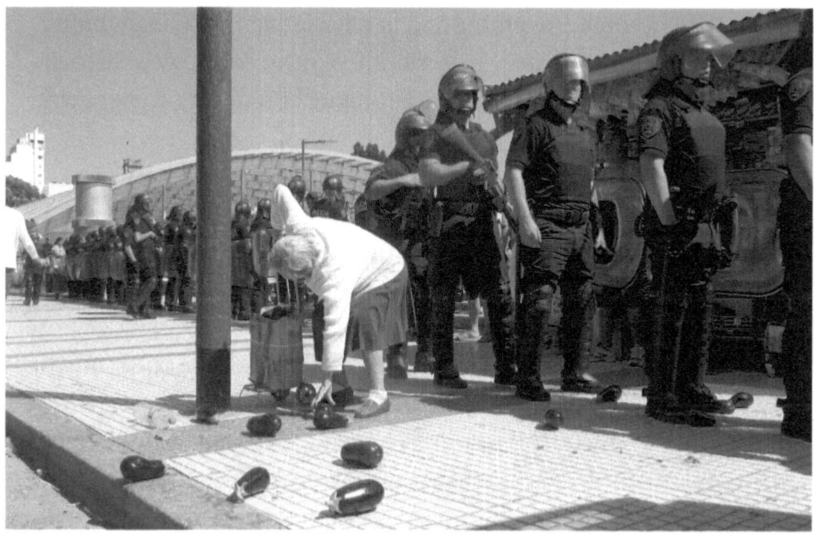

FIGURE 6.1. Police operation during a UTT *verdurazo*, 15 February 2019. Photo by Bernardino Ávila.

that resulted from it were symbolic of the wider paradigm struggle under the hegemony of extractivism. The UTT represents the small-scale, agroecological, community-oriented form of production that stands against the large-scale, glyphosate-dependent agribusiness. *Verdurazos* do not comply with the extractivist model, and because of this, they constitute a threat to the hegemony of extractivism.

## AGROECOLOGY AND PROJECTS FOR WORLDS OTHERWISE

Argentina is a leading agroecological producer in the region, producing food for both the local market and for export. However, there is not enough state support for the sector, as governments continue to champion industrial production of GMO cereals. Vanesa Rosales de la Quintana explains that agroecology in Argentina

> has a productivity that is superior to industrial agriculture . . . and it consumes 80 percent fewer resources. However, there isn't an integral state policy to support it, and there is an invisibilization of the role that it plays in public health and in the provision of food,

> in stopping climate warming and in environmental sustainability. The biggest problem for the development of agroecology is the lack of access to land, given that agroecological producers do not own the land they grow.[15]

At present time, therefore, most initiatives for small-scale agroecology emerge from the bottom up, and often, they have to battle both political and economic powers along the way.

For instance, in the midst of a pandemic, 2020 saw the emergence of Proyecto Artigas, a collaborative project that not only promotes agroecology but that also directly stands up to the corruption of the political and legal systems and the concentration of power in the agricultural sector, a form of power that manifests as patriarchal, corrupt, and feudal. Proyecto Artigas begins with the story of Dolores Etchevehere, the only daughter of Luis Etchevehere, who upon her father's death was cut out of her inheritance by her three brothers, major figures in the agribusiness sector in the province of Entre Ríos. Dolores thus began a long case against her brothers to claim her natural inheritance, and pledged 40 percent of her corresponding land, including the estate Casa Nueva, for an agroecological project that would become Proyecto Artigas.[16] The project brings together landless peasants, activists, and environmental organizations with the aim of building "an agrarian model that is sustainable, free of agrotoxics and exploitation, and different to the one that the [Etchevehere] family represents."[17] While the forty people that began the agroecological farm at Casa Nueva were evicted following a ruling in favor of Dolores Etchevehere's brothers only two weeks after the project materialized on that land in the month of October, the collectives involved said this was only the beginning of a long-term movement of agroecology for food sovereignty.[18]

Proyecto Artigas happened to emerge during the COVID-19 pandemic, a time when the matter of food production came to the forefront of the public agenda in countries across the world.[19] In Argentina, this period also saw the emergence of other agroecological initiatives, such as the first agroecological market in the suburbs of Buenos Aires, in the neighborhood of Haedo. Here, a music venue was transformed into a fruit and vegetable market through the collaboration of the venue owner, food producers, and activists, in a move that not only responded to the situation of the moment but also invited the local population to engage more closely with what they eat and where it comes from.[20] But agroecological markets had actually began to multiply in previous years across different locations, with the aim of contributing to long-term social and cultural transformations. Alejandra, an activist with the organization Tierra para Vivir in Buenos Aires, explains that urban agroecological markets are not only about the produce but are also a form of territorial action, in which the dynamic of the street and the neighborhood is transformed through the market.[21] The market in the Abasto neighborhood in Buenos Aires, for instance, hosts *cine-debates* (open movie screenings followed by debates) on subjects related to food and environmental matters, proposing in this way a shared cultural and learning experience as a vehicle for collective deconstruction of the hegemonic food model.[22]

## AGROECOLOGY AS ART

In recent years, food and agroecology have become increasingly present subjects in the work of contemporary artists in Latin America. This new wave follows from significant experiences in the 1990s, such as the work of art and environment NGO Ala Plástica, based in the city of La Plata, whose work involving the study and propagation of reeds has become a landmark reference in environmental art.

More recently in 2019, Asunción, Paraguay, was host to the public installation *Plantío Rafael Barrett*, which consisted of a plantation of corn, manioc, legumes, pumpkin, and peanut in two flowerbeds of sixty-five square yards each, opposite the Paraguayan Congress. The installation was the work of artists Mónica Millán and Adriana Bustos, who worked alongside the local Organización de Mujeres Campesinas e Indígenas Conamuri (Organization of Peasant and Indigenous Women Conamuri) to bring attention to the struggles of indigenous and peasant women over matters of land and environment. The inauguration of the installation was on November

21 and was marked by a performance that involved the sowing and watering of the flowerbeds. The work came to a close months later, with the harvest of the produce.[23]

The installation was part of an exhibition titled *Asunciones! Posiciones sobre mujer y sociedad* (Takeovers! Positions on women and society). As discussed in Chapter 2, women are often at the forefront of struggles for agroecology and food sovereignty, organizing in ways that link the matter of food to matters of gender violence, economic independence, and health. In the words of the exhibition's curator, the objective of this specific work was to "deepen and fertilize visitors' conscience on matters such as land ownership and the need for agrarian reform; the social and solidary economy [and] nutritional education and care for native seeds."[24] The work also aimed to explore the connections between land and language, as a way of delving on matters related to work, community and collective being. This is described by the artists in the following text:

> Thinking about Guaraní culture is to think about the richness of its language, in which the words *work* and *land* unfold in an admirable semantic multiplicity, which our occidental languages do not know, and have disposed of since colonial times.[25] *Pepy*, *Potiro*, and *Jopoi* are words associated to an extended notion of work: of the hands, the spirit, or the body. Work is not conceived of if it is not shared. It is a reciprocal doing, a hand that reaches out to give and to receive; it is party and celebration. It is the conscience of itself, what builds itself through the notion of the other and the land. It is a way of being an economic system that is not mere subsistence, but also a symbolic system that in its magical dynamic generates abundance.[26]

*Plantío Rafael Barrett* is comparable to early works from the tradition of ecological public art, such as *Wheatfield—A Confrontation*, the landmark piece by Agnes Denes that turned a landfill in downtown Manhattan into a temporary wheat field in 1982. It also sits alongside other contemporary works that seek to bring to the surface similar questions regarding food production, land, native knowledge, and survival. More recently, in 2016, artists from Desert ArtLAB, a duo

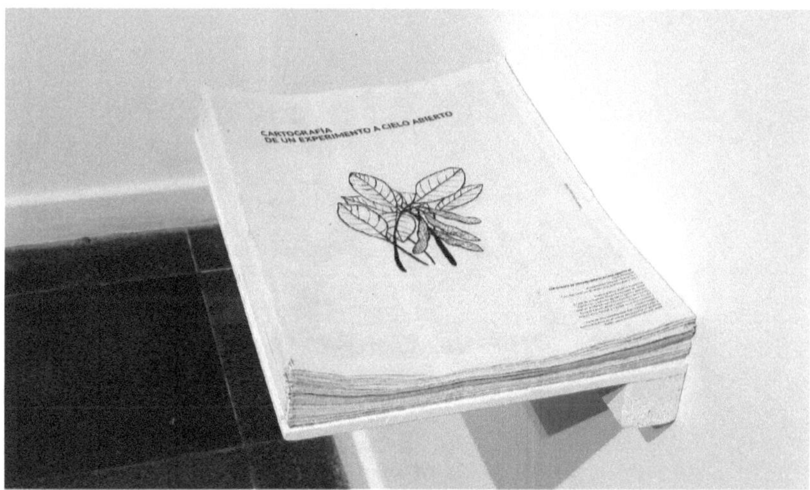


FIGURE 6.2. Julia Mensch, *Cartografía de un experimento a cielo abierto / Cartography of an Experiment under Open Sky.* Installation detail, newspaper publication, 2017. Photo by Aurelio Kopainig.

consisting of April Bojorquez and Matthew Garcia of Chicana and Rarámuri heritage, set up a long-term project in the Colorado desert that consists of transforming a parcel in the desert into a landscape composed of edible, native plants. In this way, the project responds to the forecast of widespread desertification in the Americas as a result of climate change by highlighting, nurturing, and sharing the resources of desert regions. Specifically, the project brings to the forefront valuable local, indigenous, ecological, and food practices.[27]

I now return to Argentina, where visual artist Julia Mensch has been conducting a research-based project for years, one that has no beginning or end date, titled *Cartografía de un experimento a cielo abierto / Cartography of an Experiment under Open Sky*. As part of this project, Mensch conducted fieldwork in the different agricultural regions of the country. During these trips, the artist documented the effects of the use of toxic agrochemicals and spoke to those leading the fight for agroecology and food sovereignty.[28] The body of work that makes up *Cartografía* comprises texts compiled in the form of a newspaper (fig. 6.2) as well as delicate, monochrome portraits of key players in the agricultural field, which are hand painted onto

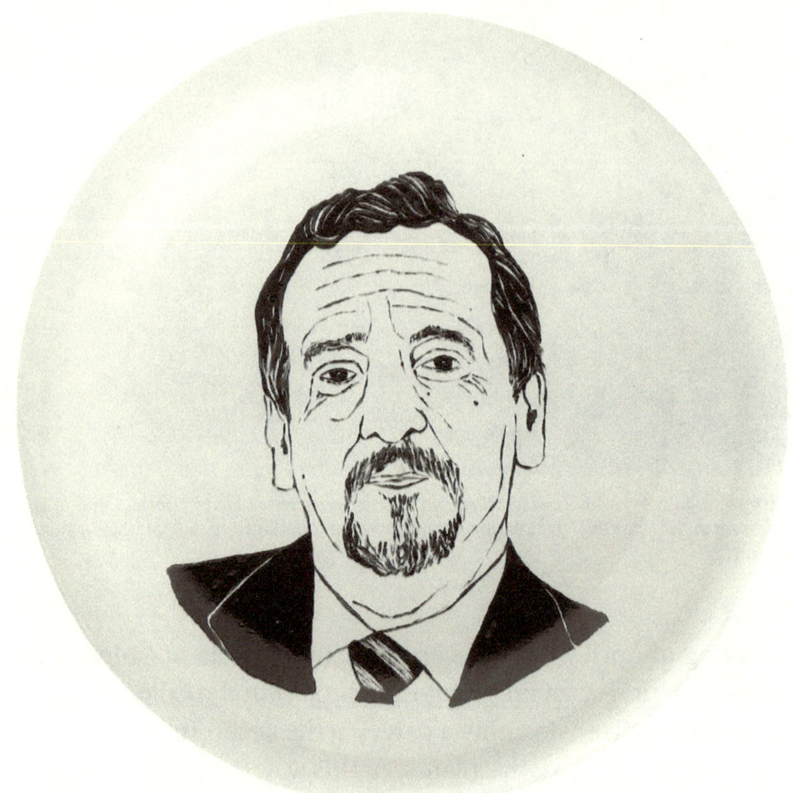

FIGURE 6.3. Julia Mensch, *Cartography of an Experiment under Open Sky (Lino Barañao).* Part of installation, painted ceramic plate, 2017. Photo by Aurelio Kopainig.

ceramic plates (figs. 6.3 and 6.4). The portraits include representatives of the movement for agroecology—including many who have passed away—as well as those that represent the hegemonic model, such as government officials, scientists, and top figures in agribusiness. The plates thus act both as objects of documentation and memorialization of those leading the struggle (much like the portraits in the *Museo del neoextractivismo* discussed in Chapter 3), and as objects of denunciation, putting names and faces to a powerful industry.

One of the places where Julia has exhibited her work in recent years is the Museo del Hambre (Museum of Hunger), an autonomous cultural space in Buenos Aires. The Museum is led by Marcos

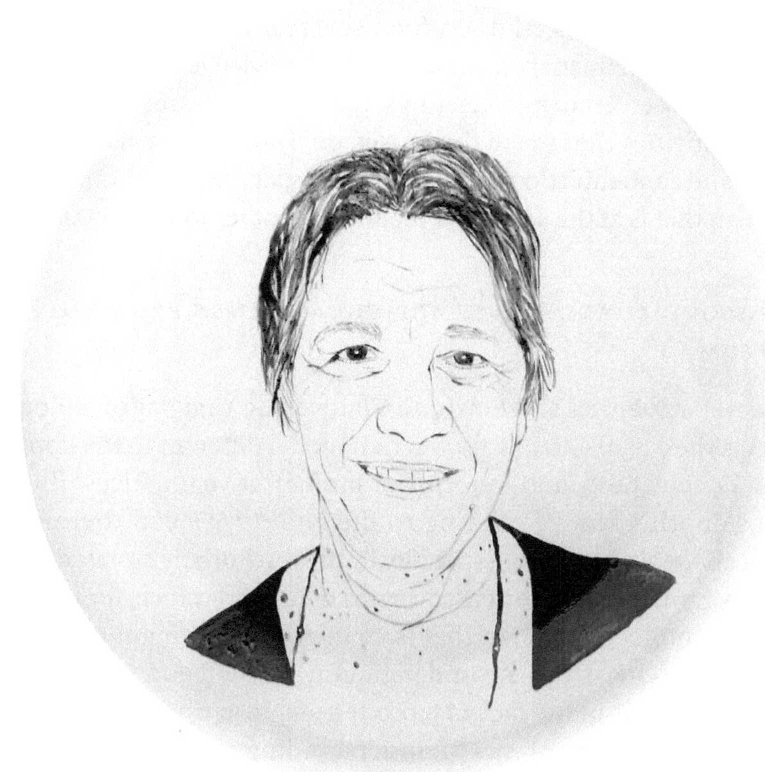

FIGURE 6.4. Julia Mensch, *Cartography of an Experiment under Open Sky (Irmina Kleiner)*. Part of installation, painted ceramic plate, 2017. Photo by Aurelio Kopainig.

Filardi, a lawyer specializing in human rights and environmental issues, who is a key player in the movement for food sovereignty in Argentina.[29] When I met Marcos he explained that the Museo del Hambre originated as a space to champion food sovereignty as the only way to eradicate world hunger. In his words, the main aim of the space is "convergence: the networking of everyone who is in some way linked to that collective struggle for food sovereignty. We can have a work of art, a film screening followed by debate, a movie, a book presentation, but the common denominator . . . is to create awareness and action and praxis and thinking around food sovereignty."[30] The museum opened in 2017, and since then it has become a gathering space for grassroots groups, a place for experiencing culture that invites reflection on food sovereignty and other issues related to postextractivism, and a hub for knowledge sharing. Workshops and seed exchange meetings, for instance, stand out as relational activities that make the Museo del Hambre a space for creativity and contemplation but also an open space for community and activism that is at the service of the movement for food sovereignty.

## ONTOLOGICAL AND EPISTEMOLOGICAL SHIFTS FROM THE BOTTOM UP

Maristella Svampa and Enrique Viale argue that "agroecology reflects the expansion of a production model different to the dominant agribusiness, and in terms of prefigurative practices, illustrates another way of relating to the land."[31] We can therefore think about agroecology—specifically the territorially situated and socially transformative oriented strand of it—as a vehicle for prefigurative, ontological design that is challenging dominant ontological foundations, from the understanding of food and territory to notions of value in the face of a profit-seeking agribusiness.

The agroecological way of understanding and relating to the land also represents for many a return to a previous way of existing in and with the rest of nature, a decolonial act. But as Escobar reminds us, in many cases it is not possible to recreate such forms of being with the earth given the current ecological (and economic and geographical) limitations resulting from centuries of colonial, capitalist extraction and expansion.[32] In response, we see forms of agroecology emerge that incorporate ancestral knowledges alongside other knowledge forms that respond to current contexts, as well as the expansion of other related praxes such as permaculture.[33] Agroecology is therefore not only about a different way of approaching agriculture, but also about a different way of viewing the world and of generating knowledge about it.[34] So how can artistic practices contribute to designing contextualized agroecological practices and to facilitating ontological shifts with regard to land, nourishment, human bonds, and ecological interdependence?

Most of the contemporary artistic practices engaging with food and food sovereignty in Argentina, Latin America, and other regions follow a relational ethic and aesthetic that centers on the relationship between humans and the soil, as well as the relationship between the artist and the public. *Plantío Rafael Barrett* for instance, brings the principles of peasant, agroecological farming to the political center of Asunción, to raise awareness of the relationships within peasant communities and between communities and their land. In the words of the artists: "work is not conceived of if it is not shared. It is a reciprocal doing, a hand that reaches out to give and to receive." Similarly, Julia Mensch's *Cartografía* is the product of conversations and shared experiences with those at the frontline of agroecology in Argentina. While the work presents an element of direct denunciation of the effects of the industrial agriculture model and points through its portraits to the human culprits, her process is inherently relational—indeed, in addition to the conversations and shared experiences that inform her oeuvre, previous exhibitions of her work have involved the sharing of agroecological food on painted plates, a continuation and extension of this process and an additional way of (re)centering food and territory.

By collaborating with peasant communities and other voices at the frontlines of the movement for agroecology, these works open up avenues of dialogue between different fields and epistemes (specifically, the arts and agriculture). These instances of dialogue facilitate the collective creation of public narratives about agroecology that incorporate multiple perspectives, position agrocecology and agribusiness historically and politically, make connections between processes and dynamics at different scales, and reach out to different publics in order to challenge and deconstruct hegemonic views on agriculture and food systems, contributing in this way to activating ontological shifts. More precisely, these dialogues between different fields and epistemes allow the design of situated relational ontologies in which land, community, and food are understood from the perspective of their interdependence. This radical notion of interdependence challenges the core assumptions and value system of an extractivist, capitalist model in which people are alienated from the production of food, and where both land and produce are primarily valued in economic terms.

Engaging with agroecology, be that directly through the production process or indirectly through the work of artists, thus provides opportunities for relearning what we know about the world, about other organisms, and about our capacity to live differently. With the importance of learning in relation to ontological shifts in mind, in what follows I look specifically at the field of environmental education. I discuss the political and epistemological positioning of Latin American environmental education as well as its material challenges and its pedagogical tools, in order to illustrate how ontological design can develop as part of this praxis, one that is key to the creation of worlds otherwise.

## *Environmental Education and the Pedagogy of Worlds Otherwise*

Latin American environmental education is invested in deconstructing the social and political roots of environmental degradation and inequality. It brings together experiences from popular education, liberation theology, and decolonial thought,[35] and it situates environmental issues within the context of development. I find it important to look at environmental education when thinking about the creation of worlds otherwise because pedagogy constitutes one of the most important bodies of work of Latin American thought and has been a historical vehicle for liberation in the region. Furthermore, education is a cornerstone of culture in its broader sense, and indeed the merger of art and education has an important role in antiextractivist struggles. In what follows, therefore, I highlight environmental education's engagement with distinct artistic practices, but I also consider its potential for ontological design beyond its artistic facet.

One of my interviewees on the matter of environmental education in Argentina was Silvina Corbetta, a committed environmental educator and political scientist who is well-regarded in the field. In her words,

> We stand in the position that education is environmental, and that we approach it from within the history of Latin American thought and its conception of the environment. From this perspective, environmental education is a type of education that is defined as critical, it is an education that is rebellious, an education that resists, an education that installs feeling uncomfortable as a way of building knowledge, of building debate, because we believe that the civilizational crisis has been a result of a rationality model that has led us here, to an ecological and humanitarian crisis.[36]

Furthermore, as argued by Valle, in response to this hegemony of extractivism, "environmental pedagogy emerges to (re)unite the desires to create a new human society capable of nurturing different creatures, other technologies, cultures, and social innovations. It recognizes the complexity of life, the interdependence of the global organic order and the differentiated knowledges, such as the ecofeminist schools of thought and ethic."[37]

While Latin American environmental education is characterized by a forceful determination for transformation, designing and sustaining forms of environmental education that can contribute to profound social transformation is far from an easy task. Indeed, the development of environmental education in Argentina has faced multiple obstacles in the last decades, from the lack of political will to the direct intervention of extractive sectors in school curricula and in universities.[38] Furthermore, much environmental education in the country emerges from the context of environmental conflicts. The problem that often arises with such initiatives, argues environmental educator Pablo Sessano, is that many so-called educational activities are not, in fact, developed from a rigorous, pedagogical perspective, but rather are assumed to form organically as part of the struggle. As a result, many of these activities end up focusing on information rather than formation. Pablo also points to the fact that often the forms of environmental education that emerge from within environmental conflicts follow the rhythms of the conflict, and as such, it is difficult to maintain consistency and think about educational programs in the long term.[39] Environmental education initiatives originating from the state on the other hand, have historically mostly emerged from the National Secretary of Environment and its equivalents at different governmental levels, rather than from the Ministry of Education. A challenge in developing a transformative environmental education in schools seems to be the ability to address environmental issues from within different disciplines as well as from a holistic perspective and engage with environmental issues from a collective position rather than the predominant individual one. As long-time Argentine environmental educator Silvia Leanza says, the key to environmental education is "to think the environmental issue from a perspective of complexity, a socio-political perspective."[40]

Despite the barriers to constructing pedagogically solid, consistent, and long-term environmental education projects, in Argentina there are several examples of valuable practice that have made important contributions to the field. One of those experiences developed as part of the national digital justice program *Conectar Igualdad* (Connect Equality) in the early 2000s. The program involved the distribution of portable computers to high school students and the training of teachers in using digital tools across different subjects and transversal areas. Silvina and Pablo were involved in the environmental education training aspect of the project. Speaking of the pedagogical design of such training instances, Silvina explained, "In this work, we gave ourselves a few central focuses, or what we call structural notions, in order to be able to provide a didactic framing for educators. These included the notion of complexity, of interdisciplinarity, transversality, the importance of an ethical perspective. . . ."[41] During this experience, added Silvina, the challenge was how to turn environmental conflicts into pedagogical opportunities. In their approach, they decided it was important to generate activities that would allow educators to discuss the conflicts they experienced in their own territories. She explained that "among these activities were collective mapping or social cartography, meaning situating the conflicts, the actors, and discussing the way people talk about the conflict, [and within this] there is also a conceptual mapping."[42] Cartographical tools are particularly well suited for such a task, as they contribute to developing the situated and territorial approach that is central to Latin American environmental education (and as argued in Chapter 1, it is also an important characteristic of collective action and artistic practice).

Another recent and ongoing, notable example of environmental education in Argentina that embodies the fruitful coming together of educators and grassroots movements is the Cátedra Libre de Soberanía Alimentaria (Open Program of Food Sovereignty). The Cátedra Libre is a free education program based at different universities and faculties in the country, and it is connected to the movement against the use of agrotoxics and the different groups and sectors that compose that movement, from doctors to activists and peasants. In our conversation Pablo highlighted this as a good example of environmental education because, he argued,

> the object of critical study is food and nourishment, and what is in crisis and what has been degraded, and what is polluted. And it is intervening precisely in our way of nourishing ourselves, and how food is so connected to health. There, a valuable space is created for deepening our reflection to the point where we are able to build pedagogical processes that are able to question the foundations of life.[43]

This illustrates how critical environmental education has the potential to engage in ontological design, as it aims to question and rebuild the foundations of our understanding of the world.

In our conversation, Silvina explained that "from the perspective of Latin American environmental thought, a critical education also has to be decolonial. It is those knowledges-other that this type of education is interested in. It is those knowledges-other that it tries to bring together to put them in conversation with scientific knowledge."[44] Indeed, environmental struggles in Latin America tend to involve a struggle for decolonization: in the first place, in their challenge of extractivism they address the modern-colonial paradigm that underpins the development project and society's extractive relation to the rest of nature,[45] and second, through their territorial approach, they confront the colonial geography that separates centers and peripheries and that tramples the rights of local populations. An environmental education, as a vehicle for transformation and worldmaking, must therefore address such issues as well, and it must engage with the decolonization of education more broadly. In the Patagonian province of Neuquén, for instance, the fight against fracking is connected to the fight for Mapuche cultural rights, and one of the central issues in both struggles is the strengthening of bilingual, intercultural education.[46]

Environmental education is not only a cultural and social matter, but it is also inescapably political in a context in which powerful sectors are invested in sustaining the status quo. From the point of view of environmental NGOs, a key strategy for the development of an environmental perspective in school education has been articulating with school teachers through their unions. Oil watchdog Observatorio Petrolero Sur has done extensive work with the teachers' union of Río Negro in Patagonia, creating a space for knowledge sharing on current issues such as the development of fracking but also for developing a critical perspective on regional and national approaches to development. Unions continue to be a stronghold of social mobilization in Argentina, and there are teachers' unions in North Patagonia that are particularly active. When schools are co-opted by extractive companies, unions act as spaces for developing alternatives to the hegemonic discourse.

The role of art and cultural production in environmental education is not unrelated to this political context. Art has been a key tool in generating awareness, explaining the technical aspects of extractive technologies, and countering the hegemonic narrative on extraction and development, one that is not only upheld by governments but also supported, fashioned, and pushed by extractive companies with significant resources. One of the ways activists and artists have pursued informational and educational aims with regard to environmental matters has been film. For instance, in the last decade Observatorio Petrol Sur has been producing animated videos explaining different issues concerning the energy system. Their videos on fracking in particular have been key instruments in distributing their research to wider audiences, and they have also been used in educational settings.[47] Another notable genre has been documentary film, including works such as *Desiertos de piedra* (Stone deserts) by Germán Ciari, based on the book *15 mitos y realidades de la minería transnacional en Argentina: Guía para desmontar el imaginario prominero* (15 myths and truths about transnational mining in Argentina: A guide for disassembling the pro-mining imaginary). In an interview, the filmmaker explained that *Desiertos de piedra* fights the battle for the arguments: "it is super long, of course, and it tackles an infinity of arguments and counterarguments. [But] we conceived it as being split into chapters precisely so that educators could use it as a tool for dialogue and debate."[48] Indeed, documentary film has become a widespread instrument for environmental education in Argentina. The format of *cine-debate*, previously mentioned in relation to agroecological markets, has been taken up in a wide range of spaces, from universities to school projects initiated by environmental educators working from within the state, to environmental assemblies across the country. In the latter, communities come together to learn about, discuss, and draw connections between their own experiences of struggle and those of other communities in the country and beyond, which become accessible through their documentation in film. Art therefore is not only a tool for communicating and explaining complex matters in an engaging and accessible way, but also a language and a vehicle for creating relational spaces that are conducive to collective, transformative experiences.

Designing a Latin American, decolonial environmental education means designing an education that is holistic, critical, transversal, situated, and in constant conversation with local conflicts. In this sense, environmental education is a key praxis in the task of creating worlds otherwise, because it is concerned with deconstruction, democratization, and design. While environmental education in Argentina has faced multiple challenges linked to political and structural issues, as well as the difficulties of sustaining any practice in a context of conflict, the ideas and examples discussed here show why and how environmental education has the capacity to facilitate deep cultural transformations. The examples and testimonies discussed point to Latin American environmental education as a prefigurative design practice, because the pedagogical principles at its core are concerned with enacting liberation and learning *with* environmental movements rather than *about* them. Furthermore, we can understand environmental education as a field of ontological (and epistemological) design because, as Pablo puts it, it is "above all a way of being, a way of learning, of learning to relearn" our place in nature.[49] Indeed, in his championing of a situated, interdisciplinary environmental rationality, Enrique Leff argues that "this new thinking and this new ethic . . . must be lived in the field of education. This involves rethinking the meaning of the educational process in the formation of the human being of our time and their future, what it means to teach and learn."[50]

Finally, education is also conceived, from this perspective, as a form of social and cultural commons, a social space from within which worlds otherwise can be collectively created.[51] In the next section, I look at cultural production from a similar perspective, to argue that prefigurative approaches to art making can enact comparable forms of ontological design.

## *Postextractivist Cultural Production and the Artist as Maker*

In previous chapters, I began to look at art from the perspective of the politics of artistic labor and production. Particularly in Chapters 4 and 5, I discussed the ethos of *autogestión* and its role in the development of contemporary politically engaged and activist art. Here, I aim to reflect specifically on the role of art and artists in a transition toward postextractivist futures, and I will do this from a perspective that draws on cultural sociology and creative industries studies and that considers the artist as worker, in addition to the concepts from art theory and aesthetics I have referenced so far.

Thinking about the role that artists can take in creating worlds invites us to think about prefiguration. Prefigurative art making involves carrying out an artistic practice that rethinks the processes, politics, and position of art making in a society marked by multiple forms of oppression, inequality, and exploitation, and in so doing contributes to creating worlds otherwise. In a move toward post-extractivist worlds, this includes challenging modern, Eurocentric ideas of art that continue to reproduce a particular perspective, designating certain expressions as "outsider" art and simultaneously undervaluing and fetishizing art forms that emerge from non-Western locations. It also involves thinking about the materials we use, their provenance, their forms of production, and their impact on our ecosystems. Such considerations inevitably determine the kinds of aesthetics that emerge, be that a move toward relational or dialogical aesthetics,[52] or toward aesthetics that are concerned with materiality, meaning works whose form is markedly influenced by the consideration of the processes and the political economy of materials, as seen in artworks that are directly engaged with matters of sustainability.

For instance, elsewhere I have looked at performance actions protesting oil sponsorship in UK museums. These performances intervene in the dynamics of a cultural space with a concrete objective (to break the relationship between the cultural sector and the fossil fuel industry), and also, by centering a prefigurative ethic and enhancing participatory and democratic processes, they put forward other ways of making art that challenge hegemonic aesthetics and conventions, including the canon of socially engaged art and the parameters of what is considered "aesthetic quality."[53] Another notable example is the publishing cooperative Eloisa Cartonera, emerging in post-2001 Argentina and briefly referenced in Chapter 5. In a context of mass unemployment, where thousands of people turned to cardboard picking as a source of income, an artists' collective designed an editorial project that would engage cardboard pickers, buying cardboard directly from them and providing them with an opportunity to be part of a creative production process by hand painting the cardboard covers of books, covers that would become icons of postcrisis Argentine aesthetics.[54]

Thinking of prefiguration in reference to the cases presented in this book, I find it necessary to revisit the work of the design and social communication duo Iconoclasistas, whose work I discussed in Chapter 1. While Iconoclasistas do not self-identify as artists, their work can be understood as a form of dialogical, relational, collective creative practice, and indeed their productions have been recognized and exhibited internationally by multiple cultural institutions. At the same time, Iconoclasistas have collaborated with the research NGO and oil watchdog Observatorio Petrolero Sur in the production of informational and educational material, one of the many ways art and creative practices intersect with environmental education in anti- and postextractivist movements.

Iconoclasistas' *mapeos collectivos* (collective mappings) generate spaces of creativity, knowledge sharing, territorialization, and democratization of conflict narratives, in which communities experiencing socioenvironmental conflicts can come together to collectively map out and represent the characteristics of a particular conjuncture. Reflecting on their work, Julia and Pablo from Iconoclasistas share that since 2018, in addition to collective mapping, they have been developing other devices for the collective construction of knowledge, which rely on deeper and longer processes of analysis:

> We call them "machines for *senti-pensar* [feeling-thinking]." . . . The graphic elements that compose these machines for *senti-pensar* propose a trip through methods that favor dialogical group work, building on each other in order to provide meaning to the complexity of situated practices and knowledges. They guide participants in discussions, offering a space of systematization that organizes the polysemy of interventions in an inventive and flexible way, and while they have a framework and a horizon, they are open and interchangeable.
>
> [. . .]
>
> For us, the collective is both a refuge and a space of potency for creating (thinking and organizing) together. We make of the collective a form of resistance to the contemporary logics of individual making, meritocracy, and competition.[55]

Iconoclasista's machines for *senti-pensar* thus activate multiple functions simultaneously. They generate spaces and provide tools for denouncing environmental incidents and conflicts, documenting events and geographical information, democratizing the public representation of conflicts, deconstructing the technocratic logic of extractive projects and producing valuable information that draws instead from people's situated knowledge of the territory, and finally, designing forms of collective organizing that are horizontal and creative.

As I anticipated earlier, rethinking art making also involves rethinking the material conditions of being a working artist in an extractive society, where the market sees a work of art as a source for generating and extracting economic value, and state support, in most places, is not sufficient. The question then emerges of whether artists that are invested in postextractivist visions should be demanding recognition as art workers from the state and argue for further support based on the cultural and social value of their creation, as many artist collectives and researchers of cultural labor have argued,[56] or whether in our recognition of the value of art in resistance, community cohesion, and worldmaking we should encourage widespread engagement with art making in our societies in the form of a cultural democracy, so that art is no longer an activity that is split between professionals and amateurs, but rather something that everyone is encouraged and supported to pursue.[57] This latter perspective often comes alongside proposals for shorter work weeks and a universal basic income, stark changes in our way of living and organizing labor that would, it is expected, free up time for us to pursue art making and other nourishing activities.

At present time, in a context of precarity, isolation, and an attack on critical thinking and revolutionary imagining, many artists find themselves fighting on multiple fronts: for the defense of their basic rights as art workers and also for the democratization of the arts as a powerful tool for resisting and breaking through neoliberal, extractivist logics. In Argentina, we can see indications of this dual approach in the work of the transdisciplinary collective and civil organization CRIA—Creando Redes Independientes y Artísticas (Creating Independent and Artistic Networks), made up of artists, independent publishers, photographers, and other arts and cultural organizations. In 2018, CRIA held the first *La criatura* (The creature), a transdisciplinary event that took the shape of a counter-summit to coincide with the gathering of the G20 in Buenos Aires. The theme for the first *La criatura* was "Pedagogías del hacer" (Pedagogies of making), a nod to feminist anthropologist Rita Segato's concept of pedagogies of cruelty, and an invitation to collectively relearn our ways of making and being.[58] In their words, the event sought to bring together "representatives from different social organizations alongside intellectuals, artists, activists, and initiatives in alternative education and popular economies."[59] The event centered around a number of key themes that spoke to the most pressing social issues of our times, including indigenous rights, feminism and trans rights, alternative economies, and extractivism. It invited participants to engage with such themes through different formats, ranging from talks to labs, projections, music, and performance. *La criatura* "is not a seminar, or a series of TEDX talks: it is a stage for collective education and the creation of solidarity networks in times of crisis. An opportunity for discovering, debating, and collectively producing new pedagogies based on making."[60]

CRIA came together in 2011 as a collective with a clearly marked position that links them to the autonomous movements in the region, and with the aim of developing cultural projects with a view to social transformation. In order to achieve this, they created a formal association (a form of NGO) that allowed them to come together as a series of independent cultural actors and jointly apply for certain forms of funding, a way of navigating the scarce and complex opportunities for financial support that the sector offers. While some artists that embrace the ethos of *autogestión* and prefiguration reject the possibility of receiving funding from the state, NGOs, or private entities on political grounds, as was the case for Casa 1234 discussed in Chapter 4, for others, creating a formal structure and applying for funding is a way of generating enough support to properly compensate the artists and cultural workers involved in their projects. In other words, participating in the uneven dynamics of the art world could be seen as a form of compromise for groups working toward structural change, but at

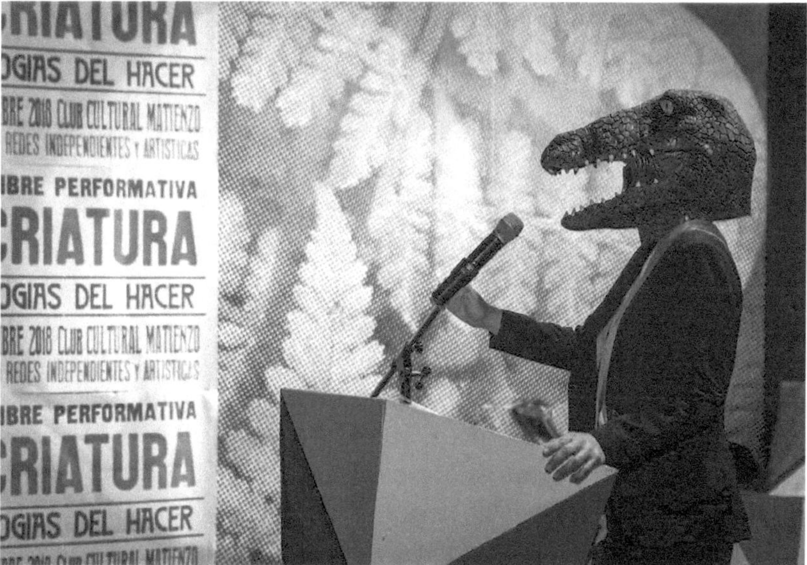


FIGURE 6.5. *La criatura* 2018. Buenos Aires, Argentina. Photo by Quilomba/ Archivo CRIA.

the same time, it allows organizations like CRIA to champion in the now a standard of paying artists for their work, something that cultural workers in Argentina have only recently began to organize for en masse. Dilemmas such as these, faced on a daily basis by activists and politically engaged artists in most places, in fact problematize the idea of prefigurative practice (which should indeed be understood as an ethos or a horizon, not a dogma): they expose the complexities of trying to work toward postextractivist futures while wanting to improve the conditions of working artists in the now, necessarily engaging with the structures and dynamics of the current system and adopting positions (e.g., "worker') that do not necessarily represent identities or long-term visions.

In 2020, in the midst of the COVID-19 pandemic, a second *La criatura* by CRIA emerged, this time in a purely online format. The restrictions of the time demanded CRIA to rethink their pedagogies of making, adapting their ethos and methods to an online format where they experimented with live music, prerecorded performances, and artistic content specially made for the screen. The theme for this new edition was "NuevAnormalidad" (New (a)normality), in reference to the changes that came about as a result of the pandemic. By experimenting with different forms of online performances, visual pieces, lectures, and the format for event programming itself, CRIA engaged in the design of new modalities of art making and experiencing, which aimed to respond to the characteristics of the time.

In the same way as they conditioned the transdisciplinary projects of CRIA, the sudden changes brought about by COVID-19 had significant impact on different forms of cultural production across the board. Especially for those of us invested in world-making practices, COVID-19 not only meant artists and creative producers had to adapt to new circumstances, but it also demanded we consider the long-term implications of this violent moment of rupture in our perception of the world, in our forms of relating to each other, and in our capacity to activate social change. For instance, what do relational and dialogical practices look and feel like when physical contact is out of bounds? How can we produce situated work when we find ourselves stranded from our territories? Should we take this opportunity to focus on transnational work, in what seems to be a sentimental return to the golden days of the internet, or focus on local initiatives within the physical restrictions of the moment? As a result of the pandemic, we saw the emergence of multiple imaginative cultural initiatives that adapted to the constraints of the times in order to make something that is shared, that is beautiful, and that contributes to socioenvironmetal change. A notable example of this was the 2020 radio drama piece *La Compañía* (The company), the product of the joint work of two cooperatives in an effort to make a cultural product of popular communication focusing on environmental issues and with a wide-reaching, federal approach. The radio drama, which involved the environmental consultancy of sociologist Maristella Svampa, sought to recuperate an old, neglected genre to reach people in a context in which the theatre and other forms of performances were out of limits.[61]

What the above examples show is the different ways art and cultural production can become ecological and engage in ontological design. *Ecological* here refers not only to art that engages directly with the subject of ecosystems, as in the case of art linked to agroecological projects, but also to practices that position themselves within a wider ecology of praxes, each contributing to enacting ontological transformations and social change in their own way.

Sometimes the approaches taken by artists sit with contradictions, as they attempt to better their conditions and those of their communities through short- and medium-term actions and organizing that operate within the prevailing logics of extractivism and in the frame of failing political systems while also working toward long-term objectives of radical transformation, contradictions that are difficult to escape given the conditions of our time. By adopting approaches that combine challenges to the hegemonic model, the creation of visions for worlds otherwise, and solutions to the material challenges faced in the now, artistic practice can act as a space of commoning, while also contributing to ontological shifts. In other words, art becomes a vehicle for generating prefigurative approaches that are at the same time responsive and that through parallel channels address the core matter of socioenvironmental justice in the short and in the long term.

## *Designing the Commons: Socioecological Transitions after COVID-19*

Struggles for the commons are present across the world. As Hardt and Negri argue, "the common is ever more central to capitalist social production and reproduction—the value that capital accumulates resides, increasingly, in the common—and yet it also designates a potential for social autonomy from capital, a potential for revolt."[62] In other words, organizing around the commons can be generative of utopian visions that, while still largely unmaterialized, are already beginning to consolidate at small scale and in certain processes and praxes, being pursued not as idealistic dreams but, as Massida and Segato argue, as concrete proposals for action.[63] In ecofeminist praxis, for instance, Veronica Gago explains that key concepts such as *cuerpo-territorio* (body-territory) put forward "another notion of possession in terms of use instead of property, thus evidencing [and rejecting] a logic of the commons as that which is being possessed and exploited."[64] Hardt and Negri propose that such struggles present huge potential for autonomous action and for the creation of postcapitalist and postextractivist ways of being: the extractivist model "preys on the various forms of the common—ecological, social and biopolitical," which is why the battle against extractivism and against the commodification of life must be fought on different arenas at the same time.[65] Some of those arenas I have presented earlier in this chapter, spaces and praxes where prefigurative design is put into action in order to create processes that are in themselves worldmaking.

The concept of the commons has been central to rethinking the basis of our societies and economies at times of ecological crisis and rising inequality and to working toward transitions to post-extractivist futures. In Latin America, groups such as the Grupo Permanente de Trabajo sobre Alternativas al Desarrollo (Permanent Working Group on Alternatives to Development) have been carrying out this work since 2011, taking as a starting point a challenge to the idea of development and generating events, texts, and other forms of knowledge production and dissemination that look to end intersecting forms of oppression and redefine our relationship to nature. In such initiatives, it is not only the concept of nature as resource that is rethought, giving way to more and less anthropocentric ideas of nature as commons. It is also management, governance, and decision-making processes that are reconceptualized as collective, democratic activities. For instance, in 2019, organizations from across Latin America came together to make a statement on the need for energy transition and sovereignty for the occasion of COP25, in which they wrote, "Our own energy transition, our popular energy project, must first go through a process of socioecological transition and be the starting point for the collective construction of cultural and political subjects that contest this arena."[66]

In 2020, the COVID-19 pandemic brought about an unprecedented opportunity for those working on transitions to postextractivism: a sudden halt in oil production and its subsequent drop in value, a decrease in nonessential consumption, and the implementation of socialist and care-centered policies by governments across the world, including those of marked neoliberal character. In other words, in the midst of a devastating pandemic that has been linked to an extractive relationship to nature, we saw things that we were once told were impossible materialize in short periods.[67] The counterpart to the fear, loss, and sorrow brought about by COVID-19 was the confirmation that many naturalized aspects of the way we live and of how societies are structured indeed could change, if there is the political will for it. The pandemic generated, among other things, an aperture for inserting the matter of the commons into public debates. Issues such as public health provision, universal income, and access to green spaces in cities were suddenly central matters of commentary, as was the matter of localizing food production.

In Argentina, activists and thinkers on the Left put forward a Gran Pacto Ecosocial y Económico (Great Ecosocial and Economic Deal), responding in some ways to the Green New Deal (GND) initiatives in the US and other Global North countries that had emerged not long before. The pact argued for "five fundamental components: a universal citizen's income; a progressive tax reform; the suspension of external debt payments; a national system of care; and a serious and radical proposal for socioecological transition."[68] A similar but region-wide response was the Pacto Ecosocial del Sur (Ecosocial Pact of the South), an initiative by activists, indigenous leaders, academics, and organizations from different parts of Latin America and the Caribbean. The pact called for social, gender, ethnic, and ecological justice, and saw the COVID-19 crisis as an opportunity to build a future based on care. It included the components promoted by the pact for Argentina and incorporated others, such as ensuring food sovereignty, strengthening community media, defending the autonomy of local societies, and building postextractivist economies. The pact states that

> It has become evident that peasant life, the senses of community, care, and reciprocity are central to the sustainment of life;

> that despite living within capitalism, we do not live for capital. We become aware of the fact that direct commerce, moneyless exchanges, networks outside of capitalist markets right now resolve many of our bare necessities; and we have experienced that they hold space and potential for the future.[69]

Such transitions initiatives emerging from Latin America are markedly different from other major initiatives in the Global North, such as the US GND. In the first place, the GND was conceived as a plan of national scale, while several of the Latin American proposals are constructed as region-wide, and/or thrive on the idea of international cooperation. Second, the GND follows a Keynesian approach that looks to increase jobs and the economy and does not actually challenge the imperative of growth that lies at the heart of the climate crisis.[70] This differs from Latin American proposals, which focus on prosperity without resorting to growth as an avenue and instead advocate for postextractivist economies. And third, proposals like the Pacto Ecosocial del Sur emphasize the significance of culture and the need to consider the viewpoints, epistemes, and traditions of different groups in order to enact transitions that are situated and socially, culturally, and ecologically just, while the GND does not challenge the modern epistemological and ontological roots of capitalism and extractivism. In other words, Latin American pacts put forward design proposals that challenge the current ontological basis of the extractivist development paradigm.

A question that emerges in response to the above proposals concerns the role of art in facilitating transitions. Is the role of art to promote these proposals, to facilitate representation, to activate the imagination, or is it to design the actual practices that materialize the proposals contained in these pacts? I propose that art can propel us to be imaginative in thinking beyond the limits of coloniality, but also, in its design capability, it can provide a space, language, and method for envisioning and enacting other ways of organizing and making. Furthermore, as a practice that engages directly and deeply with ontological issues and has the potential to contribute to ontological shifts, art can repair broken social bonds as well as the damaged connections within our ecosystems. However, as I will argue in the conclusion to this book, design is not a standalone function of art, nor is it the most relevant. Rather, all five functions of art under extractivism (denunciation, documentation, democratization, deconstruction, and design) have a role to play here, as they build on each other to facilitate different mechanisms of resistance and change that need to take place in order to be able to envision and create worlds otherwise. Socioecological transitions demand cultural transformations in addition to structural changes, and such transformations can only take place through a multistage process that responds to the different material and symbolic challenges we face.

Throughout the chapters in this book, I have built a case for the paramount role of art in struggles against extractivism and for postextractivist futures. In this chapter, however, I have purposefully widened the scope and interwoven discussions on agroecology, environmental education, and cultural production as a way of unsettling the boundaries between disciplines, demonstrating how the idea of ontological design can materialize in different praxes and offering a partial picture of how different spheres of daily life can become spaces for the creation of worlds otherwise. I highlighted the ways different fields generate spaces for ontological design but also showed the ways the boundaries of different disciplines are undone at times; while art has the capacity to engage with different fields of the social, there are movements and fusions between those practices as well (agroecology becomes art, art becomes pedagogy, activism becomes education, and so on). Put differently, we can see the combination of all these practices as constituting what T. J. Demos calls "creative ecologies—practices that make new sensible materializations and connections (aesthetic, practical, jurisgenerative) between otherwise discrete realms of experience and knowledge, and that cultivate worlds to come."[71] This kind of close and multifaceted engagement with the possibilities and challenges of different praxes, I propose, is needed in order to be able to visualize the ways that we can activate grand proposals, pacts, and manifestos for worlds otherwise. Moving beyond the theoretical and the ideal, a "dirtier" engagement with these creative praxes can allow us to grasp and learn from their potential for ontological design, and to visualize how they might be able to contribute to or enact visions and proposals for socioecological transitions, such as those discussed above.

# Conclusion

## *Art and (Post)extractivism*

THE THEORETICAL PROPOSALS elaborated in this book build on previous research I carried out on the politics and internal processes of art activism. In that work, my focus was mainly on collective, performance-based practices, and I examined and compared the work of artists, activists, and collectives who made art around different issues including queer politics, gentrification, disability, racial justice, and climate change. I proposed that art activism is a hybrid practice that is characterized by an inner tension between aesthetic and political objectives, one that is reflected in the different aspects of an action and that has the potential of being resolved when collectives adopt a holistic, prefigurative approach to achieving their political and artistic aims.[1]

In *Creating Worlds Otherwise*, I built on this line of thought but took a different avenue, focusing on art activism and other forms of creative practice that emerge from or in relation to anti- and postextractivist collective action. Art has a major role in visibilizing, platforming, and expanding both ancestral and new ideas and categories that can help us understand and confront the violence of extractivism, and this is particularly crucial at a time in which we have become increasingly aware of "the inability of established modern categories to define fully what is at stake in social struggles and conflicts."[2] Specifically, I explored the functions of art in movements that stand against extractivist forms of development and that envision and practice other ways of living instead. In this way, the book aimed to make an intervention in the field of political ecology in addition to art theory, as political ecology has only recently began to recognize the importance of artistic practices in ecological movements.[3] My findings and theoretical proposals grew out of visits, conversations, interviews, media analysis, and analysis of artwork, and culminated in a contextualized framework consisting of five functions: denunciation, documentation, democratization, deconstruction, and design.

The purpose of this framework is to describe and explain the motivations and objectives of artists and activists in extractive societies, and to help us understand how certain mechanisms and effects inherent to different art forms can be activated to those aims. By this, I mean the more universal "capabilities" of artistic practice such as the ability to generate emotional responses, to facilitate community building, to represent and visibilize complex subjects, and to contribute to pedagogical objectives, as well as others that are more specific to the context. In what follows, I return to the five functions as outlined in the introduction, and discuss them in relation to the findings from the previous chapters, to key ideas in the study of culture and politics, and to each other.

## *The Five Functions of Art under Extractivism*

The first function, denunciation, refers to the role of art as a language and space for shedding light on aspects of the extractivist model that are either ignored by governments and the media or purposefully obfuscated. This is a key function in the context of an extractive hegemony, where the means of mass communication are held in the hands of a few, and it is up to self-organized communities, artists, and alternative media practitioners to challenge hegemonic narratives on development, progress, and the economy, among other issues. Denunciation is also about making connections between historical and political factors, about pointing to those responsible, and about challenging the systems of value that deem certain events, effects, people, and territories newsworthy, and others not. Exhibitions denouncing ecocide, murals depicting the repression of environmental movements, and indigenous women's occupations with the aim of visibilizing their claims and demanding solutions to the violence exerted on their bodies and territories are all forms of denunciation under extractivism.

One of the main ways art can facilitate denunciation is through the visualization of specific issues, and the visual arts are particularly well placed for generating images that offer proof of the destructive effects of extractivism while at the same time generating alternative narratives. As a form of denunciation, visibilization is not only about making visible that which is ignored but also about exposing that which has been purposefully hidden by those in power, revealing in this way the regime of visibility of extractivism, as put by artist and researcher Eduardo Molinari.[4] This regime of visibility has a technoscientific facet that manifests in the shape of maps, graphs, and the visualization of technical information, which is often used to legitimize the position of a self-perceived extractive technocracy. The regime is also constituted of a kind of visuality that presents itself as harmonious and innocuous and covers over the destructive effects of different extractive activities. In this sense, we could compare the visual politics of extractivism to the "neoliberal sensorium" as described by Candice Amich,[5] or to the visual politics of the "war on terror," as elaborated by Ronak K. Kapadia. Kapadia explains for instance that

> The US state has, on the one hand, come to "know" the so-called human terrain of global conflict in the war on terror by using abstract vision and limitless data to map racialized "Muslim" populations and innovate surveillance and intelligence-gathering procedures. On the other hand, the US state persistently disavows imperial violence in efforts to disappear the corporeality of its wars through "black sites," redactions of classified documents, so-called touchless torture of detainees, denials of civilian death counts in drone attacks, and bans on images of the coffins of US soldiers killed in combat.[6]

In other words, contemporary hegemonic regimes of visibility are constituted by a visuality that is functional to an ideological project, one that legitimizes power and action and that includes the deliberate task of making certain things look harmless and others not visible at all.

In addition to the difficulties of breaking through hegemonic regimes of visibility, the visual denunciation of environmental conflicts presents a series of other challenges. While researchers of art and culture have highlighted the potential that the visual arts have for generating sympathy and understanding of humans and nonhuman entities in the face of a climate crisis and mass extinction, communication theorist Julie Doyle points for instance to the limitations of photography as a means for visualizing climate change.[7] Nowadays, she argues, it is common for campaigners to resort to comparative photography as a way of providing evidence of climate change, with images of glaciers shrinking making the effects of climate change visible. But, argues Doyle, such approaches also make evident the failure in action: photography seems to record everything that went wrong. Moreover, Doyle argues that the fast-paced, image-oriented reporting of new media places extra emphasis on visualizing climate news, which is not always possible. How do we, for instance, communicate the "slow violence" and less visible effects of climate change and extractivism? It is worth noting, says Doyle, that the emphasis on the visual often also comes from environmental groups themselves, who "have come to privilege visual representations of the landscape and environment as indicative of the need for its protection."[8] Many of the works discussed in this book engage in visual representation, but in fact none of them reproduce the kind of problematic visuality described by Doyle, which is fixed to a particular understanding of nature as pristine and a view of conservation at the center of the solution. Instead, the works referenced in *Creating Worlds Otherwise*, while often using visual mediums, tend to express a relational and political ontology of the territory, as artists situate themselves politically *within* the territory rather than looking at a landscape from a distance.

In addition to visual work, throughout the chapters of this book I examined several cases of site-specific performance actions that relied on the assembly of bodies and the embodied occupation of space as a form of expression. Actions that, beyond their visual character, become powerful acts of denunciation due to the presence of bodies in a particular space, the durational character, and the way that appropriation of space modifies the dynamics of a specific location. Examples of this include the performance actions of Fuerza Artística de Choque Comunicativo (FACC) outside symbolic sites of extraction and the defiant silent performances of the Mujeres del Silencio against open-pit mining in Andalgalá. These works show that there are different ways of denouncing and bearing witness, and that there are other senses and forms of experience that can be activated to those ends, beyond the visual.

The second function in the framework is documentation. There are several artists discussed in this book whose work involves the act of documenting: photojournalist Pablo Piovano, for instance, produces valuable documents of the effects of agrochemicals on human health through his images. The duo Etcétera and visual artist Julia Mensch, on their part, document the key figures in conflicts around extractivism, engaging in this way in acts of memorialization. While many artists document events and processes through their work, there are also others whose work builds on existing documents. Eduardo Molinari's Archivo Caminante (Walking Archive) is an example of an artistic practice that is research-based and that places archives and documentation at the center of a struggle for unearthing concealed truths about the extractivist model. In both cases, the function of documentation is intrinsically connected to the building of narratives, as the capturing, saving, and sharing of information provides a basis from which to develop narratives that counter the hegemonic extractivist paradigm and that overcome it.

An inclination toward documentation in artistic practice goes beyond the specific context of extractivism and has in fact been a prominent line of inquiry in both modern and contemporary art.[9]

But while much of such work is concerned with the use of archives and material from a different era, the works explored here are moved by the intention to document (and uncover) the present as it unfolds, facilitating processes of memorialization, and on occasion, generating work that acts as valuable documentation for challenging extractive projects, as in the case of Piovano's photographs being used as evidence in a legal case. Internationally, the case of Piovano can be most closely compared to the work of the research agency Forensic Architecture and their "investigative aesthetics,"[10] an aesthetic that is also built around the functions of denouncing and documenting.

The third function is democratization, and it is one that often is activated on multiple fronts. It involves, in the first place, the democratization of information and of the act of art making. In turn, these two forms of democratization give way to the building of democratic narratives and democratic spaces of struggle, which have the capacity to prefigure social configurations with a view to worlds otherwise. Democratization is thus a meaning-making activity, but it is also a social and political function.

It follows that democratization through art making and democratizing the arts are intrinsically connected processes; the modern arts have historically been part of the matrix of colonial power that forms and manipulates subjectivities, and at the same time art has also always been a language and a space for subversion.[11] I address this matter in Chapters 4 and 6, where I discuss the expediency of culture in projects of urban regeneration and the political economy of art making as work, respectively.

The cases studied in this book show how art facilitates instances of democratization of narratives, such as the murals that Claudia Tula paints in mining towns, where neighbors gather to share their views on mining and to build, collectively, a visual narrative that challenges the hegemonic myth of development espoused by mining companies and local governments alike. Other examples, such as the graphic interventions of activists from Casa 1234, demonstrate how democratizing the means of artistic production, in this case silk-screen printing, can provide struggling and marginalized groups, like the family members of victims of police violence, with a form of political agency, in turn democratizing the public narrative on crime, law, and violence. We can say the same of the collective mapping facilitated by Iconoclasistas, in which communities come together to map the conflicts in their territories and produce cartographies that are representative of their experience and that respond to their immediate needs. In this sense, democratization is a function that derives from longstanding local traditions of community-centered and politically engaged art and the ethos of *autogestión*, and it is related to what Rancière has termed the (re)distribution of the sensible. Rancière argues that art, as politics, has the potential to break through the barriers that constrain public narratives on social and political issues in the hands of the powerful.[12] Art can generate instances of expression where what presents itself to us as accepted experience is disrupted. In this sense, Rancière's theory of aesthetics and politics is related as well to the concept of a regime of visibility discussed earlier.

The fourth function is deconstruction, and I developed my use of this term from the bottom up, listening to the work of artists and activists and how they describe what they do. Throughout this book, I invoked the concept of deconstruction in order to describe the ways different artists and collectives attempt, through their practice, to challenge ingrained colonial and patriarchal ideas, such as the nature-culture divide, the hierarchical gender binary, and ideas around "civilization" and "barbarity" that have marked the development of the Argentine nation.

The use of the concept I employ here relates to and/or builds on three traditions. First, my conceptualization of deconstruction is related to, but distinct from, the work of Derrida, which challenges the hierarchical oppositions of Platonism and exposes the arbitrary nature of power.[13] I argue that artists and activists engage closely with texts (in this case, for instance, the narratives of governments and the mainstream media) to expose their fragility and inherent contradictions, effectively revealing unquestionable truths as mere constructions—for example, modernity as just one world among many others, or extractivism as an unsustainable economic project that has deep colonial roots but that is not Latin America's unquestionable destiny.

The other tradition I draw from and the one I primarily build on is feminism, specifically the militancy and theoretical work of the current feminist wave in Argentina and Latin America. Speaking of the affinities and disagreements between Derrida's deconstruction and feminism, Kate Nash notes that one of the reasons deconstruction is useful for feminism is its "commitment to the discursive construction of truth."[14] Furthermore, Derrida's work highlights the contextual character of the construction of categories, effectively assuming an anti-essentialist position that is compatible with feminist thinking on the construction of gender identities.[15] In terms of differences, she notes for instance how Derrida's (and Foucault's) versions of deconstruction fail to connect theory to the rest of the social world or to value the role of experience in knowledge construction. This is something that feminism as a praxis has successfully moved forward.

This feminist perspective on deconstruction thus calls us to consider feminist ways of mobilizing the concept. As I have established earlier in this book, my approach to theory is one that is grounded. From this position, what we can see is that the contemporary feminist call for the deconstruction of the subject, as is the case in Latin American feminisms, acts as a direct intervention on ingrained systems—such as extractivism and the patriarchy—and the ontologies and epistemologies that underpin them, and addresses not only the need to unlearn oppressive behaviors but also to relearn our place in the world and our relationship to other human and nonhuman beings. For instance, in her work on the emergence of the Ni Una Menos movement and the development of the women's strike as a constructive form of political action, Verónica Gago states on the one hand, that one of the aims of the movement is to "deconstruct the hegemony of capital," pointing in this way to the movement's overarching aspirations for profound social transformation.[16] On the other hand, she looks within the movement and explains that uncoupling the format of the assembly and the process of decision making from a centralized leadership "involves deconstructing the opposition between a horizontal social movement and a vertical leadership with the capacity of decision making."[17] In this way, she points to deconstruction as a process that is not just theoretical but rather embedded in the ways of building feminist political structures and processes.

In Latin America, deconstruction is directly linked to decolonization, as both are processes that take place—albeit not exclusively, as I have just proposed—at the epistemic and ontological level. While some decolonial theorists highlight the differences between deconstruction and decolonization, and how the first cuts short of the latter,[18] I propose to see deconstruction as a step leading to the political task of "decolonizing knowledge."[19] In artistic practice, for instance, decolonization is pursued through the deconstruction of paradigms and concepts, but also through the development of particular kinds of aesthetics (or aesthesis, as some like Mignolo and Rolando have proposed in order to differentiate the field of the sensorial from the philosophy of the Enlightenment).[20] Decolonial artistic practice is concerned with both the processes and outputs that are generally accepted as art, as well as with questioning the criteria and boundaries of that which is universally understood as aesthetics.[21] Specifically, it is about moving away from a universal conception of art and aesthetics and the boundaries and exclusionary limits imposed by such conceptions. It involves both aesthetic and epistemic disobedience, and it brings to the forefront that which Western art and aesthetics implicitly hide: the "colonial wound."[22] In addition to the works described in this book, we can see a decolonial approach to art making in the art science projects that Joanna Page discusses in *Decolonizing Science in Latin American Art,* a practice that has become increasingly widespread in recent years. Page argues that art science projects are important examples of an approach to critiquing technocratic/Western-scientific discourses through direct engagement with scientific methods. Furthermore, such projects can build bridges between science in the lab and other forms of knowledge, in this way generating *diálogos de saberes* (a dialogue between different forms of knowledge) as part of a pluriversal politics.

Finally, deconstruction relates as well to the pedagogical potential of art because, as argued in Chapter 6, Latin American environmental education begins from a decolonial epistemological, ontological, and political position. Latin American environmental education is therefore, in this sense, a deconstructive praxis, which often develops alongside or in conversation with artistic practices also aiming to activate the function of deconstruction with a view to decolonization.

The final function, design, refers to the way artistic and creative practices facilitate the imagining and implementation of alternative structures, economies, and ways of being. The conception of design I use here considers it as an activity that can be performed by everyone and can operate on multiple levels, and one of the aspects of design I have focused on is ontological design.

Building on Winograd and Flores, Escobar argues that ontological design needs to be practical not theoretical, that it needs to be relational, and that the process of designing ourselves takes place through language; this is why narratives matter.[23] The kinds of practices and praxes discussed in this book demonstrate how ontological design occurs, working on different levels and constructing meaning, socialities, and materialities at the same time: creating worlds otherwise. These kinds of ontological practices are political, as they put forward visions and methodologies that challenge universalist perspectives.[24] Indeed, "by resisting the neoliberal globalizing project, many marginalized communities are advancing *ontological struggles* for the perseverance and enhancement of the pluriverse."[25] Design thus becomes a key aspect for any worldmaking project, able to facilitate change at different levels of the individual, the collective, and the structural. Furthermore, these practices engage in forms of design that are prefigurative, because they are devising and putting into practice processes and structures that begin to enact their postextractivist visions in the now; in this way, they are directly connected to the ethos of autonomous movements that preceded them.[26] Finally, while the examples discussed reflect different positionalities, experiences, and worlds, they all display, to different degrees, ontologies that are relational in nature and an understanding of interdependence within communities and between communities and their territories and ecosystems.

The five functions described above complement each other by facilitating different kinds of interventions at the personal, collective, and structural level that are needed in order to activate holistic social transformations toward postextractivist worlds. Denunciation exposes information that has been deliberately hidden or misrepresented, and challenges as well the regime of truth and the regime of visibility upheld by actors such as governments, corporations, and the mainstream media. Documentation saves this information for posterity: the misleading representations, the recuperated information, and the testimonies that speak truth to power and put forward other imaginaries and ways of living. In this sense, documentation also allows process of memorialization of the movement. Documentation can also be a constructive act: documenting types of seeds or native flora can be an act of preservation for the future, and it can also be a constructive tool for the now, providing us with useful knowledge that has been lost, and that can allow a transformation in our way of being in the territory.

Democratization is linked to both denunciation and documentation in that it matters who speaks up, who records data, and who writes histories. Democratizing those acts means valuing multiple experiences and viewpoints and undoing knowledge hierarchies in order to create space for other narratives. Democratization in turn gives place to deconstruction: the questioning and undoing of long-held cognitive and material structures that have constrained our ability to think beyond what is presented as the only way, from a specific kind of modern epistemology to everyday manifestations of modern constructs such as forms of sexism and racism. Finally, the possibility for designing spaces, processes, practices, and ontologies that challenge and move beyond the modern-colonial, extractive paradigm emerges precisely from the deconstruction of that paradigm, which generates the apertures for new formations to emerge.

## *Moving Forward*

*Creating Worlds Otherwise* aimed to provide a deeper understanding of how the ideas of extractivism and postextractivism are constructed on a day to day basis by the actions of frontline communities, social organizations, and artists that devise different narratives in order to express the forms of injustice and violence they are experiencing, their relationship to different actors involved, and their visions for other ways of living. The focus of each chapter on a theme or narrative axis allowed me to develop those ideas in parallel to my analysis of artistic practices, in a way that brings to light how extractivism is lived, understood, and resisted as a phenomenon that permeates all aspects of life. In relation to this, I proposed the category of cultural extractivism as a useful analytical tool for understanding the multiple connections between the extractive and cultural industries. My deployment of this concept was limited to one particular case, but I believe it has much potential for helping us understand different kinds of connections between the extractive and cultural industries, including instances of cultural diplomacy, sponsorship, and the dynamics of art markets.

The cases discussed in the book also revealed how ecological matters are increasingly present in different sectors of society in Argentina, from the cultural sector to unions. The different events, artworks, and testimonies showed how matters of extraction, environment, and ecological destruction are interwoven with a variety of longstanding narratives and movements. This includes, for instance, the increasing connections between the human rights and antiextractivist movements, the ways movements against neoliberalism who are concerned with sovereignty have brought environmental issues to the center, and how popular movements for agroecology and food sovereignty have articulated matters of access to land and the right to good quality and accessible food with wider environmental, social, and political issues. The coming together of different movements, sectors, and perspectives, while each sustaining their view and project, is in a way indicative of an existing pluriverse, and of the possibility of a pluriverse with common visions concerning care, well-being, and a more attuned relationship to our ecosystems. Indeed, we are witnessing rapid moves toward intersectionality across different movements; while the Argentine mainstream media orchestrates an attack on environmentalism, dismissing it as "dumb," middle class, or imperialist, antiracist collectives like Indentidad Marrón claim "*Justicia ambiental es justicia social,*" as they highlight the connections between poverty, gender, race, and environmental injustice.

In the Global North, we have witnessed in recent years, particularly since 2018, the emergence of several new movements, networks, and groups concerned with climate action, many of these acquiring international if not global reach. Extinction Rebellion and Fridays for Future are just two examples of such initiatives that have brought the issue of climate change, ecological breakdown, and the urgent need to transition to more sustainable models to the center of public debate. However, such initiatives have also shown important limitations, and these are in great part related to a prevailing universalist approach to collective action on climate change and other ecological matters. In response to this, it is necessary to emphasize the need for action against ecological breakdown to be contextualized and in line with different countries' resources and responsibilities. But it is also paramount to consider that in many places and particularly in the Global South, environmental conflicts and concerns are not only or primarily about climate change, but rather, the most pressing matter is the direct and extreme effects that extractivism is having on communities and ecosystems. Narratives that reproduce the idea that "we are all in this together" thus sustain forms of oppression and inequality, as they gloss over gross differences in people's experiences of the climate crisis and imply an unfair, equal distribution of responsibilities. Similarly, depoliticized transition discourses often neglect extremely important issues, such as the destructive impacts of the extraction of lithium and other elements for the expansion of renewable energy, and what the costs would be of an energy transition under continued levels of growth.

Contrary to this, the forms of art and collective action explored in this book put forward contextualized approaches to opposing extractivism and transitioning to worlds otherwise that are embedded in the reality of local territories and at the same time are necessarily connected to global histories and contemporary geopolitics. This is because they stem from an awareness of how coloniality operates, how the continent's past set the basis for current imaginaries and economic models, and what external factors and interests determine Latin America's position in the global economy and in international politics.

Consequently, the main theoretical contribution I offered in this book, the five-function framework for understanding the role of art in anti- and postextractivist struggles, responds to the need for contextualized frameworks in the study of art and collective action, and aims to act as one possible framework for a postextractivist aesthetics.[27] I argued that a crucial consideration for understanding the artistic practices presented is how they respond to the challenges of their context. By this, I mean not only the violence of extraction and ecological breakdown, but also the forms of silencing and persecution, the failure of democratic mechanisms, the instances of censorship, the concentration of land and power, the construction of national histories and identities that erase entire populations and are instrumental to perpetuating an imaginary of Latin America as exporter of nature, and the continued realities of poverty, inequality, and gender-based violence. As expressed in the introduction, my study was grounded in Argentina, but in many ways the findings from this project are applicable to other contexts, given the repetition of the above dynamics across the region.

The framework I proposed in this book therefore is intended as a contribution to the study of Latin American art under extractivism. In her study on the subject, Macarena Gómez-Barris argues that in extractive societies, artistic practices make visible "submerged perspectives," ones that "perceive local terrains as sources of knowledge, vitality, and livability."[28] Submerged perspectives include the decolonial, the border perspective, the queer, the non-Western, the nondualist. My intention with the five-function framework is to provide a toolset for understanding the *how* of practices that stand against extractivism and envision other possible worlds. I proposed that there are five interrelated functions through which artists become responsive to the challenges and violences of the extractivist context and through which their work can also be constructive in a manner that is prefigurative and upholds radical visions for postextractivist worlds while also addressing pressing, everyday problems in the now with the tools that are currently at disposal.

This theoretical positioning mirrors my view on current movements of global reach such as the climate movement; while we need unifying calls and transnational networks, we also need to fight universalist approaches that erase the experiences of groups with smaller platforms and resources, those who have historically been pushed to the margins of global debates, or whose voices have been tokenized and instrumentalized in order to fulfill agendas emerging from the most powerful parts of the world. In this sense, much can be learned from Argentine and Latin American feminisms. Transnational initiatives such as the women's strike have succeeded in developing and nurturing sustained forms of international cooperation, while at the same time adapting the calls, slogans, and modality of the strike to the sociopolitical reality and needs of each country or region. As Veronica Gago recalls in reference to the first international women's strike of 2017, "We weaved, with the horizon of those days, a new internationalism."[29]

Another point to consider is how these findings contribute to an understanding of Latin America today, at a moment of multiple crises, and at the same time the surge of different forms of collective action seeking profound social transformation. What we are witnessing in 2022 is that while in certain countries a return to the Right has meant extreme forms of violence (gender-based, racial, economic, and environmental), the strongholds of neoliberalism are crumbling, and across the region the hegemony of the project of development is being challenged. In the Argentine context, some sectors at the bases of *progresismo* awakened to this reality with the window of Macri's neoliberal government from 2015 to 2019, a moment that led them to join forces with other sectors of the opposition and allowed them to realize not just the gravity of the consequences of an extractivist, development model but also the fact that there is continuity in this respect between political projects that in other aspects seem starkly different—it is worth noting, on the other hand, that parties at the left of *progresismo* such as those composing the Frente de Izquierda y de Trabajadores-Unidad (Workers' Left Front-Unity), have explicitly positioned themselves against extractivism for years. What I mean to emphasize, in other words, is that indeed, there has been a change in how environmental conflicts are understood, and this includes an incipient but growing awareness from groups affiliated to political parties that continue to champion extractivism, particularly the younger generations. What the examples in this book showcase is that, as Escobar argues, there are myriad ways those operating within modern political structures and movements can contribute to and move toward pluriversal politics for postextractivist worlds, whether or not they engage directly and explicitly with ontological matters.[30] Indeed, "pluriversal politics itself involves an entanglement of forms, inhabiting a spectrum from the radically relational to the modernist liberal."[31]

In Argentina, we have also recently seen a new wave of environmental action, one that emerged in response to global movements such as Extinction Rebellion and Fridays for Future. A great part of this movement is led by young people, and their activism has a distinct approach: unlike most of the movements and forms of action discussed across this book's chapters, this movement does not emerge from local, territorial conflicts that then adopt a broader perspective. Instead, it responds to the call of global movements emerging from the Global North, but it adapts the demands, narratives, and on occasion the aesthetics of such movements to local histories, social issues, and needs, building on decades of local organizing and the wisdom of local land defenders and environmental movements and generating connections between local and global struggles. Such is the case of the organization Jóvenes por el Clima (Young People for the Climate), formed in 2019. While joining the call of Fridays for Futures, the movement soon became involved in a range of local matters and developed a narrative and a politics that are in tune with global developments but that are situated in a Latin American, popular, and decolonial standpoint. Among their many forms of actions, they have supported grassroots projects such as the agroecological initiative Proyecto Artigas discussed in Chapter 6, and have been key actors in successfully pushing Congress to pass the Declaration of Ecologic and Climate Emergency and the Law 27520 for adaptation and mitigation of climate change in 2019, and the Environmental Education Law in 2021.[32]

While not free of growing pains, the emerging youth-led environmental movement in Argentina, alongside feminism, has the potential to become another powerful force for change. These movements' capacity to articulate different perspectives and to simultaneously think locally, transnationally, and globally in the building of worlds otherwise are fundamental for enacting the transformations we so urgently need. My hope for transformation is with art, feminist collective action, and the emerging generation of ecological activists. It is to them I dedicate this book, in the hope that my documentation and analysis of the present and recent past of the movement will contribute to inspire more imaginative and unapologetic initiatives for creating worlds otherwise.

# NOTES

## INTRODUCTION

1. Quijano, "Coloniality of Power."
2. Blaser, *Storytelling Globalization.*
3. Irwin, "Ecological Ethics," 118.
4. See Sousa Santos, *Towards a New*; Escobar, "El 'postdesarrollo.'"
5. Serafini, *Performance Action.*
6. Escobar, "Territorios de diferencia," 30; Wilson, "Energy Imaginaries," 377.
7. See for example Gudynas, "Diez tesis urgentes"; Svampa and Viale, *Maldesarrollo.*
8. See for example Gago, *La potencia feminista*; Mezzadra and Neilson, "On the Multiple."
9. Machado Aráoz, "Ecología política."
10. Ibid., 25.
11. Ibid., 17.
12. Harvey, *The New Imperialism*; Sassen, *Expulsions.*
13. Gudynas, "Más allá," 390. All translations by the author except as noted.
14. Ulloa, "Environment and Development," 320.
15. I do note that "modernity is not a single-headed process" (Swyngedouw and Ernstson, "Interrupting the Anthropo-obScene," 10). When I refer to the *modern paradigm* or *modern constructs*, I speak of the dominant ideas that emerged from modernity and underpin the sustained coloniality of knowledge.
16. Escobar, "El 'postdesarrollo,'" 19.
17. Blaser, *Storytelling Globalization*, 154.
18. Escobar, "El 'postdesarrollo,'" 20.
19. Ulloa, "Environment and Development," 321.
20. Diawara, "Globalization."
21. Svampa, "Cuatro claves," 51; GER-GEMSAL, "Bienes comunes."
22. Petras and Veltmeyer, *The New Extractivism*, 223.
23. Svampa, "Consenso de los commodities."

24. Riofrancos, "Extractivismo Unearthed."
25. While the hegemony of extractivism prevails, in recent years the shift from center-left to right-wing governments in countries like Brazil and Bolivia, and momentarily in Argentina, have generated opportunities for those on the Left to engage in critiques of extractivism (Andermann, "Turn of the tide?," 2). Indeed, the turn to the Right in Argentina, with Mautricio Macri's administration from 2015 to 2019, opened a space for supporters of the preceding progressive governments to voice their concerns about the undeniable effects of an extraction-based model, something that, in a context of strong political polarization, most had refused to do before (Svampa "Concenso de los commodities," 28). In other words, during the Macri administration, cracks began to generate in the extractivist consensus, as extractivism and neoliberalism began to be articulated as part of the same oppositional narrative.
26. For more on science and modernity see Latour, *We Have Never.*
27. Escobar, *Designs*, 89.
28. Blaser, *Storytelling Globalization*, 228.
29. Leff, "La complejidad ambiental," 4.
30. Conway and Singh, "Radical Democracy."
31. Solanas, "Menemismo: Megaminería y contaminación."
32. For a succinct yet comprehensive overview of the history of socioenvironmental movements in Argentina see Wagner, "Conflictos socioambientales."
33. D'Alo Abba, "Vienen por el oro."
34. Merlinsky, "Introducción."
35. Svampa, "Consenso de los commodities," 28.
36. Aranda, *Tierra Arrasada*; Álvarez Mullally et al., *Megaproyecto Vaca Muerta*.
37. Martínez Alier, *The Environmentalism of the Poor.*
38. Merlinsky, *Política, derechos y justicia ambiental.*
39. Escobar, *Designs*, 172.
40. Ibid., 174.
41. Svampa, "Cuatro claves," 53-54.
42. Sitrin, "Horizontalidad," 135.
43. Ibid.
44. Hardt and Zibechi, "La sociedad otra," 32.
45. "Quienes Somos," Unión de Asambleas Ciudadanas, accessed on 3 February 2020, https://asambleasciudadanas.org.ar/quienes-somos.
46. Escobar, *Designs*, 139.
47. Ibid., 140.
48. Ibid., 148.
49. Martínez and Acosta, "Los derechos de la naturaleza."
50. Escobar, *Designs*, 10.
51. Martín García, "Postextractivismo y crecimiento," 94.
52. Gudynas, "Más allá," 406.
53. Martín García, "Postextractivismo y crecimiento."
54. Irwin, "Ecological Ethics," 112.

55. Escobar, *Designs*, 147.
56. Nirmal and Rocheleau, "Decolonizing Degrowth," 471.
57. De Angelis, "Commons," 124.
58. When speaking of interdependence and the kinds of relational ontologies that underpin this notion, it is important not to see such concepts as inherently good, given that from the perspective of geoengineering they can serve "to deepen the process of capitalist enrolment of non-human and more-than human processes." Swyngedouw and Ernstson, "Interrupting the Anthropo-obScene," 10.
59. Svampa, "Consenso de los commodities," 33–34.
60. Gómez-Barris, *Beyond the Pink Tide*, 12.
61. Clarke, "Conjunctures," 119.
62. Beilin and Ares-López, "Introduction," 5.
63. Escobar, *Territories of Difference*, 21.
64. Alimonda, "Notas," 37.
65. Fagan, "Cultural Politics," 190.
66. Grosfoguel, "The Epistemic Decolonial Turn," 218.
67. Escobar, *Territories of Difference*, 14.
68. Escobar, *Designs*, 90.
69. Blaser, "Political Ontology," 877.
70. Escobar, "Territorios de diferencia," 34.
71. Dussel, "Transmodernity and Interculturality."
72. de la Cadena, "Indigenous Cosmopolitics."
73. Blaser, "Political Ontology," 879.
74. See for instance Leff, "La complejidad ambiental."
75. Escobar, *Designs*, 70.
76. Haraway, *Staying with the Trouble*, 83.
77. Hoyos, *Things with a History*, 4, 13.
78. Martínez Alier, *The Environmentalism of the Poor.*
79. Ingold, "Art and Anthropology," 660–61.
80. Demos, *Beyond the World's End*, 2.
81. Gómez-Barris, *The Extractive Zone*, 3.
82. See for example Serafini, "Subversion through Performance," "Prefiguring Performance," and *Performance Action*.
83. See for example Bishop, "Viewers as Producers," 11.
84. See for instance Gómez-Barris, *The Extractive Zone*.
85. My previous efforts in this field include the book *Arte y Ecología Política*, co-edited with Gabriela Merlinsky and resulting from an interdisciplinary symposium held in Buenos Aires in 2017.
86. See for instance Riffo, "Hidrocarburos no convencionales."
87. See for instance *Página12*, "Alberto Fernández."
88. Nixon, *Slow Violence*.
89. Serafini, *Performance Action*.
90. Doyle, "Seeing the Climate?," 283–84.
91. Polletta, "Contending Stories."
92. Blaser, *Storytelling Globalization*.

93. For more on the Political activation of relationality, see Escobar, *Sentipensar*.
94. Morton, *Ecology without Nature*, 14.
95. Derrida, *Positions*; "Force of Law."
96. Escobar, *Sentipensar*; Lorde, "The Master's Tools."
97. Escobar, *Designs*, 4.
98. Tola, "El 'giro ontológico,'" 132.
99. Zibechi, *Territories in Resistance*, 14.
100. Svampa, "Consenso de los commodities."
101. Escobar, *Designs*.
102. For a creative example of contextualized engagements with art and extraction, see Lippard, *Undermining*.
103. Gómez-Barris, *The Extractive Zone*.

## CHAPTER 1

Epigraph. Zibechi, *Territories in Resistance*, 20.

1. Ibid., 19.
2. Altschuler, "Territorio y desarrollo," 65; Escobar, "Territorios de diferencia," 7.
3. Museo de Arte Moderno de Buenos Aires, *Una historia* [exhibition brochure].
4. Raffestin, "Space, Territory."
5. Museo de Arte Moderno de Buenos Aires, *Una historia*.
6. Castro-Sotomayor, "Territorialidad" 52.
7. Zibechi, *Territories in Resistance*, 13.
8. Ibid., 17–18.
9. Lopes de Souza, "From the 'Right to the City,'" 414
10. Ibid., 411; italics in original.
11. Zibechi, *Territories in Resistance*, 14.
12. Holland "Deterritorializing Deterritorialization," cited in Elden, "The State of Territory."
13. Zibechi, *Territories in Resistance*, 15; I discuss issues surrounding autonomy and sovereignty in full in Chapter 5.
14. Sitrin, *Horizontalism*; Svampa and Pereyra, "Entre la ruta."
15. Svampa, "Consenso de los commodities," 26.
16. Svampa, *Fronteras del neoextractivismo*, 44.
17. Svampa, "Consenso de los commodities," 22.
18. *Buen vivir* (good living) is a contested concept. While some use it as a synonym of *sumak kawsay* and other Andean visions of harmonic living, the term has been incorporated and redefined by both progressive state projects and postdevelopment intellectuals, leading to different definitions and uses. See Hidalgo-Capitán and Cubillo-Guevara, "Deconstruction and Genealogy" and Cuestas-Caza, "Sumak Kawsay."
19. Svampa, "Consenso de los commodities," 23.

20. For more on this series see (in Spanish) "Territorios en Conflicto," Teatro Nacional Cervantes, accessed 21 November 2020, https://www.teatrocervantes.gob.ar/ciclo/territorios-en-conflicto.
21. Personal interview with Gabriela Massuh, 18 August 2017.
22. Cited in Yaccar, "Investigaciones."
23. Svampa, "Consenso de los commodities."
24. The notion of regimes of visibility and invisibility in colonized societies is also developed by Silvia Rivera Cusicanqui in *Oprimidos pero no vencidos*.
25. Molinari, "El manto," 22,
26. Escobar, *Designs*, 70.
27. Personal interview with Eduardo Molinari, 5 December 2017.
28. Molinari 2015, "Producción y transferencia."
29. Molinari et al., *Informe final: Arte y territorio*, 3.
30. Milder, "Teaching as Art," 13.
31. Ibid.
32. Colectivo Situaciones, *Researcher-Militant*.
33. Personal interview with Gabriela Massuh.
34. Molinari's experience is just one of the many occasions of obfuscation of critical work I encountered during my research. I discuss a similar case surrounding Pablo Piovano's images portraying the effects of agrochemicals in Chapter 3.
35. Lopes de Souza, "From the 'Right to the City,'" 417–18.
36. Blank, "Spatial Movement Strategies," 2.
37. Dinerstein, *Politics of Autonomy*; Halvorsen, "Decolonising Territory."
38. Halvorsen, "Decolonising Territory," 798.
39. Lopes de Souza, "From the 'Right to the City,'" 415; emphasis added.
40. Kwon, *Site-Specific Art*.
41. Kwon, "Notes on Site," 87–88.
42. Ibid., 95.
43. Shaughnessy, *Applying Performance*, 97.
44. Kester, *Conversation Pieces*.
45. Stallabrass, *Art Incorporated*.
46. Kester, *The One and the Many*.
47. Equipo Programa Arte y Territorio, "Arte en territorio."
48. Sack, *Human Territoriality*.
49. See the exhibition website: "Artes Visuales/ Septiembre 2017," Centro Cultural de la Memoria Haroldo Conti, accessed 7 March 2018, http://conti.derhuman.jus.gov.ar/2017/09/av-arte-territorio.php.
50. Home page, Ojo de Pez, accessed 23 February 2021, http://www.ojodepez.centroconviven.org/home.html.
51. Escobar, "Territorios de diferencia."
52. Personal interview with Julia Risler, 4 August 2017.
53. Iconoclasistas, "Mapeos colectivos," 177.
54. Personal interview with Julia Risler.
55. Iconoclasistas, "Mapeos colectivos," 182.
56. Personal interview with Julia Risler.

57. Basualdo, Domenech, and Pérez, "Territorios de la movilidad," 44.
58. Personal interview with Julia Risler.
59. Iconoclasistas, "Mapeos colectivos," 177.
60. Nouzeilles, "Patagonia as Borderland," 36.
61. Ibid., 37.
62. Svampa, *Fronteras del neoextractivismo*, 40.
63. Aliaga, "The Land 'Wars,'" 148.
64. Machado Aráoz, "Ecología política," 15.
65. While I am focusing here on the Argentine Patagonia specifically, similar conflicts resulting from extractivism can be identified in Chile, where Mapuche communities are facing extreme violence and judicialization as a result of their struggle to protect their territories.
66. Del Valle Rojas and Maldonado Rivera, "El discurso," 333.
67. Ibid., 335.
68. Polischuk, "El intento."
69. Eissa, "Construyendo al enemigo."
70. Raffestin, "Space, Territory," 128.
71. Ibid.
72. Serafini, *Performance Action*.
73. Moreno was a naturalist and border expert who travelled across Patagonia recording its fauna and flora as well as the characteristics of its indigenous inhabitants. His maps served to establish the borders with Chile and to point out the economic potential of those lands. See Nouzeilles, "Patagonia as Borderland," 38.
74. EQSNotas, "Campaña del Desierto."
75. Fanon, *The Wretched*, 83.
76. See Chandía speaking of his work: Canal4ETC, "13 11 17 Fernando Chandia - Intervencion Urbana," YouTube video, 14 November 2017, https://www.youtube.com/watch?v=s74ubBawtKU.
77. El Chubut, *Fuerte respaldo*,
78. See Puel Kona's Facebook page, https://www.facebook.com/puelkonaoficial.
79. Personal interview with Lefxaru Nawel, 28 August 2017.
80. Gutiérrez Ríos, "Kintu newen."
81. Wallmapu is the name of the territory historically inhabited by Mapuche people, which extends across the political borders of Argentina and Chile; Excerpt of lyrics by Puel Kona, cited in Gutiérrez Ríos, "Kintu newen," 172. Original in Spanish.
82. Blaser, *Storytelling Globalization*, 80–81
83. Zibechi, *Territories in Resistance*.
84. Gutiérrez Ríos, "Kintu newen."
85. Personal interview with Lefxaru Nawel.
86. Ibid.
87. Ibid.
88. Rancière, *Dissensus*.

89. The framework for antiextractivist art practice consists of five functions: denunciation, documentation, democratization, deconstruction, and design. See the Introduction and Conclusion of this book.
90. Castro-Sotomayor, "Territorialidad," 57.
91. Gómez-Barris, *The Extractive Zone*, 6.
92. Svampa, *Fronteras del neoextractivismo.*

## CHAPTER 2

1. The green scarves worn by women demanding the right to safe and free abortion have led to the movement being referred to as "the green tide."
2. Federici, *Revolution*.
3. Kunin, "Women," 6.
4. Ojeda, "Género, naturaleza," 56–57.
5. Escobar, *Designs*, 20.
6. Warren, "The Promise," 126.
7. Irwin, "Ecological Ethics," 116.
8. Carlassare, "Socialist and Cultural Ecofeminism."
9. Curtin, "Toward an Ecological"; Warren, "The Promise"; Wilson, "Energy Imaginaries."
10. Kings, "Intersectionality," 70; Mallory, "What Is Ecofeminist," 309.
11. Svampa, "Feminismos del sur"; *Abya Yala* is the way the Guna people of Colombia and Panama refer to what is now known, due to colonization, as the Americas. The term can be translated as "land of vital blood" or "land in its full maturity," and it has been adopted by indigenous groups and decolonial movements across the region. I am using the term Abya Yala alongside Latin America here with the aim of highlighting the different positionalities and epistemologies in the region.
12. Segato, *La Guerra*, 17.
13. Korol, "Somos tierra"; Ulloa, "Feminismos territoriales."
14. Pérez Prieto, "Epistemología feminista," 17.
15. Gargallo Celentani, *Feminismos desde Abya Yala*.
16. See for instance Lugones, "Decolonial Feminism"; Rivera Cusicanqui, *Violencias*.
17. Rivera Cusicanqui, "La noción de 'derecho,'" 29.
18. LaDanta LasCanta, "De la teología," 37.
19. Li, "Ecofeminism."
20. Morton, "Queer Ecology," 274.
21. Bauhardt, "Rethinking Gender," 367.
22. Singer, "Toward Intersectional Ecofeminist," 12.
23. Ibid.
24. The term *disidencias* (Spanish plural for the word dissidence) defines the political identity of collectives in Latin America that stray away from heteronormativity and feel that categories such as "gay" or "LGBT" are not representative of their experiences. They point out, for instance, the normative gender and social organization standards associated with gay

culture, and the middle class and Western perspectives that have marked much LGBT organizing across the region (González Ortuño, "Teorías," 180–81).

25. Di Liscia, "Mujeres en los movimientos"; for more on the *piquetero* movement see Chapter 1.
26. Korol, "Somos tierra."
27. Gomes, "Mujeres Afrodescendientes." See also the collectives Identidad Marrón and Cine Marrón.
28. *Travesti*, of which the literal translation would be transvestite, is a gender identity that could be broadly understood within the trans umbrella but that has a specific meaning and political weight in Latin America. *Travestis* have for long faced marginalization and violence, and the term *travesti* was initially used pejoratively. However, as Argentine *travesti* activist Lohanna Berkins explains, it has been reappropriated by the community and is currently used with the aim of destabilizing the male/female binary (cited in Aizura, *Mobile Subjects*).
29. Meyer, "Finalizó la ocupación."
30. Title of the document: "Las mujeres Mapuce hablamos desde Waj Mapu" (We Mapuche women speak from Waj Mapu). Signatory: Lofce Newen Mapu. Received via WhatsApp. Emphasis in the original.
31. Svampa, "Feminismos del sur."
32. Kunin, "Women," 12; Giarracca, "El movimiento de mujeres," 130.
33. For more on these two cases see Chapter 3.
34. Singer, "Toward Intersectional Ecofeminist," 11–12.
35. *Mate* is an infusion common in Argentina and other countries in the region, commonly drunk and shared from one cup.
36. La Alumbrera is the company behind the open-pit mine Bajo La Alumbrera, the first open-pit mine in Argentina, which began operations in Andalgalá in 1997. For more on resistance to open-pit mining, see Chapters 3 and 5.
37. Personal interview with Claudia Tula, 30 March 2018.
38. Reed, *The Art of Protest*; Serafini, *Performance Action.*
39. Bang and Wajnerman, "Arte y transformación."
40. See Cabrapan Duarte, "Comercio sexual"; Gago, "Al extractivismo."
41. Personal interview with Laura García, 30 March, 2018.
42. Wilson et al, *Petrocultures*.
43. Foucault, *The Birth of Biopolitics*.
44. Personal interview with Pao Lunch, 22 August 2017.
45. Gago, *La Potencia Feminista*, 24.
46. Lunch, "Pornopetroleo."
47. Preciado, *Testo Junkie*.
48. The series was also displayed at the Bienal Neuquén Contemporáneo (2015), the Museo de Arte Eduardo Minnicelli in the city of Río Gallego (2016), and the Feria de Arte Contemporáneo in the city of Córdoba (2016). The "model" refers here to the progressive model of the government of Cristina Kirchner, under which critiques of extractivism were few and marginal.

49. Personal interview with Pao Lunch.
50. Kunin and Simonetto, "Travas, putos y tortas."
51. Hemispheric Institute, "Mujeres Creando."
52. Interview with Julieta Paredes—now part of Mujeres Creando Comunidad—from 2013, cited in Gómez-Barris, *The Extractive Zone*, 120.
53. Galindo, *No se puede*.
54. Serafini, "Subversion through performance," 320.
55. Hemispheric Institute, *No Woman*.
56. Gómez-Barris, *The Extractive Zone*, 120.
57. Ibid., 128.
58. For a journalistic account of the reactions (in Spanish), see Cazas and Flores, "Polémico mural" for *Página Siete*.
59. Miradas Críticas del Territorio desde el Feminismo, "Sobre Nosotras."
60. Miradas Críticas del Territorio desde el Feminismo, *Mapeando el cuerpo-territorio*, 34.
61. Fals Borda, *Una sociología sentipensante*.
62. Basualdo, Domenech, and Pérez, "Territorios de la movilidad," 44.
63. For an example of counter-mapping in a different context (indigenous nations in Canada), see Kid, "Extra-activism."
64. For more on the "aesthetic of disgust," see Korsemeyer, "Gut Appreciation."
65. Gago, *La potencia feminista*, 49.
66. Ibid., 97.
67. Bauhardt, "Rethinking Gender," 367.
68. Sultana, "Emotional Political Ecology," 634.
69. Gago, *La potencia feminista*, 26.
70. For more on the practical and political implications of an ethic of care see Tronto, "An ethic of care."

## CHAPTER 3

1. Carpizo, "Los derechos humanos," 4.
2. Capella Giannattasio, "International Human Rights"; Goodale, "Toward a Critical Anthropology," 486.
3. Capella Giannattasio "International Human Rights," 522.
4. Nirmal and Rocheleau, "Decolonizing Degrowth," 468.
5. Ignatieff, "The Attack."
6. Goodale, "Toward a Critical Anthropology," 491.
7. Martínez and Acosta, "Los derechos de la naturaleza," 2929.
8. Lutz and Sikkink, "International Human Rights," 639.
9. The terms *disappeared* and *(en)forced disappearance* refer to people who are secretly detained or abducted by the state or a political organization and whose whereabouts are not disclosed. This practice was employed by military dictatorships in countries like Chile and Argentina, where thousands of people in the opposition or perceived to be political opposers were abducted, tortured, and killed.

10. Carpizo, "Los derechos humanos," 20.
11. Pautassi, "La complejidad," 623.
12. Svampa, "Cuatro claves," 62.
13. Halbwachs, *Los marcos*.
14. Crenzel, "Historia y memoria," 4.
15. See Jelin, "Política de la memoria"; Rubenstein explains that in the 1980s, "within the movement, we can distinguish between the organizations of those directly affected and other organizations. The latter include the Liga Argentina por los Derechos del Hombre established in 1937, the Servicio Paz y Justicia (SERPAJ) founded in 1974, the Asamblea Permanente por los Derechos Humanos (APDH) founded in December 1975, the Movimiento Ecuménico por los Derechos Humanos (MEDH) founded in February 1976, as well as the Movimiento Judío por los Derechos Humanos (MJDH) which appeared in 1983, and the Centro de Estudios Legales y Sociales (CELS) founded in May 1980. The organizations of people directly affected include the Familiares de Detenidos y Desaparecidos por Razones Políticas which formed toward the end of 1976 and the Madres de Plaza de Mayo (MDM) who emerged in April 1977, from which the Abuelas de Plaza de Mayo are born in October 1977." (*La sédition militaire*, 294, my translation from French).
16. Schindel, "Inscribir el pasado," 66–67.
17. Longoni, "Arte y política," 4.
18. Ibid., 7.
19. H.I.J.O.S. is the name of an organization created in 1995 by the sons and daughters of people who had disappeared during the civic-military dictatorship of 1976 to 1983. The organization was founded with the objective of pursuing justice over the yet unpunished crimes against humanity of the dictatorship, to sustain the memory of what had happened, and to maintain the social and political struggles of the many activists that were persecuted and forcibly disappeared.
20. Longoni, "Arte y política," 14.
21. Ibid.
22. Schindel, "Inscribir el pasado," 84. The *rondas* or circular marches of the Mothers began during the dictatorship, when mothers gathered at the Plaza de Mayo square to demand the whereabouts of their children. When instructed to circulate by the police, they began marching in a circle, in a defiant act of spatial appropriation.
23. Ibid., 82.
24. See Observatorio Petrolero Sur, "La CIDH."
25. See Aranda, "Una cumbre."
26. Pautassi, "La complejidad," 625.
27. See for instance CELS, "Monsanto y la privatización."
28. Personal interview with Marcos Filardi, 20 December 2017.
29. For more on food sovereignty, see La Vía Campesina, "What Is Food Sovereignty?"
30. *Página12*, "Una sola convocatoria."

31. Personal interview with Marcos Filardi.
32. Personal Skype interview with Mariana Katz, 3 February 2018. Critiques of the human rights discourse as developed by the governments of Néstor Kirchner and Cristina Fernández de Kirchner have come from both ends of the political spectrum. While the critique presented here focuses on the inconsistencies between championing human rights and perpetuating a model of development that infringes the rights of indigenous and other communities, other critiques have emerged from conservative and right-wing sectors. The latter argue that human rights are purely instrumentalized as part of populist tactics, and they have gone as far as disputing central matters in the public narrative of the civic-military dictatorship, such as the number of people disappeared during that period.
33. Ponce de León, "How to See Violence."
34. Some of the terms explored in this section, such as *genocide*, *ecocide*, and *terracide*, have been deployed before by other social movements, scholars, and even judicial systems. My intention here is not to trace a genealogy of such terms, but rather to look at the variety of frames coexisting in this moment in a particular context, and how they are mobilized.
35. Feierstein, *Genocide as Social Practice*.
36. See for instance Rubenstein *La sédition militaire*, 19–20.
37. Escobar, *Designs*, 148.
38. Martínez and Acosta, "Los derechos de la naturaleza," 2944.
39. Hardt, and Zibechi, "La sociedad *otra*," 53.
40. Blaser, "Political Ontology," 879.
41. Independent Expert Panel for the Legal Definition of Ecocide (2021), *Commentary and Core Text*, 5.
42. For more on Eduardo Molinari's work, see Chapter 1.
43. Excerpts from text by Eduardo Molinari featured in the invitation to the exhibition. My own translation.
44. This definition was included in a newsletter by Movimiento de Mujeres Indígenas por el Buen Vivir sent out on 24 January 2020 to promote a climate camp against terricide and in defense of life and territories, to take place in Chubut in February the same year.
45. Grear, "The Discourse."
46. Bavikatte and Bennett, "Community Stewardship."
47. Sajeva, "Rights with Limits."
48. Longoni, "Arte y política."
49. Agrotoxics (or *agrotóxicos* in Spanish) is a word used to refer to the industrial pesticides and herbicides used in large-scale monoculture agriculture.
50. Personal interview with Eliana, 29 March 2018.
51. Personal interview with Silvina, 4 April 2018.
52. A local precedent to FACC was the collective Costuras Urbanas, who in the late 1990s began to carry out interventions in the public space to bring attention to the privatization of state companies and services

taking place at the time. The choice of symbolic spaces, the disposition of bodies, and the stripped down aesthetics of their actions are comparable to the actions by FACC discussed in this chapter. See Alonso and Gonzáles, *Ansia y devoción*, 43. Also see the Costuras Urbanas blog, *CosturasUrbanas*, at http://costurasurbanas.blogspot.com.

53. The film is available on YouTube: *#QuiénElige (F.A.C.C)*, lavacaTV, 22 October 2017, https://www.youtube.com/watch?v=Sey_pc-4Feo.
54. Proaño Gómez, "*Artivismo* y potencia política," 50; while the governments of Néstor Kirchner and Cristina Fernández de Kirchner appropriated and championed human rights—with a specific focus on the recent dictatorial past—Mauricio Macri's term (2015–2019) was characterized by an opposite approach of negationism and erosion of memory in public institutions.
55. Ponce de León, "How to See Violence."
56. For more on the Natural History Museum, see "About," The Natural History Museum, accessed 25 January, 2022, http://thenaturalhistorymuseum.org/about.
57. Personal interview with Pablo Piovano, 17 August 2017.
58. Ibid.
59. Alvado, "El costo humano."
60. Dos Santos, "La estructura."
61. Longoni, "Arte y política," 2–3.
62. For more on rates of privatization, see Massuh, *El robo*.
63. Ponce de León, "How to See Violence," 354.
64. The case of Sandra was unique at the time but followed important precedents. In 1993, the Great Ape Project had already advocated for the recognition of the rights to life and to freedom, and prohibition of torture of nonhuman great apes. See Martínez and Acosta, "Los derechos de la naturaleza," 2932.
65. Forensic Architecture, "Ape Law."

## CHAPTER 4

1. Junka-Aikio and Cortes-Severino, "Cultural Studies of Extraction."
2. Lefebvre, *The Production of Space*.
3. Viale, "Prólogo."
4. Ibid., 16.
5. Personal interview with Julián Galeano, 4 August 2017.
6. Personal interview with Alejandra, 18 December 2017.
7. Merlinsky, *Políticas, derechos*.
8. Harvey, "The Right to the City."
9. Pintos and Narodowski, *La privatopía sacrílega*.
10. Blaseotto, "Una historia."
11. Boyce Kay, "Stay the Fuck," 3.
12. Telam, "Las voces."

13. Massidda, "Utopian Visions," 147; Merlinsky, Martín, and Tobías, "Presentación del Dossier."
14. Vásquez Duplat, "Presentación," 9.
15. Capps, "Bernie Sanders."
16. Personal interview with Susana Romero Sued, 2 December 2017.
17. Millán, "El extractivismo cultural," n.p.
18. Palma, "Museums and Mining."
19. Molinari, "El manto tóxico."
20. Sassen, *Expulsions*.
21. Yúdice, *The Expediency of Culture*, 1. For a recent study of culture as resource and the various connections between culture and extraction in a petrostate, see Plaza Azuaje, *Culture as Renewable Oil*.
22. Early critics of the cultural industries such as Horkheimer and Adorno argued, for instance, that the cultural industries function as backdrop and support of the Enlightenment project in order to ensure the domination and exploitation that lead to "progress" and "rationalization." The cultural industries capitalize on leisure, and what is supposed to be a break from work becomes an opportunity for creating consumers (Szpilbarg and Saferstein, "De la industria," 103). Benjamin, also from the Frankfurt School, highlighted instead the importance of the processes of cultural production and the positioning of artists within that process, pointing to the emancipatory potential of cultural production when the means are democratized (Benjamin, "The Author").
23. Quijano, "Coloniality of Power."
24. Sousa Santos, *Epistemologías del sur*.
25. Svampa, *El dilema argentino,* cited in Wortman, "El desafío."
26. Dinardi, "Unsettling the Role of Culture," 13.
27. Rey, *Industrias culturales*, 15.
28. Hawkes, *The Fourth Pillar*.
29. Radcliffe and Laurie, "Culture and Development," 242.
30. Buitrago Restrepo and Duque Márquez, *The Orange Economy*.
31. Oliva Abarca, "Capital Cultural"; Rey, *Industrias culturales*; Wortman, "Políticas culturales."
32. Saifer, "Research Note."
33. Benito, "Autogestión cultural," 82.
34. Maxwell and Miller, "Greening Cultural Policy."
35. Prato, Rodrigues Morais, and Segura, "La cultura comunitaria." It is important to note that the promotion of community culture on a federal level at the time was used by the government as a vehicle for strengthening the progressive platform during times of political turbulence, a reminder that culture can be instrumentalized not only by market-oriented governments and development agencies, but also by progressive governments with agendas of social inclusion.
36. Barrese and Pareja-Eastaway, "*Glocalisation* Dynamics."
37. Rodríguez and Di Virgilio, "A City for All?," 1218.
38. Saifer, "Research Note," 29.

39. Mookerjea, "Accumulated Violence," 98, cited in Saifer, "Research Note," 30.
40. See, for example, Florida, *The New Urban Crisis.*
41. Rodríguez and Di Virgilio, "A City for All?," 1219.
42. The law can be accessed here: CEDOM, *ley 4353*, 1 November 2012. http://www2.cedom.gov.ar/es/legislacion/normas/leyes/ley4353.html.
43. Barrese and Pareja-Eastaway, "*Glocalisation* Dynamics," 4.
44. Florida, *The Rise.*
45. For more on territorial work see Chapter 1.
46. Massidda, "Utopian Visions."
47. Serafini, "Cultural Production."
48. Radcliffe and Laurie, "Culture and Development," 242.
49. Serafini, "Cultural Production," 58.
50. Personal interview with Natalia Quinto, 5 April 2018
51. Ibid.
52. *The Wiley Blackwell Encyclopedia of Consumption and Consumer Studies*, s.v. "Cultural Omnivores," by Jennifer Smith Maguire, first published 24 March 2015. DOI: 10.1002/9781118989463.wbeccs085.
53. Zukin, "Gentrification," 143.
54. Florida, *The Rise*; Rodríguez, "Estado, clases y gentrificación."
55. Serafini, "Cultural Production," 59.
56. Lees, Bang Shin, and López-Morales, *Planetary Gentrification.*
57. Serafini, "Cultural Production," 59.
58. Personal interview with Natalia Quinto.
59. Ciudad del Deseo, "Qué-Quiénes," accessed 13 January 2021, https://www.ciudaddeldeseo.com/que-quienes.
60. Personal interview with Manuel, 3 December 2017. Manuel is a pseudonym.
61. See Grupo de Arte Callejero, *Pensamientos, prácticas, acciones.*
62. *Chicha* is a kind of Peruvian *cumbia* known for a specific aesthetic that sets apart the graphics and promotional materials that surround it. *Chicha* posters are usually printed using the silk-screen technique, and tend to feature a distinctive large and elaborate font, and contrasting colors (although Casa 1234's posters about police brutality are often printed in black and white). *Chicha* has become widespread in parts of Argentina as a result of cultural exchange and migration from Andean countries.
63. Personal interview with Manuel.
64. Personal interview, 3 December 2017. Analía is a pseudonym.
65. For more on Heraldo and the vegetable garden of Villa La Maternidad see *La Tinta*, "La memoria de Heraldo hecha semilla: La huerta de la maternidad resiste," 27 February 2018, https://latinta.com.ar/2018/02/heraldo-resistencia-verdura-maternidad.
66. Personal interview with Manuel.
67. Sitrin, "Horizontalidad, autogestión."
68. Maeckelbergh, "Doing Is Believing."

69. Benito, "Autogestión cultural," 75.
70. *Autogestión* emerges from autonomous politics. For more on autonomy, see the introduction and Chapter 5.
71. Proyecto Squatters, "About," Facebook, accessed 2 June 2019, https://www.facebook.com/ElSquatt/about.
72. Serafini, "Mediating Identities."
73. Proyecto Squatters, "La plaza es nuestra!!"
74. Personal conversation with Julián Pellegrini, 3 August 2017.
75. Pellegrini, "Contrapublicidad."
76. Benito, "Autogestión cultural," 81.
77. Ibid., 84.
78. Lekakis, "Culture Jamming," 14.
79. Zukin, "Gentrification."
80. See the UN resolution "International Year of Creative Economy for Sustainable Development, 2021," doc. number A/C.2/74/L.16/Rev.1, here: https://undocs.org/A/C.2/74/L.16/Rev.1

## CHAPTER 5

1. Escobar, "Territorios de diferencia," 35.
2. Escobar, *Designs*, 175, emphasis in the original.
3. Dinerstein, *The Politics of Autonomy*.
4. Serafini, *Performance Action*.
5. Pautasso, "Apuntes."
6. Petroni, "Estrategias de resiliencia," 312–13.
7. The group took its name from the 1968 collective artistic action *Tucumán Arde*, which denounced the critical economic situation of the province of Tucumán at the time.
8. Feldman, "Los colectivos artísticos."
9. Giunta, *Poscrisis*.
10. Bell, "Recycling Materials."
11. Wortman, "Políticas culturales."
12. See for instance Zamorano, "La transformación."
13. "Modelo" here refers to the progressive political project of *Kirchnerismo*.
14. Hardt and Negri, *Empire*.
15. Hardt and Negri, "Empire, Twenty Years On," 67.
16. Harvey and Paik, "How Capital Operates."
17. Elden, "The State of Territory," 56.
18. Conway and Singh, "Radical Democracy," 689.
19. Goñi, "Argentina Gets Biggest Loan."
20. Carta Abierta is a space that emerged in 2008 during the progressive government of Cristina Fernández de Kirchner during the time of the so-called "conflict of the countryside," when the government attempted to increase import taxes on agriculture and farming and met strong resistance from large-scale producers. The collective expressed their support for the government's proposed measures, and since then they

have published a series of open letters responding to social and political events, which have been adhered to by supporters of *Kirchnerismo* as well as nonaligned intellectuals. The collective had different commissions including one for artists and writers, and was eventually disbanded in 2019.

21. Carta Abierta, "Un freno."
22. Carta Abierta, "Un freno."
23. Medina, "Malvenido FMI."
24. Personal interview with Mario and Bettina, 9 August 2017. Mario is a pseudonym.
25. Personal interview with Mario.
26. See a video recording the action and featuring the participating artists here: La Ala Accionista, *Procesión pagana del Plumero de La Pampa - Cumbre de los Pueblos -* , 2 December 2019, https://www.facebook.com/laalaaccionista/videos/2404746733111614.
27. Serafini, *Performance Action*.
28. Conway and Singh, "Radical Democracy," 700.
29. Svampa, "Cuatro claves," 52.
30. Assies, "Los pueblos indígenas," 242.
31. Svampa, "Cuatro claves," 53.
32. Assies, "Los pueblos indígenas," 230; Svampa, "Cuatro claves," 55.
33. Tola, "El 'giro ontológico,'" 137.
34. Personal interview with Lefxaru Nahuel, 28 August 2017.
35. Ramos, "Los caminos," 63–64.
36. Machado Aráoz, "Ecología política," 23. Emphasis in the original.
37. Personal interview with Silvina and Ricardo, 4 April 2018.
38. Personal interview via Skype with Mariana Katz, 3 February 2018.
39. Personal interview with Sergio, 29 March 2018.
40. Personal interview with Sergio.
41. Serafini, "Community Radio."
42. Personal interview via telephone with Ruth, 10 March 2018.
43. Aranda, "Una cumbre."
44. Resumen Latinoamericano, "Argentina: Cumbre latinoamericana."
45. Bakhtin, *Rebelais*; Graeber, *Possibilities*; Tancons, "Occupy Wall Street."
46. Ponce de León, *Another Aesthetics*, 244.
47. Ibid., emphasis in the original.
48. Hardt and Negri, "Empire Twenty Years On," 68.

## CHAPTER 6

1. Jeffrey and Dyson, "Geographies," 2, 5.
2. Escobar, *Designs*.
3. Svampa and Viale, *El colapso ecológico*, 19.
4. Tlostanova, "On Decolonizing Design," 51.
5. Illich, *Tools for Conviviality*; Escobar, *Designs*, 118.
6. Tlostanova, "On Decolonizing Design," 52–53.

7. See for instance Escobar, *Designs*, 90, 96.
8. Tsing, "Arts of Inclusion," 201.
9. Jeffrey and Dyson, "Geographies," 3.
10. Altieri and Toledo, "The Agroecological Revolution."
11. Goulet et al., "La agroecología," 141.
12. Ibid., 144.
13. See the UTT's Facebook page for their account of the incident: "Gas y balas contra el Verdurazo en capital," Facebook, 16 February 2019, https://www.facebook.com/trabajadoresdelatierra/posts/1029542270569348.
14. Unión de Trabajadores de la Tierra, "¿Quiénes Somos?"
15. Rosales de la Quintana, "La agroecología como política,"
16. Proyecto Artigas received support from many sectors of the antiextractivist movement. However, there were also critiques around the fact that Dolores's fight for her inheritance (which would include the donation of 40 percent to the project) was still perpetuating a system that allows the concentration of land and wealth and its sustainment across time.
17. Proyecto Artigas, *Modelo agrario sostenible.*
18. Risso, "Fortalecidas."
19. See for instance the *Decalogue for the Post Covid-19 Era*, in which United Cities and Local Governments (UCLG) included a section on proximity models of global consumption and production. It proposes that "a territorial approach to food systems should guarantee not only security but also greater sustainability models in which many small producers and small processors, respectful of the environment, would restore life to our territories and encourage job creation and local development." (United Cities and Local Governments, *Decalogue*).
20. Grasso, "Crean el primer mercado agroecológico."
21. Personal interview with Alejandra, 18 December 2017.
22. For more on *cine-debate* and socioenvironmental issues see Fernández Bouzo, "Escenas."
23. CONAMURI, "Plantío Rafael Barrett."
24. Curator Fernando Moure quoted in *ABC*, "Una Huerta."
25. The Guaraní are indigenous people native to Paraguay, Argentina, Brazil, and parts of Bolivia and Uruguay.
26. Adriana Bustos and Monica Millán, quoted in CONAMURI, "Plantío Rafael Barrett."
27. Sgaramella, "Ecologías sensibles," 673. See also Desert ArtLAB, "The Desertification Cookbook - In Progress . . . ," accessed 17 May 2020, http://www.desertartlab.com/p/cookbook.html.
28. For more on Julia's work, see her blog, *Mensch*, at http://julia-mensch.blogspot.com.
29. For Marcos's description of food sovereignty and its relation to human rights, see Chapter 3.
30. Personal interview with Marcos Filardi, 20 December 2017.
31. Svampa and Viale, *El colapso ecológico*, 19.

32. Escobar, *Designs*.
33. Permaculture collapses distinct approaches to building and resource management in urban and rural settings, from environmental engineering and similar fields of knowledge toward a more transdisciplinary approach that also involves art and design. What is notable in the permaculture approach is its principle of interactive observation of the environment, which shifts the weight from theoretical knowledge to situated approaches that begin with interaction and knowledge of the environment. See Beilin and Aras-López, "Introduction," 18; Goulet et al., "La agroecología," 142.
34. Goulet et al., "La agroecología," 144.
35. Corbetta, "Pensamiento ambiental latinoamericano," 166.
36. Personal interview with Silvina Corbetta, 10 August 2017.
37. Valle, "El ecofeminismo," 32.
38. Álvarez Mullally, "El resurgir del consenso."
39. Personal interview with Pablo Sessano, 3 April, 2018
40. Personal interview with Silvia Leanza, 24 August 2017.
41. Personal interview with Silvina Corbetta.
42. Ibid.
43. Personal interview with Pablo Sessano.
44. Ibid.
45. Galano, "Entrevista," 27.
46. See Chapter 5 for more on the Mapuche cultural and socioenvironmental struggles.
47. Personal interview with Fernando Cabrera, 28 August 2017.
48. Personal interview via Skype with Germán Ciari, 8 March 2017.
49. Sessano, "La educación ambiental," 108.
50. Leff, "La complejidad ambiental," 8.
51. As I was completing this chapter, in May 2021 the Argentine Senate approved the Environmental Education Law, after decades of failed attempts at such projects. It remains to be seen how the integral environmental education program it stipulates is implemented across different education levels, and to what effects.
52. Kester, *Conversation Pieces*.
53. Serafini, *Performance Action*.
54. Banks and Serafini, "Towards Post-Growth Creative Economies?"; Bell, "Recycling Materials."
55. Iconoclasistas, "Mapeos colectivos," 192.
56. For discussions and genealogies of the organizing of artists as workers see Sholette, *Dark Matter*; Serafini, Holtaway, and Cossu, *artWORK*.
57. Gross and Wilson, "Cultural Democracy."
58. Segato, *Contra-pedagogías*.
59. CRIA, "Sobre la Criatura."
60. Ibid.
61. Cabezas, "Radioteatro La Compañía."
62. Hardt and Negri, "Empire, Twenty Years On," 79.

63. Massidda, "Utopian Visions," 145; Segato, *La guerra*, 26.
64. Gago, *La potencia feminista*, 98.
65. Hardt and Negri, "Empire, Twenty Years On," 81.
66. Observatorio Petrolero Sur, "En América Latina."
67. See for instance Sultana, "Climate Change, COVID-19"; Merlinsky, "La pandemia como crisis ecopolítica."
68. Svampa and Viale, "A View."
69. Pacto Ecosocial del Sur, "Inicio."
70. Jordana, "False Hopes."
71. Demos, *Beyond the World's End*, 18.

## CONCLUSION

1. Serafini, *Performance Action*.
2. Escobar, *Pluriversal Politics*, xiii.
3. See, for instance, the issue on art of the magazine *Ecología política* (no. 57), published in 2019, and the book *Arte y ecología política* by Merlinsky and Serafini from 2020.
4. Molinari, "El manto."
5. Amich, *Precarious Forms*, 4.
6. Kapadia, *Insurgent Aesthetics*, 12. For more on visuality and regimes of visibility see also the work of Nicholas Mirzoeff.
7. Ballard, "New Ecological Sympathies"; Doyle, "Seeing the Climate?"
8. Doyle, 285.
9. Stallabrass, *Documentary*.
10. Forensic Architecture, *Hacia una Estética*. Part art, part academic research, and with a social and technical purpose in mind, the work of Forensic Architecture uses architectural knowledge, archives and documentation of cases involving human rights and environmental violations, and a series of visualization techniques to generate knowledge that can help viewers better understand certain cases, or even act as official evidence in legal procedures. For more on Forensic Architecture see Chapter 1.
11. Gómez and Mignolo, *Estéticas decoloniales*, 8.
12. Rancière, *Dissensus*.
13. Derrida, "Force of Law"; Glendinning, "Derrida."
14. Nash, "The Feminist Production," 66.
15. Ibid., 67.
16. Gago, *La potencia feminista*, 131.
17. Ibid., 187.
18. Mignolo and Vázquez, "Decolonial AestheSis."
19. Castro-Gómez and Grosfoguel, *El giro decolonial*; Sousa Santos, *Epistemologías del sur*.
20. Mignolo and Vázquez, "Decolonial AestheSis."
21. Gómez and Mignolo, *Estéticas decoloniales*, 8.
22. Ibid., 9.
23. Winograd and Flores, *Understanding Computers*; Escobar, *Designs*, 113.

24. Tola, "El 'giro ontológico,'" 131.
25. Escobar, *Designs*, 70.
26. See Sitrin, "Horizontalidad," and Maeckelbergh, "Doing Is Believing."
27. For a brief but insightful proposal for postextractivist aesthetics see Roesch, "Propuesta para un regimen estético post-extractivista."
28. Gómez-Barris, *The Extractive Zone*, 1.
29. Gago, *La potencia feminista*, 46.
30. Escobar, *Pluriversal Politics.*
31. Ibid., xvii.
32. Svampa and Viale, *El colápso ecológico*, 14.

# BIBLIOGRAPHY

*ABC*. "Una huerta para convocar a la reflexión sobre la tierra." 20 December 2019. https://www.abc.com.py/edicion-impresa/artes-espectaculos/2019/12/20/una-huerta-para-convocar-a-la-reflexion-sobre-la-tierra.

Aizura, Aren Z. *Mobile Subjects: Transnational Imaginaries of Gender Reassignment*. Durham, NC: Duke University Press, 2018.

Aliaga, Cristian. "The Land 'Wars' in Twenty-First Century Patagonia." *Journal of Latin American Cultural Studies* 28, no. 1 (2019): 139–51.

Alimonda, Héctor. "Notas sobre la ecología política latinoamericana: Arraigo, herencias, diálogos." *Ecología Política*, no. 51 (2016): 36–42.

Alonso, Rodrigo, and Valeria Gonzáles. *Ansia y devoción*. Buenos Aires: Fundación Proa.

Altieri, Miguel, and Victor M. Toledo. "The Agroecological Revolution of Latin America: Rescuing Nature, Securing Food Sovereignty and Empowering Peasants." *Journal of Peasant Studies* 38, no. 3 (2011): 587–612.

Altschuler, Bárbara. "Territorio y desarrollo: Aportes de la geografía y otras disciplinas para repensarlos." *Theomai*, no. 27–28 (2013): 64–79.

Alvado, María Alicia. "'El costo humano de los agrotóxicos,' fotografías que proponen 'abrir los ojos.'" *Telam*, 9 March 2019. https://www.telam.com.ar/notas/201603/138955-agrotoxicos-muestra-fotografica.html.

Álvarez Mullally, Martín. "El resurgir del consenso del fracking: Publicitar no es educar (Parte II)." *Observatorio Petrolero Sur*, 27 June 2018. https://opsur.org.ar/2018/06/27/el-resurgir-del-consenso-del-fracking-publicitar-no-es-educar-parte-ii.

Álvarez Mullally, Martín, Lisandro Arelovich, Fernando Cabrera, and Diego Di Riso. *Megaproyecto Vaca Muerta: Informe de externalidades*. Buenos Aires: EJES–Enlace por la Justicia Energética y Socioambiental, 2017. https://ejes.org.ar/InformeExternalidades.pdf.

Amich, Candice. *Precarious Forms: Performing Utopia in the Neoliberal Americas*. Evanston, IL: Northwestern University Press.

Andermann, Jens. "Turn of the Tide? Cultural Critique and the New Right." *Journal of Latin American Cultural Studies* 27, no.1 (2018): 1–3.

Aranda, Darío. *Tierra arrasada: Petróleo, soja, pasteras y megaminería: Radiografía de la Argentina del siglo XXI*. Buenos Aires: Sudestada, 2015.

———. "Una cumbre por el derecho al agua." *Página12*, 17 September 2018. https://www.pagina12.com.ar/142737-una-cumbre-por-el-derecho-al-agua.

Assies, Willem. "Los pueblos indígenas, la tierra, el territorio y la autonomía en tiempos de globalización." In *Pueblos indígenas y política en América Latina: El reconocimiento de sus derechos y el impacto de sus demandas a inicios del siglo XXI*, edited by S. Martí i Puig, 227–46. Barcelona: Fundación CIDOB, 2007.

Bakhtin, Mikhail. *Rabelais and His World*. Cambridge, MA: MIT Press, 1968.

Ballard, Susan. "New Ecological Sympathies: Thinking about Contemporary Art in the Age of Extinction." *Environmental Humanities* 9, no. 2 (2018): 255–79.

Bang, Claudia, and Carolina Wajnerman. "Arte y transformación social: La importancia de la creación colectiva en intervenciones comunitarias." *Revista argentina de psicología*, no. 48 (2010): 89–103.

Banks, Mark, and Paula Serafini. "Towards Post-Growth Creative Economies? Building Sustainable Cultural Production in Argentina." In *The Industrialization of Creativity and Its Limits*, edited by Iliya Kiriya, Yiannis Mylonas, and Panos Kompatsiaris, 17–28. Cham: Springer, 2020.

Barrese, Lía, and Montserrat Pareja-Eastaway. "*Glocalisation* Dynamics: The Appropriation of the 'Creative Turn' Discourse in Buenos Aires, Argentina (2007–2015)." *City, Culture and Society*, no. 21 (2020): 1–4.

Basualdo, Lourdes, Eduardo Domenech, and Evangelina Pérez. "Territorios de la movilidad en disputa: Cartografías críticas para el análisis de las migraciones y las fronteras en el espacio." *Revista interdisciplinar da mobilidade humana* 27, no. 57 (2019): 43–60.

Bauhardt, Christine. "Rethinking Gender and Nature from a Material(ist) Perspective: Feminist Economics, Queer Ecologies and Resource Politics." *European Journal of Women's Studies* 20, no. 4 (2013): 361–75.

Bavikatte, Kabir Sanjay, and Tom Bennett. "Community Stewardship: The Foundations of Biocultural Rights." *Journal of Human Rights and the Environment* 6, no. 1 (2015): 7–29.

Beilin, Kata, and Daniel Ares-López. "Introduction: Environmental Cultural Studies as a Transdisciplinary Field: Latin American and Iberian Studies." In *Environmental Cultural Studies through Time: The Luso-Hispanic World*, edited by Kata Beilin, Kathleen Connolly, and Micah McKay, 1–26. Hispanic Issues On Line, vol. 24. Minneapolis: College of Liberal Arts, University of Minnesota, 2019. https://cla.umn.edu/hispanic-issues/online/environmental-cultural-studies-through-time-luso-hispanic-world.

Bell, Lucy. "Recycling Materials, Recycling Lives: Cardboard Publishers in Latin America," In *Literature and Sustainability: Concept, Text and Culture*, edited by Adeline Johns-Putra, John Parham, and Louise Squire, 76–96. Manchester: Manchester University Press, 2017.

Benito, Karina. "Autogestión cultural en la ciudad de Buenos Aires." *European Review of Artistic Studies* 8, no. 1 (2017): 74–91.

Benjamin, Walter. "The Author as Producer." *New Left Review* 1, no. 62 (1970): 83–96.

Bishop, Claire. "Introduction: Viewers as Producers," In *Participation: Documents of Contemporary Art*, edited by Claire Bishop, 10–17. London: Whitechapel Ventures Limited, 2006.

Blank, Martina. "De-Fetishizing the Analysis of Spatial Movement Strategies: Polymorphy and *trabajo territorial* in Argentina." *Political Geography*, no. 50 (2016): 1–9.

Blaseotto, Azul. "Una historia de abajo hacia arriba." In Merlinsky and Serafini, *Arte y ecología política*, 57–80.

Blaser, Mario. "Political Ontology." *Cultural Studies* 23, no. 5–6 (2009): 873–96.

———. *Storytelling Globalization from the Chaco and Beyond*. Durham, NC: Duke University Press, 2010.

Boyce Kay, Jilly. "'Stay the Fuck at Home!': Feminism, Family and the Private Home in a Time of Coronavirus." *Feminist Media Studies* 20, no. 6 (2020): 883–88. DOI: 10.1080/14680777.2020.1765293.

Buitrago Restrepo, Pedro Felipe, and Iván Duque Márquez. *The Orange Economy: An Infinite Opportunity*. Bogota: Inter-American Development Bank, and Puntoaparte Bookvertising, 2013.

Cabezas, Erika Eliana. "Radioteatro La Compañía: Una ficción federal de la comunicación popular." *Radio Gráfica*, 2 August 2020. https://radiografica.org.ar/2020/08/02/radioteatro-la-compania-una-ficcion-federal-de-la-comunicacion-popular.

Cabrapan Duarte, Melisa Gisel. "Comercio sexual en contextos extractivos: La casita de chapa de YPF y la prostitución reglamentada." *Identidades* 14, no. 8 (2018): 97–118.

de la Cadena, Marisol. "Indigenous Cosmopolitics in the Andes: Conceptual Reflections beyond 'Politics.'" *Cultural Anthropology* 25, no. 2 (2010): 334–70.

Capella Giannattasio, Arthur Roberto. "International Human Rights: A Dystopian Utopia." *Archives for Philosophy of Law and Social Philosophy* 100, no. 4 (2014): 514–26.

Capps, Kriston. "Bernie Sanders and AOC Unveil a Green New Deal for Public Housing." *Grist*, 16 November 2019. https://grist.org/politics/bernie-sanders-and-aoc-unveil-a-green-new-deal-for-public-housing.

Carlassare, Elizabeth. "Socialist and Cultural Ecofeminism: Allies in Resistance." *Ethics and the Environment* 5, no. 1 (2000): 89–106.

Carpizo, Jorge. "Los derechos humanos: Naturaleza, denominación y características." *Cuestiones constitucionales: Revista mexicana de derecho constitucional*, no. 25 (2011): 3–29.

Carta Abierta. "Un freno al acuerdo con el FMI." *Página12*, 11 June 2018. https://www.pagina12.com.ar/120773-un-freno-al-acuerdo-con-el-fmi.

Castro-Gómez, Santiago, and Ramón Grosfoguel, eds. *El giro decolonial: Reflexiones para una diversidad epistémica más allá del capitalismo global.* Bogotá: Siglo del Hombre Editores- Universidad Central-Pontificia Universidad Javeriana, 2007.

Castro-Sotomayor, José. "Territorialidad as Environmental Communication." *Annals of the International Communication Association* 44, no. 1 (2020): 50–66.

Cazas, Anahì, and Eliana Flores. "Polémico mural de Mujeres Creando provoca protestas." *Página Siete*, 12 October 2016. https://www.paginasiete.bo/cultura/2016/10/12/polemico-mural-mujeres-creando-provoca-protestas-113075.html.

CELS. "Monsanto y la privatización de las semillas," 19 June 2018. https://www.cels.org.ar/web/2018/06/monsanto-y-la-privatizacion-de-las-semillas.

Ciudad del Deseo. "Qué/Quiénes," accessed 13 January 2021. https://www.ciudaddeldeseo.com/que-quienes.

Clarke, John. "Conjunctures, Crises, and Cultures: Valuing Stuart Hall." *Focaal*, no. 70 (2014): 113–22.

Colectivo Situaciones. *On the Researcher-Militant.* Translation by Sebastian Touza, 2003. http://eipcp.net/transversal/0406/colectivosituaciones/en.

CONAMURI. "Plantío Rafael Barrett," 18 December 2019. https://www.conamuri.org.py/plantio-rafael-barrett.

Conway, Janet, and Jakeet Singh. "Radical Democracy in Global Perspective: Notes from the Pluriverse." *Third World Quarterly* 32, no. 4 (2011): 689–706. DOI: 10.1080/01436597.2011.570029.

Corbetta, Silvina. "Pensamiento ambiental latinoamericano y educación ambiental." *Voces en el fénix* 6, no. 43 (2006): 160–67.

Crenzel, Emilio. "Historia y memoria: Reflexiones desde la investigación." *Aletheia* 1, no. 1 (2010).

CRIA. "Sobre La Criatura 2018," accessed 12 January 2021. https://lacria.org/criatura18-statement.

Cuestas-Caza, Javier. "Sumak Kawsay Is Not Buen Vivir." *Alternautas* 5, no. 1 (2018): 51–65.

Curtin, Deane. "Toward an Ecological Ethic of Care." *Ecological Feminism* 6, no. 1 (1991): 60–74.

D'Alo Abba, Pablo. "Vienen por el oro, vienen por todo: Retrato cinematográfico del pueblo de Esquel en su lucha contra la megaminería." In Merlinsky and Serafini, *Arte y ecología política*, 129–42.

De Angelis, Massimo. "Commons." In *Pluriverse: A Post-Development Dictionary*, edited by Ashish Kothari, Ariel Salleh, Arturo Escobar, Federico Demaria, and Alberto Acosta, 124–26. Delhi: Tulika Books, 2019.

Del Valle Rojas, Juan Alfredo, and Claudio Andrés Maldonado Rivera. "El discurso del periódico digital mapuche Werken.cl en torno al territorio:

Una aproximación semiótico-decolonial." *Chasqui: Revista latinoamericana de comunicación*, no. 132 (2016): 329–50.

Demos, T. J. *Beyond the World's End: Arts of Living at the Crossing*. Durham, NC: Duke University Press, 2020.

Derrida, Jacques. *Positions*. Translated and annotated by Alan Bass. Chicago: University of Chicago Press, 1982.

———. "Force of Law: The 'Mystical Foundations of Authority.'" In *Deconstruction and the Possibility of Justice*, edited by Drucilla Cornell, Michel Rosenfeld, and David Carlson, 3–67. London: Routledge, 1992.

Di Liscia, María Herminia Beatriz. "Mujeres en los movimientos sociales en Argentina: Un balance del último siglo." *Cuadernos de estudios latino-americanos*, no. 6 (2008): 141–80.

Diawara, Mamadou. "Globalization, Development Politics and Local Knowledge." *International Sociology* 15, no. 2 (2000): 361–71.

Dinardi, Cecilia. "Unsettling the Role of Culture as Panacea: The Politics of Culture-Led Urban Regeneration in Buenos Aires." *City, Culture and Society*, no. 6 (2015): 9–18.

Dinerstein, Ana C. *The Politics of Autonomy in Latin America: The Art of Organizing Hope*. Basingstoke: Palgrave Macmillan, 2015.

Dos Santos, Theotonio. *La estructura de la dependencia*. Buenos Aires: Ediciones Periferia, 1975.

Doyle, Julie. "Seeing the Climate?: The Problematic Status of Visual Evidence in Climate Change Campaigning." In *Ecosee: Image, Rhetoric, and Nature*, edited by Sidney Dobrin and Sean Morey, 279–98. Albany: State University of New York Press, 2009.

Dussel, Enrique. "Transmodernity and Interculturality: An Interpretation from the Perspective of Philosophy of Liberation." *TRANSMODERNITY: Journal of Peripheral Cultural Production of the Luso-Hispanic World* 1, no. 3 (2012): 28–59.

Eissa, Sergio G. "Construyendo al enemigo: La securitización del reclamo mapuche (agosto-diciembre de 2017)." *Perspectivas revista de ciencias sociales* 3, no. 5 (2018): 35–61.

El Chubut. *Fuerte respaldo del equipo directivo del IES 818 a la intervención artística de Chugo*, 20 November 2017. https://www.elchubut.com.ar/nota/2017-11-19-23-45-33-fuerte-respaldo-del-equipo-directivo-del-ies-818-a-la-intervencion-artistica-de-chugo.

Elden, Stuart. "The State of Territory under Globalization: *Empire* and the Politics of Reterritorialization." *Thamyris/Intersecting*, no. 12 (2006): 47–66.

EQSNotas. "Campaña del Desierto: Un artista intervino monumentos en Esquel," 13 November 2017. https://www.eqsnotas.com/campana-del-desierto-un-artista-intervino-monumentos-en-esquel.

Equipo Programa Arte y Territorio. "Arte en territorio." *El Conti*, 2017. http://conti.derhuman.jus.gov.ar/2017/09/av-arte-territorio.php.

Escobar, Arturo. "El 'postdesarrollo' como concepto y práctica social." In *Políticas de economía, ambiente y sociedad en tiempos de globalización*, edited by Daniel Mato, 17–31. Caracas: Facultad de Ciencias Económicas y Sociales, Universidad Central de Venezuela, 2005.

———. *Territories of Difference: Place, Movements, Life, Redes*. Durham, NC: Duke University Press, 2008.

———. *Sentipensar con la tierra: Nuevas lecturas sobre desarrollo, territorio y diferencia*. Medellín: Ediciones UNAULA, 2014.

———. "Territorios de diferencia: La ontología política de los 'derechos al territorio.'" *Cuadernos de Antropología Social*, no. 41 (2015): 25–38.

———. *Designs for the Pluriverse: Radical Interdependence, Autonomy and the Making of Worlds*. Durham, NC: Duke University Press, 2018.

———. *Pluriversal Politics: The Real and the Possible*. Durham, NC: Duke University Press, 2020.

Fagan, G. Honor. "Cultural Politics and (Post)Development Paradigm(s)." In *Critical Development Theory: Contributions to a New Paradigm*, edited by Ronaldo Munck and Denis O'Hearn, 178–95. London: Zed Books, 1999.

Fals Borda, Orlando. *Una sociología sentipensante para América Latina*. Buenos Aires: CLACSO, 2009.

Fanon, Franz. *The Wretched of the Earth*. New York: Grove Weidenfeld, 1991 [1963].

Federici, Silvia. *Revolution at Point Zero: Housework, Reproduction, and Feminist Struggle*. Oakland: PM Press, 2012.

Feierstein, Daniel. *Genocide as Social Practice: Reorganizing Society under the Nazis and Argentina's Military Juntas*. New Brunswick: Rutgers University Press, 2014.

Feldman, Jonathan. "Los colectivos artísticos y una mirada acerca de la crisis de 2001: El caso de Arde! Arte, 2001–2006." *Artilugio*, no. 5 (2019): 115–32.

Fernández Bouzo, Soledad. "Escenas de la cuestión ambiental en Argentina: El proceso de producción, circulación y uso de documentales ambientales y su impacto en la construcción socio-política del ambiente (2007–2014)." *Quid 16*, no. 6 (2016): 333–37.

Florida, Richard. *The Rise of the Creative Class*. New York: Basic, 2002.

———. *The New Urban Crisis*. London: Oneworld, 2017.

Forensic Architecture. "Ape Law." 22 October 2016. https://forensic-architecture.org/investigation/ape-law.

———. *Hacia una estética investigativa*. Barcelona: MACBA, 2017.

Foucault, Michel. *The Birth of Biopolitics: Lectures at the Collège de France, 1978–1979*. Edited by Michel Senellart. New York: Palgrave MacMillan, 2010.

Fry, Tony. "Design for/by 'the Global South.'" *Design Philosophy Papers* 15, no. 1 (2017): 3–37.

Gago, Carla. "Al extractivismo, un puño feminista." *Revista Cítrica*, 26 December 2019. https://www.revistacitrica.com/al-extractivismo-un-puno-feminista.html.

Gago, Verónica. *La potencia feminista: O el deseo de cambiarlo todo*. Madrid: Traficantes de Sueños, 2019.

Galano, Carlos. "Entrevista a Carlos Galano: Educación ambiental: Morada de la vida." *Anales de la Educación Común* 3, no. 8 (2007): 26–33.

Galindo, María. *No se puede descolonizar sin despatriarcalizar: Teoría y propuesta de la despatriarcalización*. La Paz: Mujeres Creando, 2013.

Gargallo Celentani, Francesca. *Feminismos desde Abya Yala: Ideas y proposiciones de las mujeres de 607 pueblos en nuestra América*. Mexico City: Editorial Corte y Confección, 2013.

GER-GEMSAL. "Bienes comunes en la hegemonía extractivista: Disputas y resistencias." In *Actividades extractivas en expansión: ¿Reprimarización de la economía argentina?*, edited by Norma Giarracca, and Miguel Teubal, 413–22. Buenos Aires: Antropofagia, 2013.

Giarracca, Norma. "El movimiento de mujeres agropecuarias en Lucha: Protesta agraria y género durante el último lustro en Argentina." In *Una nueva ruralidad en América Latina*, edited by Norma Giarracca, Edelmira C. Pérez, María de Nazareth Baudel Wanderley, and Miguel Teubal, 129–51. Buenos Aires: CLACSO, 2001.

Giunta, Andrea. *Poscrisis: Arte argentino despues de 2001*. Buenos Aires: Siglo XXI, 2009.

Glendinning, Simon. "Derrida and the Philosophy of Law and Justice." *Law and Critique* 27, no. 2 (July 2016): 187–203.

Gomes, "Mujeres afrodescendientes en la Argentina." *Haroldo*, 25 July 2020. https://revistaharoldo.com.ar/nota.php?id=495.

Gómez, Pedro P., and Walter Mignolo. *Estéticas decoloniales*. Bogotá: Universidad Distrital Francisco José de Caldas, 2012.

Gómez-Barris, Macarena. *The Extractive Zone: Social Ecologies and Decolonial Perspectives*. Durham, NC: Duke University Press, 2017.

Gómez-Barris, Macarena. *Beyond the Pink Tide: Art and Political Undercurrents in the Americas*. Oakland, CA: University of California Press.

González Ortuño, Gabriela. "Teorías de la disidencia sexual: De contextos populares a usos elitistas: La teoría queer en América latina frente a las y los pensadores de disidencia sexogenérica." *De raíz diversa: Revista especializada en estudios latinoamericanos* 3, no. 5 (2016): 179–200.

Goñi, Uki. "Argentina Gets Biggest Loan in IMF's History at $57bn." *Guardian*, 27 September 2018. https://www.theguardian.com/world/2018/sep/26/argentina-imf-biggest-loan.

Goodale, Mark. "Toward a Critical Anthropology of Human Rights." *Current Anthropology* 47, no. 3 (2006): 485–511.

Goulet, Frédéric, Danièle Magda, Nathalie Girard, and Valeria Hernández. "La agroecología y la cuestión de la convivencia de modelos de desarrollo agrícola." In *La agroecología en Argentina y en Francia: miradas cruzadas*, edited by Valeria Hernández, Frédéric Goulet, Danièle Magda, and Nathalie Girard, 141–47. Buenos Aires: INTA, 2014.

Graeber, David. *Possibilities: Essays on Hierarchy, Rebellion and Desire*. Oakland, CA: AK Press, 2007.

Grasso, Agustina. "Crean el primer mercado agroecológico del Conurbano que busca ser referente en el país." *Perfil*, 9 June 2020. https://www.perfil.com/noticias/sociedad/crean-primer-mercado-agroecologico-del-conurbano-busca-ser-referente-en-argentina.phtml.

Grear, Anna. "The Discourse of 'Biocultural' Rights and the Search for New Epistemic Parameters: Moving beyond Essentialisms and Old Certainties in an Age of Anthropocene Complexity?" *Journal of Human Rights and the Environment* 6, no. 1 (2015): 1–6.

Grosfoguel, Ramón. "The Epistemic Decolonial Turn." *Cultural Studies* 21, no. 2–3 (2017): 211–23.

Gross, Jonathan, and Nick Wilson. "Cultural Democracy: An Ecological and Capabilities Approach." *International Journal of Cultural Policy* 26, no. 3 (2020): 328–43, DOI: 10.1080/10286632.2018.1538363.

Grupo de Arte Callejero. *Pensamientos, prácticas, acciones*. Buenos Aires: Tinta Limón, 2009.

Gudynas, Eduardo. "Diez tesis urgentes sobre el nuevo extractivismo: Contextos y demandas bajo el progresismo sudamericano actual." In *Extractivismo, política y sociedad*, by Jürgen Schuldt, Alberto Acosta, Alberto Barandiarán, Anthony Bebbington, Mauricio Folchi, CEDLA–Bolivia, Alejandra Alayza, and Eduardo Gudynas, 187–225. Quito, Ecuador: CAAP and CLAES, 2009.

———. "Más allá del nuevo extractivismo: Transiciones sostenibles y alternativas al desarrollo." In *El desarrollo en cuestión: Reflexiones desde América Latina*, edited by Fernanda Wanderley, 379–410. La Paz: Oxfam and CIDES UMSA, 2011.

Gutiérrez Ríos, Felipe. "Kintu newen, buscando la fuerza: La recuperación de la voz mapuche en el conflicto energético a partir de la experiencia de la banda Puel Kona." In Merlinsky and Serafini, *Arte y ecología política*, 163–76.

Halbwachs, Maurice. *Los marcos sociales de la memoria*. Barcelona: Anthropos, 2004 [1925].

Halvorsen, Sam. "Decolonising Territory: Dialogues with Latin American Knowledges and Grassroots Strategies." *Progress in Human Geography* 43, no. 5 (2019): 790–814.

Haraway, Donna. *Staying with the Trouble: Making Kin in the Chthulucene*. Durham, NC: Duke University Press, 2016

Hardt, Michael, and Antonio Negri. *Empire*. Cambridge, MA: Harvard University Press, 2000.

———. "Empire, Twenty Years On." *New Left Review*, no. 120 (Nov/Dec 2019): 67–92.

Hardt, Michael, and Raúl Zibechi. "La sociedad *otra* en América Latina." In *Preservar y compartir: Bienes comunes y movimientos sociales* by Raúl Zibechi and Michael Hardt. Buenos Aires: Mardulce, 2013: 15-66.

Harvey, David. *The New Imperialism*. Oxford: Oxford University Press, 2003.

———. "The Right to the City." *New Left Review*, no. 53 (Sept/Oct 2008): 23–40.

Harvey, David, and Paik Nak-chung. "How Capital Operates and Where the World and China Are Going: A Conversation Between David Harvey and Paik Nak-chung." *Inter-Asia Cultural Studies* 18, no. 2 (2017): 251–68. DOI: 10.1080/14649373.2017.1309501.

Hawkes, Jon. *The Fourth Pillar of Sustainability: Culture's Essential Role in Public Planning*. Melbourne: Cultural Development Network, 2001. http://www.culturaldevelopment.net.au/community/Downloads/HawkesJon(2001)TheFourthPillarOfSustainability.pdf.

Hemispheric Institute, "Mujeres creando," accessed 2 March 2022. https://hemisphericinstitute.org/en/hidvl/hidvl-int-wips/itemlist/category/235-mujeres-creando.html.

———. "No Woman Is Born to Be a Whore (2007)," accessed 2 March 2022, https://hemisphericinstitute.org/en/hidvl-collections/item/2215-mujeres-puta.html.

Hidalgo-Capitán, Luis, and Ana Patricia Cubillo-Guevara. "Deconstruction and Genealogy of Latin American Good Living (Buen Vivir): The (Triune) Good Living and Its Diverse Intellectual Wellsprings." In *Alternative Pathways to Sustainable Development: Lessons from Latin America*, edited by Gilles Carbonnier, Humberto Campodónico, and Sergio Tezanos Vázquez, 23–50. Leiden: Brill | Nijhoff.

Holland, Eugene W. "Deterritorializing Deterritorialization: From the Anti-Oedipus to A Thousand Plateaus." *Substance* 20, no. 3 (1991): 55–65.

Hoyos, Héctor. *Things with a History: Transcultural Materialism and the Literatures of Extraction in Contemporary Latin America.* New York: Columbia University Press, 2019.

Iconoclasistas. "Mapeos colectivos sobre extractivismos y resistencias en Latinoamérica." In Merlinsky and Serafini, *Arte y ecología política*, 177–92.

Ignatieff, Michael. "The Attack on Human Rights." *Foreign Affairs* 80, no. 6 (2001): 102–16.

Illich, Ivan. *Tools for Conviviality.* New York: Harper and Row, 1973.

Ingold, Tim. "Art and Anthropology for a Sustainable World." *Journal of the Royal Anthropological Institute* 25, no. 4 (2019): 659–75.

Independent Expert Panel for the Legal Definition of Ecocide (2021) Commentary and Core Text. Amsterdam: Stop Ecocide Foundation.

Irwin, Ruth. "Ecological Ethics in the Context of Climate Change: Feminist and Indigenous Critique of Modernity." *International Social Science Journal* 64, no. 211-210 (2013): 111–23.

Jeffrey, Craig, and Jane Dyson. "Geographies of the Future: Prefigurative Politics." *Progress in Human Geography* 45, no. 4 (2020): 641-58. DOI: 10.1177/0309132520926569.

Jelin, Elizabeth. "La política de la memoria: El Movimiento de Derechos Humanos y la construcción democrática en la Argentina." In *Juicio, castigos y memorias: Derechos humanos y justicia en la política Argentina*, by Carlos Acuña, Inés González Bombal, Elizabeth Jelin, Oscar Landi, Luis Alberto Quevedo, Catalina Smulovitz, and Adriana Vacchieri, 101–46. Buenos Aires: Editorial Nueva Visión, 1995.

Jordana, Rufus. "False Hopes for a Green New Deal." *Open Democracy*, 29 August 2019. https://www.opendemocracy.net/en/oureconomy/false-hopes-green-new-deal.

Junka-Aikio, Laura, and Catalina Cortes-Severino. "Cultural Studies of Extraction." *Cultural Studies* 31, no. 2–3 (2017): 175–84.

Kapadia, Ronak K. *Insurgent Aesthetics: Security and the Queer Life of the Forever War.* Durham NC: Duke University Press, 2019.

Kester, Grant H. *Conversation Pieces: Community and Communication in Modern Art*. Berkeley: University of California Press, 2004.

———. *The One and the Many: Contemporary Collaborative Art in a Global Context*, Durham, NC: Duke University Press, 2011.

Kidd, Dorothy. "Extra-activism: counter-mapping and data justice." *Information, Communication & Society* 22, no. 7 (2019): 954-70.

Kings, A. E. "Intersectionality and the Changing Face of Ecofeminism." *Ethics and the Environment* 22, no. 1 (2017): 63–87.

Korol, Claudia. "Somos tierra, semilla, rebeldía: Mujeres, tierra y territorios en América Latina." GRAIN, Acción por la Biodiversidad, and América Libre, 5 December 2016. https://grain.org/es/article/entries/5563-somos-tierra-semilla-rebeldia-mujerestierra-y-territorios-en-america-latina.

Korsemeyer, Carolyn. "Gut Appreciation: Possibilities for Aesthetic Disgust." *Lebenswelt*, no. 3 (2013): 186–99.

Kunin, Johana. "'Women Are Those Who Lose Their Sense of Shame': Resistance and Fulfilment of Gender Expectations in Dissident Initiatives in a Rural District of Argentina." *L'Ordinaire des Amériques*, no. 224 (2019). DOI: 10.4000/orda.4705.

Kunin, Johana, and Patricio Simonetto. "Travas, putos y tortas en el reino de la soja." *Anfibia*, 14 January 2020. http://revistaanfibia.com/ensayo/travas-putos-y-tortas-en-el-reino-de-la-soja.

Kwon, Miwon. "One Place after Another: Notes on Site Specificity." *October*, no. 80 (1997): 85–110.

———. *One Place after Another: Site-Specific Art and Locational Identity.* Cambridge, MA: MIT Press, 2002.

La Vía Campesina. "What Is Food Sovereignty?," 15 January 2003. https://viacampesina.org/en/food-sovereignty.

LaDanta LasCanta. "De la teología a antiextractivismo: ecofeminismos en Abya Yala." *Ecología Política*, no. 54 (2017): 37–43.

Latour, Bruno. *We Have Never Been Modern.* Translated by Catherine Porter. Cambridge, MA: Harvard University Press, 1993.

Lees, Loretta, Hyun Bang Shin, and Ernesto López-Morales. *Planetary Gentrification.* Cambridge, UK: Polity Press, 2016.

Lefebvre, Henri. *The Production of Space.* Oxford: Blackwell, 1991.

Leff, Enrique. "La complejidad ambiental." *Polis: Revista latinoamericana* 6, no. 16 (2007): 1–10.

Lekakis, Elefteria. "Culture Jamming and Brandalism for the Environment: The Logic of Appropriation." *Popular Communication* 15, no. 4 (2017): 311–27.

Li, Huey-li. "Ecofeminism as a Pedagogical Project: Women, Nature and Education." *Educational Theory* 57, no. 3 (2017): 351–68.

Lippard, Lucy R. *Undermining: A Wild Ride through Land Use, Politics, and Art in the Changing West.* New York: New Press, 2014.

Longoni, Ana. "Arte y política: Políticas visuales del movimiento de derechos humanos desde la última dictadura: Fotos, siluetas y escraches." *Aletheia* 1, no. 1 (2010): 1–23.

Lopes de Souza. "From the 'Right to the City' to the Right to the *Planet:* Reinterpreting Our Contemporary Challenges for Socio-Spatial Development." *City* 19, no. 4 (2015): 408–43.

Lorde, Audre. "The Master's Tools Will Never Dismantle the Master's House." *Sister Outsider: Essays and Speeches*, 110–14. Berkeley, CA: Crossing Press. 2007 [1984].

Lugones, María. "Toward a Decolonial Feminism." *Hypatia* 25, no. 4 (2010): 742–59.

Lunch, Pao. "Pornopetroleo: Transcripciones y traducciones desobedientes." *Pao Lunch* (blog), 20 March 2015. https://paolunch.wordpress.com/2015/03/20/pornopetroleo-transcripciones-y-traducciones-desobedientes.

Lutz, Ellen L., and Kathryn Sikkink. "International Human Rights Law and Practice in Latin America." *International Organization* 54, no. 3 (2000): 633–59.

Machado Aráoz, Horacio. "Ecología política de los regímenes extractivistas: De reconfiguraciones imperiales y re-exsistencias decoloniales en nuestra América." *Bajo el Volcán* 15, no. 23 (2015): 11–51.

Maeckelbergh, Marianne. "Doing Is Believing: Prefiguration as Strategic Practice in the Alterglobalization Movement." *Social Movement Studies* 10, no. 1 (2011): 1–20.

Mallory, Chaone. "What Is Ecofeminist Political Philosophy?: Gender, Nature and the Political." *Environmental Ethics* 32, no. 3 (2010): 305–22.

Martín García, Facundo. "Postextractivismo y crecimiento en América Latina: Historias, problemas y desafíos hacia una agenda de luchas comunes." In *La espacialidad crítica en el pensamiento político-social latinoamericano: Nuevas gramáticas de poder, territorialidades en tensión*, edited by Marcela Rosales, Zenaida Garay Reyna, and Carla Pedrazzani, 77–100. Buenos Aires: CLACSO, 2016.

Martínez, Esperanza, and Alberto Acosta. "Los derechos de la naturaleza como puerta de entrada a otro mundo posible." *Dereito e Práxis* 8, no. 4 (2017): 2927–61.

Martínez Alier, Joan. *The Environmentalism of the Poor: A Study of Ecological Conflicts and Valuation.* Cheltenham: Edward Elgar, 2002.

Massidda, Adriana L. "Utopian Visions for Buenos Aires Shantytowns: Collective Imaginaries of Housing Rights, Upgrading and Eviction (1956–2013)." *Bulletin of Latin American Research* 37, no. 2 (2018): 144–59.

Massuh, Gabriela. *El robo de Buenos Aires: La trama de corrupción, ineficiencia y negocios que le arrebató la ciudad a sus habitantes.* Buenos Aires: Sudamericana, 2014.

Maxwell, Richard, and Toby Miller. "Greening Cultural Policy." *International Journal of Cultural Policy* 23, no .2 (2017): 174–85.

Medina, Cecilia. "Malvenido FMI," 11 October 2019. https://www.cecilia medina.art/single-post/2019/10/11/MALVENIDO-FMI.

Merlinsky, Gabriela. "Introducción: La cuestión ambiental en la agenda pública." In *Cartografías del conflicto ambiental en Argentina*, edited by Gabriela Merlinsky, 19–60. Buenos Aires: Fundación CICCUS, 2013.

———. *Políticas, derechos y justicia ambiental: El conflicto del Riachuelo.* Buenos Aires: Fondo de Cultura Económica, 2013.

———. "La pandemia como crisis ecopolítica: Desafíos de investigación." Consejo Latinoamericano de Ciencias Sociales (CLACSO), 16 June 2020. https://www.clacso.org/en/la-pandemia-como-crisis-ecopolitica-desafios-de-investigacion.

Merlinsky, Gabriela, Facundo Martín, and Melina Tobías. "Presentación del Dossier #13: Hacia la conformación de una ecología política del agua en América Latina: Enfoques y agendas de investigación." *Quid 16*, no. 13 (2020): 1–11.

Merlinsky, Gabriela, and Paula Serafini. *Arte y ecología política.* Buenos Aires: IIGG-CLACSO, 2020.

Meyer, Adriana. "Finalizó la ocupación de las mujeres indígenas en el Ministerio del Interior." *Página12*, 19 October 2019. https://www.pagina12.com.ar/226223-finalizo-la-ocupacion-de-las-mujeres-indigenas-en-el-ministe.

Mezzadra, Sandro, and Brett Neilson. "On the Multiple Frontiers of Extraction: Excavating Contemporary Capitalism." *Cultural Studies* 31, no. 2–3 (2017): 185–204.

Mignolo, Walter, and Rolando Vázquez. "Decolonial AestheSis: Colonial Wounds/Decolonial Healings." *Social Text*, July 15, 2013. https://socialtextjournal.org/periscope_article/decolonial-aesthesis-colonial-wounds decolonial-healings.

Milder, Patricia. "Teaching as Art: The Contemporary Lecture-Performance." *PAJ: Journal of Performance and Art* 33, no. 1 (2010): 13–27.

Millán, Moira. "El extractivismo cultural es la sustracción de un saber o arte ancestral para destruirlo." *Revista Resistencias*, 24 February 2020. https://revistaresistencias.wixsite.com/resistencias/post/el-extractivismo-cultural-es-la-sustracci%C3%B3n-de-un-saber-o-arte-ancestral-para-destruirlo.

Miradas Críticas del Territorio desde el Feminismo. "Sobre Nosotras," accessed 12 January 2021. https://territorioyfeminismos.org/about..

———. *Mapeando el cuerpo-territorio: Guía metodológica para mujeres que defienden sus territorios.* Quito: Miradas Críticas del Territorio desde el Feminismo; Red Universitaria de Mujeres Defensoras de Derechos Sociales y Ambientales; Instituto de Estudios Ecologistas del Tercer Mundo; CLACSO, 2017.

Molinari, Eduardo. "Producción y transferencia de saberes y conocimientos desde el Taller Proyectual Pintura." In *Investigación y construcción de pensamiento con herramientas artísticas: Cuadernos de investigación*, by Eduardo Molinari, Mario Bolchinsky, Mercedes Fidanza, and Paula Arellano, 7–22. Buenos Aires: Universidad Nacional de las Artes, 2015.

———. "El manto: Nuevas noticias de la República Unida de la soja." In *Territorios en conflicto*, edited by Fabián Díaz, Ariel Farace, Andrés Gallina, Carlos Gamerro, Gabriela Massuh, and Alejandro Tantanian, 19–34. Buenos Aires: Teatro Nacional Cervantes, 2017.

———. "El manto tóxico." In Merlinsky and Serafini, *Arte y Ecología Política*, 43–56.

Molinari, Eduardo, Estefanía Bellucci, Cristian Espinoza, Florencia Fernández Frank, Josefina Francia, Santiago Fredes, Carla Hebe Gorbalán, Martín Medina, Paolo Pérez Polar, Pablo Rozengardt, María Schwartz Lozada, and Florencia Stáffora. *Informe final: Arte y territorio: Gramáticas, topografías, cuerpos y poderes.* Universidad Nacional de las Artes [unpublished, n.d.].

Mookerjea, Sourayan. "Accumulated Violence, or, The Wars of Exploitation: Notes toward a Post-Western Marxism." *Mediations* 32, no. 1 (2018): 95–114.

Morton, Timothy. *Ecology without Nature: Rethinking Environmental Aesthetics.* Cambridge, MA: Harvard University Press, 2007

———. "Queer Ecology." *PMLA* 125, no. 2 (2010): 273–82.

Museo de Arte Moderno de Buenos Aires. *Una historia de la imaginación en la Argentina: Visiones de la pampa, el litoral y el altiplano desde el siglo XIX a la actualidad* [exhibition brochure], 2019.

Nash, Kate. "The Feminist Production of Knowledge: Is Deconstruction a Practice for Women?" *Feminist Review* 47, no. 1 (July 1994): 65–77.

Nirmal, Padini and Rocheleau, Dianne. "Decolonizing Degrowth in the Post-Development Convergence: Questions, Experiences, and Proposals from Two Indigenous Territories." *ENE: Nature and Space* 2, no. 3 (2019): 465–92.

Nixon, Rob. *Slow Violence and the Environmentalism of the Poor*. Cambridge, MA: Harvard University Press, 2011.

Nouzeilles, Gabriela. "Patagonia as Borderland: Nature, Culture, and the Idea of the State." *Journal of Latin American Cultural Studies* 8, no. 1 (1999): 35–48.

Observatorio Petrolero Sur. "La CIDH recibió con preocupación denuncias sobre el fracking en América," 4 October 2018. https://opsur.org.ar/2018/10/04/la-cidh-recibio-con-preocupacion-denuncias-sobre-el-fracking-en-america.

Observatorio Petrolero Sur. "En América Latina está latiendo un mundo nuevo y la energía va a ser el corazón de ese latido," 4 December 2019. https://opsur.org.ar/2019/12/04/en-america-latina-esta-latiendo-un-mundo-nuevo-y-la-energia-va-a-ser-el-corazon-de-ese-latido.

Ojeda, Diana. "Género, naturaleza y política: Los estudios sobre género y medio ambiente." *Historia Ambiental Latinoamericana y Caribeña* 1, no. 1 (2011): 55–73.

Oliva Abarca, Jesús Eduardo. "Capital cultural, creatividad y desarrollo sustentable: Retos y desafíos actuales de la producción cultural." *Revista estudios*, no. 33 (2016): 343–67.

Pacto Ecosocial del Sur. "Inicio," 2020. https://pactoecosocialdelsur.com.

Page, Joanna. *Decolonizing Science in Latin American Art*. London: UCL Press, 2021.

*Página12*. "Una sola convocatoria, el mismo escenario y dos documentos," 20 March 2018. https://www.pagina12.com.ar/102783-una-sola-convocatoria-el-mismo-escenario-y-dos-documentos.

———. "Alberto Fernández: 'Ningún negocio puede ser más importante que el lugar donde vivimos,'" 22 September 2020. https://www.pagina12.com.ar/293586-alberto-fernandez-ningun-negocio-puede-ser-mas-importante-qu.

Palma, Karla. "Museums and Mining Technologies." *Cultural Studies* 33, no. 5 (2019): 802–22.

Pautassi, Laura Cecilia. "La complejidad de articular derechos: Alimentación y cuidado." *Salud Colectiva* 12, no. 4 (2016): 621–34.

Pautasso, Jimena. "Apuntes de un cambio en la relación arte/política: La incorporación de los *grupos políticos de arte* en la cultura nacional posterior a 2001." *Revista lindes*, no. 6 (May 2013): 1–8.

Pellegrini, Julián. "Contrapublicidad: Una respuesta creativa al monólogo del poder." In Merlinsky and Serafini, *Arte y Ecología Política*, 193–201.

Pérez Prieto, Laura. "Epistemología feminista y conocimientos desde el sur global." *Ecología Política*, no. 54 (2017): 14–17.

Petras, James, and Henry Veltmeyer. *The New Extractivism: A Post-Neoliberal Development Model or Imperialism of the Twenty-First Century?* London: Zed Books, 2014.

Petroni, Ilze Gabriela. "Estrategias de resiliencia: Prácticas de gestión autónoma de arte contemporáneo en la Argentina post-crisis de 2001." *Revista de estudios globales y arte contemporáneo* 3, no. 1 (2015): 302–21.

Pintos, Patricia, and Patricio Narodowski, eds. *La privatopía sacrílega: Efectos del urbanismo privado en los humedales de la cuenca baja del río Luján.* Buenos Aires: Imago Mundi, 2012.

Plaza Azuaje, Penélope. *Culture as Renewable Oil. How Territory, Bureaucratic Power and Culture Coalesce in the Venezuelan Petrostate*. London: Routledge, 2018.

Polischuk, Sebastián. "El intento de aplicar la Ley Antiterrorista sobre el pueblo mapuche en Argentina." *Resumen Latinoamericano*, 25 April 2015. https://www.resumenlatinoamericano.org/2015/04/25/el-intento-de-aplicar-la-ley-antiterrorista-sobre-el-pueblo-mapuche-en-argentina-el-caso-de-la-comunera-relmu-namku.

Polletta, Francesca. "Contending Stories: Narrative in Social Movements." *Qualitative Sociology* 21, no. 4 (1998): 419–46.

Ponce de León, Jennifer. "How to See Violence: Artistic Activism and the Radicalization of Human Rights." *ASAP/Journal* 3, no. 2 (2018): 353–76.

Ponce de León, Jennifer. *Another Aesthetics Is Possible: Arts of Rebellion in the Fourth World War.* Durham, NC: Duke University Press, 2021.

Prato, Anna Valeria, Isa Paula Rodrigues Morais, and María Soledad Segura. "La cultura comunitaria y los gobiernos progresistas: Políticas y participación social en Argentina y Brasil entre 2003 y 2015." *Época III* 24, no. 48 (2018): 9–41.

Preciado, Paul B. *Testo Junkie: Sex, Drugs, and Biopolitics in the Pharmacopornographic Era*. New York: Feminist Press, 2013.

Proaño Gómez, Lola. "*Artivismo* y potencia política: El colectivo Fuerza Artística de Choque Comunicativo: Cuerpos, memoria y espacio urbano." *Telóndefondo*, no. 26 (2017): 48–62.

Proyecto Artigas. *Modelo agrario sostenible, libre de agrotóxicos y explotación*, 2020. https://www.proyectoartigas.ar.

Proyecto Squatters. "La plaza es nuestra!! Encuentro de artistas y activistas." Facebook, April 22, 2018. https://www.facebook.com/events/8223836779 72825.

Quijano, Anibal. "Coloniality of Power, Eurocentrism, and Latin America." *Nepantla: Views from South* 1, no. 3 (2000): 533–80.

Radcliffe, Sarah A., and Nina Laurie. "Culture and Development: Taking Culture Seriously in Development for Andean Indigenous People." *Environment and Planning D: Society and Space* 24, no. 2 (April 2006): 231–48.

Raffestin, Claude. "Space, Territory, and Territoriality." *Environment and Planning D: Society and Space* 30, no. 1 (Feb. 2012): 121–41.

Ramos, Ana Margarita. "Los caminos sinuosos del *kizugüneun* (autonomía). Reflexiones situadas en las luchas mapuche." *Publicar* 15, no. 23 (2017): 53-72.

Rancière, Jacques. *Dissensus: On Politics and Aesthetics*. Edited and translated by Steven Corcoran, London: Continuum International Publishing Group, 2010.

Reed, T. V. *The Art of Protest: Culture and Activism from the Civil Rights Movement to the Streets of Seattle*. Minneapolis: University of Minnesota Press, 2005.

Resumen Latinoamericano. "Argentina: Cumbre latinoamericana del agua para los pueblos," 16 September 2018. https://www.resumenlatinoamericano.org/2018/09/16/argentina-cumbre-latinoamericana-del-agua-para-los-pueblos.

Rey, Germán. *Industrias culturales, creatividad y desarrollo*. Madrid: Agencia Española de Cooperación Internacional para el Desarrollo, 2009.

Riffo, Lorena. "Hidrocarburos no convencionales y conflictos socioambientales. Análisis crítico de la escena enunciativa en el diario Río Negro sobre el acuerdo Chevron-YPF S.A." *(En)clave Comahue* 23 (2017): 61-84.

Riofrancos, Thea. "Extractivismo Unearthed: A Genealogy of a Radical Discourse." *Cultural Studies* 31, no. 2–3 (2017): 1–30.

Risso, Natalí. "Fortalecidas pese al traspié judicial para Dolores Etchevehere. 'El Proyecto Artigas sigue en marcha.'" *Página 12*, 1 November 2020. https://www.pagina12.com.ar/302971-el-proyecto-artigas-sigue-en-marcha.

Rivera Cusicanqui, Silvia. *Oprimidos pero no vencidos: Luchas del campesinado Aymara y Qhechwa de Bolivia, 1900–1980*. La Paz: La Mirada Salvaje, 1984.

———. "La noción de 'derecho' o las paradojas de la modernidad postcolonial: Indígenas y mujeres en Bolivia." *Temas Sociales*, no. 19 (1997): 27–52.

———. *Violencias (re)encubiertas en Bolivia*. La Paz: Piedra Salvaje/ Editorial Piedra Rota, 2010.

Rodríguez, María Carla. "Estado, clases y gentrificación: La política urbana como campo de disputa en tres barrios de la Ciudad de Buenos Aires." In *Perspectivas del estudio de la gentrificación en México y América Latina*, edited by Victor Delgadillo, Ibán Díaz, and Luis Salinas, 205–27. Mexico: Universidad Nacional Autónoma de México, 2015.

Rodríguez, María Carla, and María Mercedes Di Virgilio. "A City for All? Public Policy and Resistance to Gentrification in the Southern Neighborhoods of Buenos Aires." *Urban Geography* 37, no. 8 (2016): 1215–34.

Roesch, Anaïs. "Propuesta para un régimen estético post-extractivista." *Index, revista de arte contemporáneo*, no. 7 (2019): 176–84.

Rosales de la Quintana, Vanesa. "La agroecología como política de salud pública." *Página 12*, 15 January 2020. https://www.pagina12.com.ar/241765-la-agroecologia-como-politica-de-salud-publica.

Rubenstein, Jérémy. "La sédition militaire de Semana Santa de 1987: Le peuple au secours du régime démocratique argentin." PhD diss., Université Panthéon-Sorbonne-Paris I, 2014.

Sack, Robert D. *Human Territoriality: Its Theory and History*. Cambridge: Cambridge University Press, 1986.

Saifer, Adam. "Research Note: Reimagining Creative Economy through the Lens of Multiple Colonialisms." *Review in Cultural Theory* 8, no. 1 (2018): 23–38.

Sajeva, Giulia. "Rights with Limits: Biocultural Rights—between Self-Determination and Conservation of the Environment." *Journal of Human Rights and the Environment* 6, no. 1 (2015): 30–54.

Sassen, Saskia. *Expulsions: Brutality and Complexity in the Global Economy*. Cambridge, MA: Harvard University Press, 2014.

Schindel, Estela. "Inscribir el pasado en el presente: Memoria y espacio urbano." *Política y Cultura*, no. 31 (2009): 65–87.

Segato, Rita Laura. *La guerra contra las mujeres*. Madrid: Traficantes de Sueños, 2016.

———. *Contra-pedagogías de la crueldad*. Buenos Aires: Prometeo Libros, 2018.

Serafini, Paula. "Subversion through Performance: Performance Activism in London." In *The Political Aesthetics of Global Protest: The Arab Spring and Beyond*, edited by Pnina Werbner, Kathryn Spellman-Poots, and Martin Webb, 320–40. Edinburgh: Edinburgh University Press, 2014.

———. "Prefiguring Performance: Participation and Transgression in Environmentalist Activism." *Third Text* 29, no. 3 (2015): 195–206.

———. *Performance Action: The Politics of Art Activism*. London: Routledge, 2018.

———. "Mediating Identities: Community Arts, Media, and Collective Identity in the Frontline Resistance to Fracking." *Journal of Cultural Analysis and Social Change* 3, no. 2 (2018): 11.

———. "Community Radio as a Space of Care: An Ecofeminist Perspective on Media Production in Environmental Conflicts." *International Journal of Communication*, no. 13 (2019): 1–18.

———. "Cultural Production beyond Extraction? A First Approach to Extractivism and the Cultural and Creative Industries in Argentina." In *Cultural Industries and the Environmental Crisis: New Approaches for Policy*, edited by Kate Oakley and Mark Banks, 51–63. Cham: Springer, 2020.

Serafini, Paula, Jessica Holtaway, and Alberto Cossu. *artWORK: Art, Labour and Activism*. London: Rowman and Littlefield International, 2017.

Sessano, Pablo. "La educación ambiental: Un modo de aprender." *Anales de la Educación Común* 2, no. 3 (2006): 102–11.

Sgaramella, Chiara. "Ecologías sensibles: Arte de enfoque colaborativo y crisis ecosocial en el contexto americano." Paper presented at IMAGEN [N] VISIBLE. IV Congreso Internacional de Investigación en Artes Visuales: ANIAV 2019. Valencia, Spain, July, 2019. DOI: 10.4995/ANIAV.2019.8981.

Shaughnessy, Nicola. *Applying Performance: Live Art, Socially Engaged Theatre and Affective Practice.* London: Palgrave Macmillan, 2012.

Sholette, Gregory. *Dark Matter: Art and Politics in the Age of Enterprise Culture.* London: Pluto Press, 2011.

Singer, Ross. "Toward Intersectional Ecofeminist Communication Studies." *Communication Theory* 30, no. 3 (2020): 268–289. DOI: 10.1093/ct/qtz023.

Sitrin, Marina, ed. *Horizontalism: Voices of Popular Power in Argentina.* Oakland, CA: AK Press, 2006.

———. "Horizontalidad, autogestión y protagonismo en Argentina." *Historia actual online*, no. 21 (2010): 133–42. https://historia-actual.org/Publicaciones/index.php/hao/issue/view/28.

Solanas, Fernando 'Pino.' "Menemismo: Megaminería y contaminación." *Página12*, 2 January 2010. https://www.pagina12.com.ar/diario/sociedad/3-137921-2010-01-02.html.

Sousa Santos, Boaventura de. *Towards a New Legal Common Sense.* London: Butterworth, 2002.

———. *Epistemologías del sur.* Mexico DF: Siglo XXI, 2010.

Stallabrass, Julian. *Art Incorporated: The Story of Contemporary Art.* Oxford: Oxford University Press, 2004.

———. *Documentary (Whitechapel Documents of Contemporary Art).* Cambridge, MA: MIT Press, 2013.

Stallybrass, Peter, and White, Allon. *The Politics and Poetics of Transgression.* Ithaca, NY: Cornell University Press, 1986.

Sultana, Farhana. "Emotional Political Ecology." In *The International Handbook of Political Ecology*, edited by Raymond Bryant, 633–45. Cheltenham: Edward Elgar, 2015.

———. "Climate Change, COVID-19, and the Co-production of Injustices: A Feminist Reading of Overlapping Crises." *Social and Cultural Geography* 22, no. 4 (2021): 447–60.

Svampa, Maristella. *El dilema argentino: Civilización o barbarie: De Sarmiento al revisionism peronista.* Buenos Aires: El Cielo por Asalto, 1994.

———. "Consenso de los commodities, giro ecoterritorial y pensamiento crítico en América Latina." *Observatorio Social de América Latina*, no. 32 (2012): 15–38.

———. "Feminismos del Sur y ecofeminismo." *Nueva Sociedad*, no. 256 (2015): 127–131.

———. "Cuatro claves para leer América Latina." *Nueva Sociedad*, no. 268 (2017): 50–64.

———. *Las fronteras del neoextractivismo en América Latina: Conflictos socioambientales, giro ecoterritorial y nuevas dependencias.* Guadalajara: CALAS, 2019.

Svampa, Maristella, and Sebastián Pereyra. *Entre la ruta y el barrio: La experiencia de las organizaciones piqueteras*. Buenos Aires: Editorial Biblos, 2003.

Svampa, Maristella, and Enrique Viale. *Maldesarrollo: La Argentina del extractivismo y el despojo*. Buenos Aires: Katz, 2014.

———. *El colapso ecológico ya llegó: Una brújula para salir del (mal)desarrollo.* Buenos Aires: Siglo XXI, 2020.

———. "A View of the Green New Deal from Argentina." *Jacobin*, 17 June 2020. https://jacobinmag.com/2020/6/green-new-deal-argentina-gran-pacto.

Szpilbarg, Daniela, and Ezequiel Saferstein. "De la industria cultural a las industrias creativas: Un análisis de la transformación del término y sus usos contemporáneos." *Estudios de filosofía práctica e historia de las ideas* 16, no. 2 (2014): 99–112.

Swyngedouw, Erik, and Henrik Ernstson. "Interrupting the Anthropo-obScene: Immuno-biopolitics and Depoliticizing Ontologies in the Anthropocene." *Theory, Culture, and Society* 35, no. 6 (2018): 3–30.

Tancons, Claire. "Occupy Wall Street: Carnival against Capital? Carnivalesque as Protest Sensibility." *e-flux*, no. 30, December 2011. https://www.e-flux.com/journal/30/68148/occupy-wall-street-carnival-against-capital-carnival esque-as-protest-sensibility .

Telam. "Las voces que se oponen a la privatización de Costa Salguero," 30 November 2020. https://www.telam.com.ar/notas/202011/536966-voces-se-oponen-privatizacion-costa-salguero.html.

Tlostanova, Madina. "On Decolonizing Design." *Design Philosophy Papers* 15, no. 1 (2017): 51–61.

Tola, Florencia. "El 'giro ontológico' y la relación naturaleza/cultura: Reflexiones desde el Gran Chaco." *Apuntes de investigación del CECYP*, no. 27 (2016): 128–39.

Tronto, Joan C. "An ethic of care." *Generations: Journal of the American Society on Aging* 22 (1998): 15–20.

Tsing, Anna. "Arts of Inclusión, or, How to Love a Mushroom." *Mānoa* 22, no. 2 (2010): 191–203.

Ulloa, Astrid. "Environment and Development: Reflections from Latin America." In *The Routledge Handbook of Political Ecology*, edited by Tom Perreault, Gavin Bridge, and James McCarthy, 320–31. London: Routledge, 2015.

———. "Feminismos territoriales en América Latina: Defensas de la vida frente a los extractivismos." *Nómadas*, no. 45 (2016): 123–29.

Unión de Asambleas Ciudadanas. "Quienes Somos," accessed 3 February 2020. https://asambleasciudadanas.org.ar/quienes-somos.

Unión de Trabajadores de la Tierra. "¿Quiénes Somos?," accessed 16 March 2021. https://uniondetrabajadoresdelatierra.com.ar/quienes-somos.

United Cities and Local Governments. *Decalogue for the Post Covid-19 Era*, 2020. Barcelona: United Cities and Local Governments. ttps://www.uclg.org/sites/default/files/decalogue_for_the_post_covid-19_era.pdf.

Valle, Luísa de Pinho. "El ecofeminismo como propulsor de la expansión de la racionalidad ambiental." *Ecología Política*, no. 54 (2017): 28–36.

Vásquez Duplat, Ana María. "Presentación." In *Extractivismo urbano: Debates para una construcción colectiva de las ciudades*, edited by Ana María Vásquez Duplat, 9–14. Buenos Aires: Editorial El Colectivo, 2017.

Viale, Enrique. "Prólogo: El extractivismo urbano." In *Extractivismo urbano: Debates para una construcción colectiva de las ciudades*, edited by Ana María Vásquez Duplat, 15–20. Buenos Aires: Editorial El Colectivo, 2017.

Wagner, Lucrecia. "Conflictos socioambientales por megaminería en Argentina: Apuntes para una reflexión en perspectiva histórica." *Áreas: Revista Internacional de Ciencias Sociales*, no. 35 (2016): 87–99.

Warren, Karen. "The Promise and Power of Ecofeminism." *Environmental Ethics* 12, no. 2 (1990): 125–46.

Wilson, Sheena. "Energy Imaginaries: Feminist and Decolonial Futures." In *Materialism and the Critique of Energy*, edited by Brent Ryan Bellamy and Jeff Diamanti, 377–412. Chicago: MCMPrime Press, 2018.

Wilson, Sheena, Adam Carlson, and Imre Szeman, eds. *Petrocultures: Oil, Politics, Culture*. Montreal: McGill-Queen's University Press, 2017.

Winograd, Terry, and Fernando Flores. *Understanding Computers and Cognition: A New Foundation for Design*. Boston: Addison Wesley, 1986.

Wortman, Ana. "El desafío de las políticas culturales en Argentina." In *Estudios Latinoamericanos sobre cultura y transformaciones sociales en tiempos de globalización 2*, edited by Daniel Mato, 251–67. Buenos Aires: CLACSO, 2001.

———. "Políticas culturales y legitimidad política en tiempos de crisis: El caso del Programa Puntos de Cultura en Argentina." *Políticas culturais em revista* 10, no. 1 (2017): 138–60.

Yaccar, María Daniela. "Investigaciones que suben a escena." Página12, 4 April 2017. https://www.pagina12.com.ar/29627-investigaciones-que-suben-a-escena.

Yúdice, George. *The Expediency of Culture: Uses of Culture in the Global Era*. Durham, NC: Duke University Press, 2003.

Zamorano, Mariano Martín. "La transformación de las políticas culturales en Argentina durante la primera década Kirchnerista: Entre la hegemonía y la diversidad." *Aposta*, no. 70 (2016). https://www.redalyc.org/jatsRepo/4959/495952432003/html/index.html.

Zibechi, Raúl. *Territories in Resistance: A Cartography of Latin American Social Movements*. Translated by Ramor Ryan. Oakland, CA: AK Press, 2012.

Zukin, Sharon. "Gentrification: Culture and Capital in the Urban Core." *Annual Review of Sociology*, vol. 13 (1987): 129–47.

# INDEX

www.ingramcontent.com/pod-product-compliance
Lightning Source LLC
LaVergne TN
LVHW091113080826
845145LV00008B/1897
* 9 7 8 0 8 2 6 5 0 4 5 5 5 *